# Studies in Australian Literary History

By Brian Kiernan

*Images of Society and Nature: Seven Essays on Australian Novels*

*Criticism*, Australian Writers and Their Work

*Henry Lawson*, Australian Authors (ed.)

*The Most Beautiful Lies : A Collection of Stories by Five Major Contemporary Fiction Writers* (ed.)

*Considerations: New Essays on Kenneth Slessor, Judith Wright and Douglas Stewart* (ed.)

*Patrick White*

*The Essential Henry Lawson* (ed.)

*David Williamson: A Writer's Career* (two editions)

# Studies in Australian Literary History

Brian Kiernan

SYDNEY STUDIES
SHOESTRING PRESS

Studies in Australian Literary History


Sydney Studies in Society and Culture 17

ISSN 0812-6403
ISBN 0-949405-15-9

Published in Australia by the
Sydney Association for Studies in Society and Culture
University of Sydney, NSW 2006

Distributed by Sydney Studies
PO Box 575 Leichhardt
Sydney, NSW 2040
(02) 9569 1452

Published in the United Kingdom by Shoestring Press
19 Devonshire Avenue, Nottingham NG9 1BS

Formatting and design by Annette Krausmann

Printed in Australia by Berget Pty Ltd

Published with the support of
the Faculty of Arts, University of Sydney, and
the Australian Academy of the Humanities

For Michael Wilding,
Always a stimulating writer of fiction,
scholar, and friend.

# Contents

# Preface

The first essay here, 'Literature, History, and Literary History', was written in the mid-1970s. My impression then was that literary history was regarded, unfairly, as at best a mustily antiquarian pursuit; at worst as a questionable hybrid which attempted to reconcile mundane 'extrinsic' matters of bibliographical and biographical fact with criticism's higher, 'intrinsic' purposes—the interpretation and evaluation of individual poems, fictions and plays.

That general impression changed utterly when *The Oxford History of Australian Literature*, edited by Leonie Kramer, appeared in 1981. Hostile reactions to it, alleging that its 'intrinsic' appraisals of fiction, poetry and drama ignored a range of contexts and other forms of writing, showed that literary history was anything but a musty pursuit to be relegated to a less critically or theoretically aware past. Instead it provided a focus for an otherwise seemingly disparate range of contemporary concerns.

These hostile reactions culminated in a counter-history, *The Penguin New Literary History of Australia*, written by members of the then still fledgling Association for the Study of Australian Literature under the general editorship of Laurie Hergenhan, and published in 1988, the Bicentennial year. This volume (to which I contributed one of the 'contextual' chapters) manifested no anxiety about hybridity—feminist, multicultural and cultural-materialist approaches were prominent among the range of cross-disciplinary interests it incorporated; and, from around the time it appeared, revisionist varieties of literary history became the dominant mode of what used to be called 'literary criticism'.

When the editors of the Sydney Studies series invited me to contribute a selection from the shorter studies I had written over the past twenty years or so years, I thought that a choice from those which related to some variety of literary history might provide a thread through the labyrinth of occasional essays, articles and introductions commissioned by various editors, for different readerships, in Australia, the U.S. and the U.K. If I have chosen some which seem more preoccupied with individual writers than with wider contexts, then I would appeal to Emerson—'There is properly no history; only biography' (*History*, 1841)—and argue, as I do in the last essay here, that literary biography can also be a mode of cultural historiography.

# Literature, History and Literary History: Perspectives on the Nineteenth Century in Australia

*To trace the growth of letters in the community, from the earliest period of our history to the present time, and to show in what manner that growth had been influenced by the productions of the Mother Country ... would amount to a literary history of the country, and it was hoped that such a history would serve more than one useful service. It would enable the reader to form an exact idea of the progress, extent and prospects of literary enterprise among us, more readily than could be done by means of any general statement; it would constitute a bibliographical account that might be practically useful, not only to those who are interested in our literature, but also to those who may hereafter be engaged in historical enquiries; it would serve to throw some light, from a new point of view, on our social history; and lastly, it would preserve the memory, and give some notion of the achievement, of men whose name could scarcely be expected to survive their generation.*

So wrote G. B. Barton, Reader in English at the University of Sydney, in the introduction to his *Literature in New South Wales* (1866). This and his critical anthology, *The Poets and Prose Writers of New South Wales* (also 1866), were the first books on Australian literature. Although Barton recorded much valuable bibliographical information, he did not provide any systematic review along the lines he suggests in the above passage; however, his ideal of what literary history ought to provide comprehends the intentions of many who were to follow him with their accounts of the 'growth of letters' in this country.

Barton's intention of enabling the reader to form an opinion of the 'progress' of literature in this country reminds us that he was writing in the mid-Victorian period—and three years after the first appearance

---

First published in Leon Cantrell, ed., *Bards, Bohemians and Bookmen: Essays in Australian Literature* (University of Queensland Press, St Lucia, 1976); reprinted in *Twentieth Century Literary Criticism* (Gale, Detroit, 1993).

of Taine's *History of English Literature*. 'Progress' in accordance with the universal laws of evolution was assumed by most nineteenth-century (and perhaps later) commentators on Australian literature. As a new society, a new race, evolved in response to the new environment, so would a new literature, which (ambiguously) would be an agent in and a product of this evolution.[1] And 'prospects' had a particular poignancy for the scholar turning his attention to the literature of his own colony; what he surveyed could be only the first fruits plucked from a vine that had scarce taken root in this thin soil; it would be a later age that reaped the harvest. Later literary historians have traced the extent of the Mother Country's influence on local writing, and of Europe's and America's. Bibliographies have been compiled, and the memories of men whose names could scarcely be expected to survive their generation have been preserved. Here, I want to consider the success with which Barton's other, and elusive, aim—that of throwing some light 'from a new point of view' on our social history—has been fulfilled.

Broadly, one can imagine a literary 'history' that has no awareness of social history at all. The various 'Histories of English Literature' written for schools and civil service examinations in England last century approach this extreme, being chronological listings of authors and descriptions of their works, located in time by reference to ruling monarchs or wars. Then there is the 'social history' of literature itself: literary movements, literary influences, even the lives of writers do not always correspond with the periods postulated on economic or other grounds. But at the point that even the most ahistorical of literary historians move beyond texts and chronology to considerations of conditions of authorship, the writer's expression of social values, or other relationships between the writer, his work, and his society, they are encountering history and, consciously or otherwise, offering an interpretation of the past and of the nature of these cultural relationships. At the opposite extreme from the literary chronicle would be a work —such as Taine's—highly aware of literature as a social institution. In Australia, although there were no attempts to provide inclusive literary histories between Barton's books and H. M. Green's *Outline of Australian Literature* in 1930, many of the problems, assumptions

1 See Brian Kiernan, *Criticism*, Australian Writers and Their Work (Oxford University Press, Melbourne, 1974), pp.8–12.

and issues of Australian literary history had emerged by then.

The first of these problems was that of defining the field—what is *Australian* literature? ('What is Australian *literature?'* and the issue of whether historians should confine themselves to an Arnoldian notion of literature or adopt an anthropological approach to literary culture did not, for obvious reasons, preoccupy a pioneer like Barton.) Although we most usually think of the concept of a national literature emerging in the eighties and nineties of last century, it is a concept that was present almost from the beginning of the century in literary expectations—expectations because these all but preceded the literature. Romantic literary theory in England and on the Continent had seen literature as the history of the national mind and as the expression of the genius of the individual race. The peculiar problems of a country sharing the language and cultural heritance of the English but encountering and mastering a different environment, and developing a new culture, had been experienced in America. There the issue of a national literature—the issue, simply of whether a writer's obligations were to be American or a writer first of all—remained contentious at least until the Civil War; and the contention was not diminished by English observers such Sidney Smith enquiring in the *Edinburgh Review* in 1820: 'Who in the four quarters of the globe reads an American book?' William Ellery Channing, who felt that it were 'better to have no literature than form ourselves unresistingly on a foreign one' addressed the issue in 1830 in his lecture *The Importance and Means of a National Literature*. In this he defined literature as 'the expression of a nation's mind' and claimed that 'literature is plainly among powerful methods of exalting the character of a nation, of forming a better race of men'.

Such exalted views of literature's function were quite orthodox on both sides of the Atlantic—and soon after on the other side of Pacific. For as George Nadel documents in *Australia's Colonial Culture,* these were also the principles of those who took upon themselves the education and moral improvement of the Australian colonies. Literature and culture were virtually co-extensive terms, and the propagation of literature was expected to alleviate the depressingly materialistic tone of the Australian colonies, restore a lost sense of community, and morally elevate the masses. Nadel shows how, from the 1830s onwards, literary culture was related to nationalism: 'In whatever fashion the argument was disseminated the basic point seemed to be that sheep and acres did not give a country nationality, but that literature did: indeed there could be no patriotism without literature' and he quotes the essay 'Literature—Its Advancement and Results' from the first issue of the *Australian Era* (1850). The author of the essay saw Australia 'standing on the brink of nationality ... Literature created nationality, because nationality presupposed national thought and a national intelligence, themselves the product of literature'.[2]

The connection between literature and nationality came early—we might say it was imported before much imaginative writing had appeared in Australia. One of the first (of many, as it turned out) to proclaim the emergence of a national literature was William Walker in his lecture 'Australian Literature' delivered at the Windsor School of Arts in 1864. His historical survey, he felt, showed that Australia had 'a literature of her own of a progressive and promising character', and one, his title implied, that transcended colonial borders and jealousies. So impressed was Walker with the progress already made that he felt another lecture would be necessary to do full justice to the poetry, and that there was every probability that Australia would produce writers worthy to be placed alongside Bacon, Shakespeare, Byron, and Scott. Such optimism reminds one of Melville's in America earlier—'Believe me, my friends, men not very inferior to Shakespeare are being born this day on the banks of the Ohio'[3]—and the American parallel was one that occurred naturally to critics as Australia enjoyed its own debate over a national literature in the last quarter of the nineteenth century. While 'universalists' agonised over whether one could meaningful speak of American literature (if a work were good enough it surely belonged to English literature?), the 'nationalists' were inspired with confidence, as were the republicans in politics, by the American precedent. The confident national literature they saw as emerging with Hawthorne, Longfellow, Bret Harte, and others seemed an important indication of the most likely course of Australia's own literary maturation. The invariable analogies between literary and biological or organic growth (mothers and daughters, trees and branches, with America always at a

2 George Nadel, *Australia's Colonial Culture: Ideas, Men and Institutions in Mid-Nineteenth Century Eastern Australia* (Harvard University Press, Cambridge, Mass., 1957), p.69.

3 Herman Melville, 'Hawthorne and His Mosses', *Literary World* [New York], August 17 and 14, 1850.

later stage of development) fitted the general belief in the inevitability of evolutionary progress and must have seemed, subconsciously, to guarantee eventual social and literary maturation. The American parallel provided the historical model which was to be employed by later historians of Australian literature. After a colonial period in which immigrant writers discovered a strange new land, native-born writers would emerge to express their acceptance of this land and society as their own; eventually, after a period of nationalistic self-consciousness, a mature, assured, unselfconsciously national literature would be established. Consistently, from about 1870 onwards (and well into the twentieth century) Australian critics were proclaiming the beginning of this second stage, the emergence of distinctively Australian writers; just as in the twentieth century they have proclaimed the achievement of the final stage, the coming of age.

Although there could be no full-scale histories of Australian literature written in the nineteenth century, critical discussions in books and periodicals presupposed views of the development of Australia and literature's relationship to this. Australia had done well for a pioneering country with a small population which, of necessity, had to get on with more immediate matters than pursuing culture; on the other hand, Australia was too materialistic (a view that Barton questioned) and its prosperous class that could afford time and money for culture was too philistine, too nouveau-riche to offer the traditional patronage of the European aristocracy and haute-bourgeoisie. Whichever way the argument ran, this sense of literature as an index of cultural attainment and social history was common to a number of books that appeared around the turn of the century. These were not literary histories in the sense that they pretended to any systematic inclusiveness, but their assumptions concerning the relationships between literature and the society in which it was produced, like those in many other studies of particular writers or partial views of Australian writing in the periodicals, contributed to an awareness of literature as part of our general or cultural history. Indeed, the most frequent assumptions, issues, and phrases, of later literary history can be found in these books which appeared within a brief space of time at the end of last century: Patchett Martin's *The Beginnings of Australian Literature* (1898), a pamphlet originally delivered in London as a lecture by a former editor of the *Melbourne Review;* Desmond Byrne's *Australian Writers* (1896), a collection of biographical and critical discussions of Clarke, Kingsley, Cambridge, Gordon, Boldrewood, Praed and 'Tasma' introduced by a general discussion; and Turner and Sutherland's *The Development of Australian Literature* (1898), the only one to be published in Australia with primarily an Australian audience in mind.

Turner's introductory 'General Sketch of Australian Literature', (which is then followed by Sutherland's biographies of Clarke, Gordon, and Kendall) expresses the conventional literary historical assumptions about the relationship between the size of the population, the country's stage of development, and its literature. Turner, writing at a time when the population was four million, says that the growth of a large population sharing local experience 'must inevitably bring strength and maturity to a national literature'. The present stage in cultural development Turner sees as restricted by the necessity for culture to take a second place in a pioneering community and the lack of national feeling. Until leisure is possible and a national spirit is developed ('as it will be unless the tradition of our race suffers decay') we must be content 'with the productions of local literature, essentially English in its characteristics, but moulded by climatic and scenic surroundings into a form that gives it sufficient distinctiveness to justify the term "Australian".'

Scepticism towards this attitude that linked the 'development' of Australian literature with the expansion of society, and its corollary that what literature had been produced was admirable for a society at such an early stage of its development, was also expressed. Professor T. G. Tucker, an editor of the *Australasian Critic,* constantly attacked this attitude, as also did Byrne in his introduction to *Australian Writers.* Taking up the parallel with America which had been used so often to prophesy the inevitable emergence of an Australian literature, Byrne inverts it to question its assumptions (Benjamin Franklin, he points out, appeared considerably before America achieved nationhood) and to shatter any complacency about Australian cultural life. Australians, he says, take no pride in creative intellectual work; despite Government provision of education and cultural establishments public taste has not improved; clubs and societies devoted to literature are elitist; the lack of support for local periodicals and books, because of public preference for what is approved by the English public, has meant that it is impossible to live by writing in Australia. These facts, Byrne suggests: 'may not be found to explain why there is yet no sign of the coming of an Antipodean Franklin or Irving, or Hawthorne or Emerson; but they will help to show why the literature of the country grows so unevenly, why it is chiefly of the objective order and leaves large tracks of the lives of the people untouched.'

In later literary historical accounts, the years in which these views of the relationships between society and culture in Australia were being advanced were also the years when a national feeling (and a politically unified nation) was emerging, and finding expression, particularly in the Sydney *Bulletin.* Byrne, writing in England, seemed unaware of the *Bulletin* writers; the others however were not, though their contemporary view was not that of later generations. Turner's conservatism made him critical of Lawson's radicalism and wary of exaggerating the place of the *Bulletin* writers; Patchett Martin was more warmly disposed towards them as indicating the commencement of an Australian school of writing; Francis Adams employed by the *Bulletin* in the late eighties was contemptuous of local poetry and prose. It would be interesting to establish when the view of the *Bulletin's* central role in the development of a national literature—a view shared by many of its writers and, presumably, readers also—became a historical view. Nettie Palmer's *Modern Australian Literature* (1924) would seem to have been very influential here.

As its title suggests, it is concerned with the first quarter of the twentieth century, and its necessarily summary treatment of the previous century became orthodox in many later accounts. Nettie Palmer was among the first to take a historical view of the decades before and after Federation and to draw a sharp division between the 'colonial' literature which presented Australia through the eyes of expatriate Englishmen (or 'bias-bleared spectacles' as A. G. Stephens had expressed it characteristically in 1901) and the 'Australian' literature that had emerged with the new nation. Of course writers involved in the conscious movement to establish a national literature—Stephens, Lawson, Vance Palmer—felt that the *Bulletin* schools had achieved those long anticipated characteristics by which the national literature would be recognised: a lack of self-consciousness in the use of Australian experience and the assumption of a local rather than an English audience. As Jose wrote in his *History of Australasia* in 1909: 'during the last twenty years there has sprung up a school of young Australians who tell of their own life in their own natural way, and describe their own country as men who love it; so that through them a stranger can get at the heart of the people, not merely at the ideas about the people formed by interested outsiders.'[4] *Modern Australian Literature* endorsed such contemporary views as historically accurate. The long-awaited nationhood and national literature had been achieved. For the literary historian the task was to reveal what was essentially Australian in the literature, and the elusive relationships between the land, the people, and the literature that for a long time it had been presupposed would emerge.

Although literary historical issues had been discussed for the best part of a century, it was not until 1930 that the first attempt to provide a comprehensive account of imaginative writing appeared with H. M. Green's *An Outline of Australian Literature.* It was presented, in its introduction, as preliminary to 'a short history of Australian literature' in which an attempt would be made 'to relate the literature of each period to its social, political and other conditions'. As we now know, it was to be another thirty years before that work, which attempted the higher literary historical aim of exploring the relationships between literature and society, appeared. The earlier *Outline,* however, is conceptually unadventurous. It is a 'pure' literary history, and a history of 'pure' literature, which makes only passing references to historical events and developments and is concerned only with 'high' literary culture. The interpretative framework remains vague and general, and its opening sentence retains the favourite metaphor and the guarded stance of the 'colonial' critic: 'Australian literature is a branch of English literature, and however great it may become and whatever characteristics it may develop, it will remain a branch.' For Green, as for so many of the nineteenth century critics, 'the literature of a country is obviously an expression of the characteristic qualities of its life', and he lists the characteristics he discerns:

> Most apparent are the qualities, positive and negative, which one would expect to find in the literary work of any young and comparatively undeveloped country, such as vigour and freshness, crudity and lack of architecture and craftsmanship generally; these

4 A. W. Jose, *History of Australasia* (third edition, Angus and Robertson, Sydney, 1909), p.236.

> last, however, no longer mark the best Australian work. But there is also apparent at times a richness, an almost tropical warmth and colouring which may be noticed particularly in the verse of Hugh McCrae and Dorothea Mackellar. More widely spread are certain other qualities which are only in part literary, since their presence in any work which involves representation of character will be derived from the characters represented as well as from the temperament and experience of the writer and their result upon his literary method and point of view. These qualities are an independence of spirit, a kind of humorous disillusion, a careless willingness to take a risk, a slightly sardonic good nature and a certain underlying hardness of texture.[5]

The first two sets of characteristics are conventionally evolutionist and synthesise much nineteenth century discussion which emphasised the difficulties encountered by a pioneering society, and which speculated that climatic and other environmental factors would mould the people and their culture. The third set relates to national character and its expression through literature, and although Green does not develop these here it is these characteristics and their relationship to historical experience and social institutions, including literature, that were to become so important in later accounts, including his own.

In the same year as the *Outline* another book appeared which was to affect views of Australian social history, culture, and literary history for generations to come—W. K. Hancock's *Australia.* Like Tocqueville, who 'tried to explain to cultivated Europeans the characteristics of democracy in a "new" country', Hancock tried to explain to cultivated Europeans the paradoxes of Australian life. His success can be gauged from the fact that *Australia* has assumed something of the same classic status for historians and commentators on society here as *Democracy in America* has in that country. Although not a history, being as much concerned with what could be considered separately as politics, economics, culture, or sociology (for each of which areas it contributed concepts), it was the first study to seek 'dominant themes' in Australian life that would relate the past to the present. It provided an interpretative

5 H. M. Green, *An Outline of Australian Literature* (Whitcombe and Tombs, Sydney, 1930), pp.14–15.

framework that related the social, economic, and cultural in bold hypotheses which many later scholars have examined. For example, the statement that 'Australian nationalism took definite form in the class struggle between the landless majority and the land monopolising squatters', although it synthesises attitudes that had been expressed many times at various stages in the past, confers a historical validation upon them, and anticipates the major theme of Australian historians in later decades.[6]

Hancock's influence on historians and social commentators has been discussed and criticised by R. W. Connell:[7] here I want only to draw attention to its similar influence on the concept of history found in the work of literary critics. Again as an example of the bold generalisation that anticipates or stimulated later writers we could take his statement that 'Recurrent in Australian poetry is a note of renunciation, sometimes regretful, sometimes defiant ... and a note of expectation, of waiting upon the future for an Australia which has not been known to the past ...'[8] which accords with Judith Wright's later study of the preoccupations with exile and utopia in Australian poetry.[9]

Hancock sees literature as part of the total cultural development he traces and analyses, and sees it as expressing 'the prevailing ideology of Australian democracy': 'in Lawson and Collins [Furphy], and almost every other writer of the *Bulletin* school, Australian nationalism expressed itself as a repudiation of English conventions and standards, as a vindication of equality and democracy and an assertion of the supreme worth of the average man.'[10] Hancock is synthesising the nationalism and egalitarian democracy that were expressed (however more complexly) by these writers. But he is also defining in social and political terms what was 'characteristic' of Australian literature and providing the literary historian with the link between literature and society in terms of the values expressed in the literature of the nationalist period. These were not the links perceived, or so explicitly formulated, by literary historians (for example, Nettie Palmer or H. M. Green) up to

6 W. K. Hancock, *Australia* (1930; Jacaranda Press, Brisbane, 1961), p.44.

7 R. W. Connell, *Quadrant* 12, 2 (1968), 9–19.

8 Hancock, p.43.

9 Judith Wright, *Preoccupations in Australian Poetry* (Oxford University Press, Melbourne, 1965).

10 Hancock, p.257.

this time. However, the tradition Hancock postulated was to be elaborated by historians and critics from then on. It provided the opportunity to interpret the development of literature in terms of social history and to use literature to illustrate the formation of an egalitarian national culture and character. By the time H. M. Green's full history appeared this had become an orthodoxy—though already an orthodoxy under attack—which provided in numerous summaries a stereotyped view of literature developing in accordance with national consciousness. It is also an orthodoxy that clearly affects Green's consideration of the relationship of 'the literature of each period to its social, political and other conditions'.

His *History of Australian Literature* (1961) opens with much more confidence in its subject as an entity than does his *Outline* with its branch-of-the-tree image: 'It is scarcely necessary to argue nowadays that the literature of Australia is worth discussing on its own account, and not merely as part of the great literature in English, of which it is an outgrowth. This great literature is like a banyan-tree, whose branches bend down, and, striking the ground, take root and grow up as independent individuals.'[11] And the *History* reflects the growth of interest in, and re-interpretation of, the nineteenth century that had developed since 1930. Green in his concluding section mentions key contributors to this greater awareness of the past, as much historical and broadly cultural as specifically literary: Russel Ward, A. A. Phillips, Cecil Hadgraft, whose own history of Australian literature had appeared in 1960, Vincent Buckley, and others. A. A. Phillips in *Meanjin* (in essays later collected in *The Australian Tradition*) and other contributors to that journal including Manning Clark had elaborated the connections between literature and society Hancock had discerned. Vance Palmer, whose first essay on an Australian national literature had appeared in 1905, and Russel Ward had both explored the social historical bases of the 'legend' that linked the past to the present in a national consciousness. And in the criticism of Buckley and others a reaction against the democratic nationalist interpretation of literature and social history had emerged, so that Green in introducing his discussion of the period 'Self-Conscious Nationalism' could observe 'a tendency nowadays to underrate the

11 H. M. Green, *A History of Australian Literature: Pure and Applied*, two vols (Angus and Robertson, Sydney, 1961), p.xi. Subsequent page references, included in the text in parentheses, refer to this edition.

achievement of the third Period of Australian literature'.

In the *History* Green's sympathies are on the side of those who had expounded an Australian social and literary tradition. He confesses, in a footnote, of having made the mistake in his *Outline* of 'concentrating too much upon literature in its more aesthetic aspect'. This 'aesthetic' writing in earlier periods was thin and nostalgic in comparison with the 'rough spun' indigenous material: 'beyond the world of books ... material was accumulating that was to form the basis of important elements in the literature to be ... yarns and anecdotes ... old bush songs ... sketches ... recollections, diaries, memoirs ...' (pp.8–9). Following Russel Ward and other historians, Green perceives in the popular culture of the earlier nineteenth century the bases of an Australian tradition. In dealing with the nineties, his analysis seems to owe more to Hancock and his influence than to what had already been written in the *Outline:* 'In Australia, the spirit of the nineties and early nineteen-hundreds was a spirit ... which took the form in literary as well as in the social and political worlds, of a fervent democratic nationalism: it was based upon a broad social consciousness, a feeling of mutual relationship, that found its most characteristic expression in Lawson's doctrine of mateship' (p.348). Here, the characteristics of a distinctive Australian literature are defined in social and political terms, although the vaguer perceptions of the pre-Hancock *Outline* are retained also—'a kind of warmth and glow which seems to be a reflection of heat and light and the colour-effects of the landscape' (p.335). After his period of 'Self-Conscious Nationalism', Green abandons the attempt to relate social and literary developments closely. His promise to discuss national types and characteristics at the end is not fulfilled; perhaps because, as the introduction to the 'Modern Period' suggests, the democratic idealism of those earlier decades had become dissipated in cosmopolitanism and superficiality.

The *History of Australian Literature* most fully achieves the aims Barton had suggested nearly a century before. The mass of information it assembles on the press, the social groupings of writers, and the economics of authorship make it an important contribution to social and cultural history as well as a more narrowly literary study. So comprehensive, in fact, is Green that the broad interpretation he offers on social and literary relationships in the nineties is qualified by his recognition that there were many periodicals other than the *Bulletin,* writers like Brennan, Baylebridge, and Richardson as well as Lawson, Furphy, and Paterson, and the influences of the Celtic twilight as well as democratic nationalism on a host of minor writers. In these ways, the *History* avoids the stereotyped account of the development of a national literature that had been advanced by wedding Hancock's social analysis to literary history.

Now that the major role for the literary historian was no longer to provide the basic biographical and bibliographical information (as had been necessary in 1930), critical interpretations of the stereotypes appeared. Cecil Hadgraft's *Australian Literature* was published the year before Green's *History.* It concentrates on 'pure' literature and the methodological problems of establishing 'periods' that will reconcile the temper of a particular time with the literary works of distinction produced within it. Thus on his first period, Hadgraft writes: 'The name Colonial Period has been suggested for these seventy years. If poetry alone is considered then the name is pertinent. But to apply it to a period that includes Clarke's masterpiece seems almost defamatory. It is worth noting, however, that the literature of the period does not much express Australian ideals.'[12] For his second period 1880–1930 Hadgraft postulates two 'subperiods', 1880–1914 and 1900–1930, to account for the diversity of writing, some consciously nationalistic, some unconcerned with issues of nationality, and for the stubborn refusal of facts to fit the stereotypes neatly: 'the nineties, often thought of as prolific in valuable and representative works are really rather thin. Only two volumes of Lawson's tales and one of his verse and only one volume of Paterson's verse, for instance, appeared before 1900' (p.169).

A similar awareness that the courses of literary and social history did not always run parallel had already been expressed by G. A. Wilkes, in his essay 'The Eighteen Nineties':

> Was there a literary period 'the nineties' in Australia? The stages of Australian literary history have still to be determined. The present tendency is to fix them in accordance with existing political or economic divisions, so that a new age is dated from the gold-rushes of 1851, for instance, another from the nineties or the

12 Cecil Hadgraft, *Australian Literature: A Critical Account to 1995* (Heinemann, London, 1960), p.53.

> attainment of Federation in 1901, and another from the Great War of 1914–18. This is to determine periods of literary development by reference to non-literary criteria, and the boundaries that result are often fallacious.[13]

Wilkes sees the literature of the period having been distorted by the emphasis placed on democratic and nationalistic writing, which was not the only kind of writing, was not necessarily the best—and was certainly not the best because it was democratic. He combines a historian's responsibility to take account of all relevant evidence with a critic's attention to the interpretation of texts (for example, what Furphy was concerned with) and their artistic quality (the best of Lawson's work would not include his political verse).

'The Eighteen Nineties' is the first critically conscious discussion of the hybrid nature of literary history by an Australian critic, and the same awareness of conceptual and methodological problems is found in Wilkes's later *Australian Literature: A Conspectus,* (1969). Like Hadgraft's *Australian Literature* this admirably fulfils the literary historian's traditional role of providing a guide for the non-specialist, while establishing an interpretative framework that is critical of received and stereotyped formulations. By implication, the opening sentence which sees the continual interaction of two cultural strands—European and indigenous—as operating throughout the course of Australian literature, dismisses as irrelevant the riddle 'What is *Australian* literature' with which most previous historians had felt compelled to begin. There is no attempt at an explanation of literary developments in social terms, and wariness of such explanations is suggested by the observation on Neilson and McCrae that they remind us how 'literature at any period may escape parochialism through the artist with the vitality and perception to create his own imaginative world'.[14]

As well as these comprehensive literary histories there have been other studies which suggest that the earlier nineteenth century was not as discontinuous with the nineties and the twentieth century as earlier accounts had assumed. Historical studies such as George

13 *Arts* 1 (1958), 17–26, reprinted in Grahame Johnston, ed., *Australian Literary Criticism* (Oxford University Press, Melbourne, 1962), p.30.

14 G. A. Wilkes, *Australian Literature: A Conspectus* (Angus and Robertson, Sydney, 1969), p.50.

Nadel's *Australia's Colonial Culture* (1957), Michael Roe's *The Quest for Authority in Eastern Australia* (1965), Henry Mayer's *Marx and Engels in Australia* (1964), and the first volume of Manning Clark's *History of Australia* (1962) made it clear that Australia had a more complex and vital culture than the stereotype of generations awaiting the coming of the *Bulletin* allowed. It was, of course, a 'literary' culture in the fullest sense of that word, and most of its literature assumes most interest for us today in relation to that culture and its issues. Judith Wright in her *Preoccupations in Australian Poetry* (1965), which searches for correspondences between literary attitudes towards Australia and the historical social reality, also questions assumptions of cultural discontinuity. The dual vision she traces as a recurrent theme of poets throughout the nineteenth century and later sees Australia as a land of exile and a utopia simultaneously in each period, rather than each aspect representing a different stage of development.

Other reinterpretations of a deliberately provocative kind have followed. Humphrey McQueen's *A New Britannia* (1970) although not a literary study (despite its title) impinges on literary history because of his attack on Russel Ward's *The Australian Legend* (1958), the democratic egalitarianism of the social and literary tradition postulated by critics and historians in the forties and fifties, and his iconoclastic assault on its most 'representative' literary figure, Henry Lawson. After the appearance of the third volume of Manning Clark's *History* (1973), it seemed that any point in McQueen's diatribe against Australian society as capitalist, racist and militaristic which was relevant to Australian culture in the first half of the nineteenth century had found more substantial and responsible expression in Clark's analysis of the conflicts within this period and the ensuing dominance of bourgeois values in Australian society. Coral Lansbury's *Arcady in Australia* (1970) argues that recurrent images of Australia in literature before the 'nationalist' period were formed in fact in England and represented expectations there that the colonial writer here observed. The facts Coral Lansbury adduces have been questioned; her argument is partial, but it has the virtue of suggesting the complexity of social forces that enter into the forming of literary images and conventions. The image of idyllic possibilities of life in the Australian landscape is a persistent one that her study stimulatingly draws attention to—even though the stimulus might be to disagreement and qualification.

Barry Argyle's *The Australian Novel: 1830–1930* (1972) is also partial, reckless in its procedures, and desperate to assert a continuity in Australian literature and society of the violence and cruelty established in the convict era; but like the others it is most interesting in manifesting a concern to revalue the past, to discover continuities with the present, and to depart from received stereotypes (though both of these writers seem equally anxious to establish their own).

The attitudes of historians, literary or otherwise, towards culture in nineteenth century Australia have acquired a history of their own by now. The closing decades of the century especially provide a focal point for any general account of Australian culture, so that, today, we cannot look back directly to the nineteenth century itself without being conscious of the interpretations and evaluations of it that have been offered in the interval between its close and our own vantage point in time. The 'colonial' period probably seems more interesting now than it has in earlier decades this century. Its literature may not be granted any intrinsically higher value than it has been accorded previously, but when the different later perspectives are taken into account, the period raises interesting issues for cultural history. These issues concern the social ramifications of literature and culture generally, and here most later commentators have much in common with nineteenth century critics, who were similarly concerned with relating social and cultural development and with suggesting formative and causal connections. The basic assumptions here, and the forms of the arguments advanced, have not changed essentially over more than a century, and these are valuably rehearsed in Geoffrey Serle's *From Deserts the Prophets Come* (1973), the first book to provide a comprehensive cultural history of Australia.

One of the many virtues of Serle's outline is that, like Desmond Byrne's earlier analysis, it brings into the open assumptions which prefer to shelter shyly behind a hedge of organicist analogies. 'Culture is a highly perishable growth which, transplanted, cannot bloom as before', Serle himself writes, and quotes from Henry James's *Hawthorne* (1879), the now classic statement about the thinness of the soil in which the American novelist found himself planted.[15] The analogy, implicit in

15 Geoffrey Serle, *From Deserts the Prophets Come: The Creative Spirit in Australia 1788–1972* (Heinemann, Melbourne, 1973), p.52.

our uses of the word 'culture', between man's cultivation of the natural world and his 'cultivation' of what he has created himself begs many questions. Talk of 'transplanting', of tending slips or seedlings in the new soil in the expectation of a later harvest, follow naturally—such tropes come as second nature to the literati. But what sort of growth is being presupposed—qualitative or quantitative—and is there any essential relationship between the two? What ensures this growth—are 'natural' processes involved, is time essential? Or is this a pseudo-explanation that disguises only a confidence that what has happened elsewhere will happen here, eventually? What is the 'soil'—the people, all the people, or culturally conscious groups and individuals? James's emphasis on the need for 'an accumulation of history and custom ... a complexity of manners and types, to form a fund of suggestion for a novelist' has been very influential in later discussions of the relationship of the individual talent to a social tradition. It tells us a lot about the position James felt himself to be in, but he was clearly wrong about the writer in mid-nineteenth century America: not only was there Hawthorne, there were Emerson, Melville, Whitman, Dickinson, Poe, and others producing one of the most vital periods in any national literature in that century. These writers did not go unobserved in Australia, by Harpur, by Kendall, by many critics. As Frederick Sinnett intimated in 1856, in his essay 'The Fiction Fields of Australia', the Australian writer, deprived of such properties of romance as ivied ruins or even a house with seven gables, could better concentrate on the serious concerns of fiction.

The need for Australia to grow in scale and diversity and to move towards nationhood Serle also lists as important factors in the 'theory of cultural growth' he advances. Again, nineteenth century critics (for example, the historian Turner in 1898) had nominated these as essential for the eventual development of a national literature; but are these 'essential factors', do they contribute to an explanation of how culture 'grows', or do they provide a description of the social conditions against which it grew in America or Australia? If, as did the majority of Australian critics in the nineteenth century, we assume a natural evolution or growth at work, how do we explain the relative lack of 'progress' in the 1920s in Australia? Was the federationist and nationalist idealism which has been seen as the stimulus behind the literature of the preceding decades in advance of actual social conditions, and did this become apparent in the twenties? Are the arts really active agents in social change or are they, like seeds waiting for the right season, soil, and water, passively dependent on fertile social conditions? Serle himself sees not only 'growth' but 'maturity' as important, and argues that the delayed development in literature and painting in the twenties is related to the delayed development of national independence and to the continuation of cultural isolation. This is a succinct, accurate expression of one's 'sense' of the period but how is 'maturity' (as distinguished from 'growth', which is thereby assigned a more quantitative or descriptive role) determined: is *For the Term of His Natural Life,* by all accounts the finest novel of the 'colonial' period, necessarily a lesser achievement than the novels (all of them, or the best of them) that were produced at a more 'mature' stage of our cultural development?

A general pattern of links connecting literature and society in a causal way remains as elusive as ever. At one level there are the abstractions of 'society', 'culture', and 'literature', at another level the particular works of individual writers (in dealing with these critics and biographers can also contribute to our historical understanding, by bringing these abstractions to life in the case of their chosen subjects). Too much insistence on social and economic conditions, publishing outlets and markets, political ideology and established conventions can lead to a deterministic sense that the 'age' has produced the literature; at the other extreme too great an insistence on the autonomy of imaginative literature can ignore the involvement, direct or indirect, of writers with their society.

In confronting this dilemma and attempting to find a point of balance, Australian literary historians have thrown, in Barton's words, 'some light, from a new point of view, on our social history'. They have contributed to our awareness of the culture of the past and raised issues of its interpretation from a later vantage point in time and its relevance to the present. These are not issues that can be disposed of finally, because they reconstitute themselves for each generation. Beyond recording biographical and bibliographical facts, what literary historians do most successfully is register their generation's understanding of the past. In this way literary historians themselves have some claim on posterity: for later generations the best of them will become part of what they have described, part of literary history.

# Cultural Transmission and Australian Literature: 1788-1998

Although Dr Johnson had died four years before the First Fleet arrived, his loyal Boswell was still alive, as was Edward Gibbon, the author of *The Decline and Fall of the Roman Empire*. So also were many others whose names suggest that, for English literary culture, the later eighteenth century was an age (like all ages) of transition. Among these were James 'Ossian' McPherson, whose liberal 'translations' from the Gaelic in the 1770s had aroused curiosity about a mysteriously remote, heroic past, and Bishop Percy, whose *Reliques of Ancient British Poetry* (1765) had stimulated a revival of traditional popular forms. When Australia was settled, on the eve of the French Revolution, Robert Burns was still enjoying the first success of his Kilmarnock poems. A romantic 'revival' was already well underway, though what the later nineteenth century was to see as a romantic revolution still lay ahead, with William Wordsworth and Samuel Taylor Coleridge's *Lyrical Ballads* (1798), Walter Scott's *Lay of the Last Minstrel* (1805) and *Waverley* (1814), and Lord Byron's *Childe Harold* (first two cantos, 1812)—a revolution that was to have its impact on writers in the infant colonies.

The weight that literature contributed to the 'cultural baggage' accompanying the garrison and their convict charges is not known precisely, though the thousands of religious books the chaplain, Richard Johnson, brought with him suggest it was considerable. It certainly included copies of those key literary texts, the Bible, *The Book of Common Prayer* and hymnals; and most likely copies of Shakespeare

---

First published as 'Literature and Language' in Neville Meaney, ed., *Under New Heavens: Cultural Transmission and the Making of Australia* (Heinemann, Melbourne, 1989). This collection draws on the proceedings of the University of Sydney Bicentennial History Project, a series of inter-university and cross-disciplinary seminars held in 1986–87.

and *Paradise Lost*, or, if not actual copies, memories of these and other classic texts which helped form the thoughts of the better educated, such as Watkin Tench, on their arrival. The first dramatic production in the new colony was of Farquhar's *The Recruiting Officer*, and in his journal Ralph Clark recorded reading *The Tragedy of Douglas*. Robert Dixon has deduced from other journals that Adam Ferguson's *Essay on the History of Civil Society* and Oliver Goldsmith's *A History of the Earth and Animated Nature* must have been among the books brought by the First Fleet, and we could assume more works of natural history or philosophy.[1] As well as the religious literature (which included Swedenborgian tracts), practical handbooks, accounts of travels and voyages, and George Johnston's volumes of the *Spectator* there could also have been, in an age of rising literacy, almanacs, chapbooks, and other popular forms of information and amusement. Again, if there were not actual copies, there would have been memories, for by this time print was a familiar supplement to oral culture, even for illiterate auditors.

A hand printing press was included in the equipment provided for the settlement, even though no one could use it, and it was not until early in the next century that the first book (*New South Wales General Standing Orders*, 1802) and the first newspaper (the *Sydney Gazette*, 1803) were produced on it—well after accounts of the settlement and the first book written for an Australian audience (chaplain Richard Johnson's address to the inhabitants of the new colonies) had been published in London. But what arrived physically with the First Fleet was less important an influence on the written expression of experience in the new land than the literary culture that had been left behind and which continued to be transmitted. As the influences that Wordsworth, Coleridge, Scott and Byron were to have on writers in the Australian colonies demonstrate, cultural transmission was not (in one of the metaphors of the kind favoured by later literary historians) an initial planting of acorns from the mighty oak of English literature in an alien soil, but a continuing, and changing, process.

The concept of 'English literature' was still relatively recent.

1 Michael Richards, People, *Print and Paper: A Catalogue of a Travelling Exhibition Celebrating the Books of Australia, 1778–1988* (National Library of Australia, Canberra, 1988); Robert Dixon, *The Course of Empire: Neo-Classical Culture in New South Wales* (Oxford University Press, Melbourne, 1986), p.3.

Traditionally, and etymologically, literature referred to letters, or writing generically. In the universities it meant primarily the study of classical authors, whether poets and dramatists, or historians and philosophers. Since the Renaissance, it had been argued that writers in English had as much right to be seen as contributing in their language to the tradition of letters and poetry since the ancients as the most admired French and Italian models. Indeed, Sir Philip Sidney had claimed that English had literary advantages over the romance vernaculars. Later, Dryden and Johnson had argued that Shakespeare deserved to be ranked with the bards of other languages, ancient and modern, and Johnson's *Dictionary* was an endeavour consistent with such claims for England's national literature. Although, it went without saying, a gentleman did not need to study authors in his own tongue (unless he were interested in its origins), it was assumed he would appreciate Chaucer and Shakespeare, enjoy Fielding, Smollett and Sterne, and take a lively interest in contemporary authors. A galaxy of editors, including Johnson, had restored Shakespeare's text according to the principles of classical emendation and, out of an initially antiquarian set of interests, a historical sense of the national literary tradition emerged in the later eighteenth century. This was manifested in the three volume *History of English Poetry* by William Warton, poet laureate and Professor of History at Oxford, and in Johnson's *Lives of the English Poets* which postulated a canon and set the terms for much subsequent critical discussion (the publication of both was completed in 1781).

On the eve of thc machine printing age—another eve on which Australia was settled—the concept of English literature, in a sense approaching our understanding of literature as aesthetically valued imaginative writing, was established and being propagated by a flourishing periodical press and the production of histories, biographies and collections of reprints for an expanding reading public. Advances in print technology made the national literature popularly available, especially for education. Shakespeare, Milton and Dryden were seen as the pre-eminent figures in a literary tradition that expressed the common culture of a people sharing the same language, environment (climate was held to be particularly important) and historical development. Romantic perceptions of literature as the expression of the 'genius' of the 'race' were to intensify the patriotic appeal of this tradition throughout the nineteenth century. George Nadel's *Australia's Colonial Culture*

(1957) gives numerous examples from the 1820s of how the idea of literature was central to concerns about the colonies' cultural, as distinct from merely material, progress: 'Britain, it was frequently asserted, was great not because of her might but because of Shakespeare and Milton; her glory lay in her poets'.[2]

The excesses of bardolatry in the high Victorian period epitomised the perception of England's national literature at the height of imperial power. This was the perception institutionalised also in the Australian colonies, where cities were graced with statues of the Swan of Avon, public buildings and private mansions displayed scenes from his plays in stained glass and ceramic tile, suburbs had networks of streets named after characters and settings in them, and his works themselves, bound Bible-like, dignified respectable suburban parlours. Even when names for the federal capital were being considered, King O'Malley, who was generally credited with being responsible for its founding, preferred that it be called after Shakespeare, 'the greatest Englishman ever born' or failing that, Burns or even Longfellow.[3] Successful Scots ensured that their national poet, Burns was memorialised as often as the Bard; and expressed their love of Scott by bestowing names like Abbotsford, Ivanhoe and Waverley on suburbs.

Whatever books had arrived with the First Fleet, it was soon apparent that the ideal of the mother country's literature (selectively perceived by English, Scots, and Irish settlers) had been imported to the new country. But so, simultaneously, had the idea of a national literature itself. If the colonies were to advance, if expectations of a future nation were to be fulfilled, then literature would have to take root and flourish in them. Admittedly it would be in the same language and forms as English literature, but it would reflect Antipodean differences in the key cultural determinants of climate, environment and social development.

2 Nadel, p.73.

3 *Commonwealth Parliamentary Debates*, vol. LXV, p. 1809, 7 August 1912; O'Malley's speech at the Dedication ceremony on 12 March 1913, published in *Concerning Canberra: The Christening and Dedication of Australia's National Capital and Its Dire Neglect* (Excell Press, Melbourne, 1936) p.9. It is in this speech that O'Malley refers to Shakespeare as the 'greatest Englishman ever born'; O'Malley was apparently disappointed when his Cabinet colleagues declined his alternative suggestion of Burns and Longfellow. See A. R. Hoyle *King O'Malley: 'The American Bounder'* (Macmillan, South Melbourne, 1981) p.120.

## Neoclassicism and Romanticism

Most of the writing produced during the first half century of settlement in New South Wales and Van Diemen's Land was not literature in the more recent and educationally institutionalised sense, but chronicles, journals of exploration, and handbooks for prospective immigrants, which were published mainly in London. Yet, as some of the more original literary history of recent years has shown, literary preconceptions could enter documentary writing. Paul Carter observes of Major Thomas Mitchell, the mid-nineteenth century explorer, that he

> ... arranged his landscapes to meet certain literary rather than geographical criteria ... for aesthetic, rather than scientific reasons, he treated the mountains and rivers as so many 'topoi' [conventional topics] in an epic poem, as familiar themes about which to cultivate his own reflections.[4]

As a translator of the *Lusiads*, Mitchell was an exceptionally literary explorer—though one who instructed the surveyors under him to retain Aboriginal names for features whenever these could be established[5]—and the Portuguese national epic provided him with a model for his account of his expeditions, and affected his observations. His literariness, though, was only an extreme instance of a more general tendency. Leichhardt's Port Essington log, for example, was thought by King to be too routine and he edited it, adding the requisite classical allusions and expressions of elevated sentiment to make it accord better with readers' expectations.[6]

In *The Course of Empire* (1986), Robert Dixon observes that

> From about 1815—the year of Governor Macquarie's spectacular progress through Cox's Pass to Bathurst—it seemed increasingly possible that Australia, too [like the United States], might become

4 Paul Carter, 'River of Dreams', *Age Monthly Review* 2 (September 1982), 5–6.

5 C. W. Salier, 'Thomas Livingston Mitchell', *Journal of the Royal Australian Historical Society* 17 (1931), p.37.

6 Paul Carter, 'Major Mitchell and Triangles of Life', *Scripsi* 4 (November 1986), 213–50; *The Road to Botany Bay* (Faber, London, 1987), pp.99–135.

> a continental empire. By that time the composition of journals of inland exploration had become a matter of negotiation between the geographical facts of the country traversed and the requirements of an increasingly epic form.[7]

These epic conventions, coming down through poetic tradition from Lucretius and Virgil, were also ideological: they presupposed a world-historical view of the ever-westward course of civilisation as empires rose, flourished, decayed, and the process began all over again. As Adam Smith has it in *The Wealth of Nations*, a nation passed through four stages: the nomadic, pastoral, agricultural and commercial before returning to barbarism. The explorer seeking the site of some future Athens or Rome, reversed these stages as he moved westward from the commercial centre, through agricultural then pastoral districts into the interior where the Aborigines pursued their primitive way of life.

The same topoi, or commonplaces, about 'the history of civil society' were shared by those more manifestly literary figures, the early colonial poets. The closing lines of W. C. Wentworth's non-prize winning poem at Cambridge, *Australasia* (1826) have often been quoted this century, usually with amusement at what seems their precocious bluster.

> And, oh Britannia! shouldst thou cease to ride
> Despotic Empress of old Ocean's tide;— ...
> May this, thy last-born infant,—then arise,
> To glad thy heart, and greet thy parent eyes:
> And Australasia float, with flag unfurled,
> A NEW BRITANNIA IN ANOTHER WORLD!

Yet the topos of the inexorable decline and fall of empire, as conventional as Wentworth's heroic couplets, justifies any apparent presumption on the part of the 'currency lad' poet. The consolation he offers for Britain's

7 Dixon, pp.79–80. This section is heavily indebted to Dixon's researches, and those of other members of the 'Sydney school' of literary history, including G. A. Wilkes and G. A. Turnbull's editions of Charles Tompson's *Wild Notes, From the Lyre of a Native Minstrel* (Sydney University Press, Sydney, 1973) and Wilkes's *The Colonial Poets* (Angus and Robertson, Sydney, 1974). See also Richard White's review of Dixon, 'History's Epic', *Age Monthly Review* 6 (September 1986), 7–19.

inevitable decline, the corollary that Australia will assume its imperial role, is an assertion of British-Australian loyalty.

Whereas at first most colonial writing in book form was documentary and published in England (as later most Australian novels were also published in London or Edinburgh), contributors to local newspapers and magazines embraced a very elevated conception of literature.[8] Despite apologies throughout the century for the colonies being at an early stage in their development, and necessarily preoccupied with material considerations, locally published verse was anything but 'primitive' or naive. Michael Massey Robinson, a convict commissioned by Macquarie to deliver patriotic odes on public occasions, was proclaimed by the Sydney Gazette to be 'the laureate bard of the colony'. His 'ODE for the Queen's Birthday, 1816' celebrates in very mannered couplets the crossing of the Blue Mountains, and predicts the prosperity soon to follow.

> Where yon Blue Mountains, with tremendous Brow,
> Frown on the humbler Vales that wind below,
> Where scarcely human footsteps ever trac'd
> The craggy Cliffs that guard the ling'ring Waste;
> O'er the wild Surface of the Western Plains,
> Aerst the lorn Range of Isolated Trains:—
> Where from the Birth of Time the slumbering Soil
> Had born no Traces of the Peasant's Toil—
> Behold, where Industry's encourag'd Hand
> Has chang'd the lurid Aspect of the Land;
> With Verdure cloathed the solitary Hills,
> And pour'd fresh Currents from the limpid Rills;
> Has shed o'er darken'd Glades a social Light,
> And BOUNDLESS REGIONS OPEN TO OUR SIGHT!

This passage could serve well to illustrate an orthodox view of the colonial artist as lacking the appropriate diction and forms (or the

8 Elizabeth Webby, 'Writers, Printers, Readers: The Production of Australian Literature to 1855', in Laurie Hergenhan, ed., *The Penguin New Literary History of Australia* (Penguin, Ringwood, 1988), pp.113–25 makes the point that most 'imaginative' literature in the period was published in Australia, the 'non-imaginative' in London.

palette and technique in the case of painters) to render the actual with fidelity. While Robinson names the Blue Mountains, there is nothing in his categorising Augustan diction to locate his setting in the Antipodes. One legacy of romanticism was the assumption that literatures in new societies developed like individuals: after an initial imitative phase, followed by adolescent assertiveness, came eventual maturity and confident individuality. According to this assumption Robinson's clearly imitative ode exemplifies colonial artistic immaturity (though if we are to employ such psychological criteria, it is also paradoxically quite sophisticated). Scholars who, rather than dismissing such poems as imitative, have asked what they were imitative of—for neo-classical poetry was by definition imitative—have revealed some of the complexities of cultural transmission and adaptation as they affected colonial poets.

Since the Renaissance, English poets had aspired to create epics in the vernacular that would provide their literature with its equivalents of Homer and Virgil. American and Australian poets imbued with neo-classical understandings of imitation were aspiring to record their country's part in that universal history epics represented. By the early nineteenth century there had been a number of long patriotic odes celebrating the discovery, settlement and future of America as the culmination of history. These could serve very aptly as models for patriotic Australian versifiers with epic visions and ambitions; and Robinson's ode begins not, as quoted above, with the approach to the Blue Mountains and the revelation from their westward slopes of God's providence, but with Columbus's discovery of the new world.

The first collection of verse from a 'currency lad' was Charles Tompson's *Notes of a Native Minstrel* (1826). As some of his contemporaries were unkind enough to observe, the young Tompson's poems were also highly imitative. His 'Black Town', located where Governor Macquarie had established an institution for Aborigines is, like Goldsmith's *The Deserted Village*, an elegiac contemplation of a once idyllic social setting that has suffered the depredations of time and change. It is filled with formal apostrophe as the poet contemplates the ruins.

> Ill-fated hamlet; from each tott'ring shed,
> Thy sable inmates perhaps for ever fled

(Poor restless wand'rers of the woody plain!
The skies their covert—nature their domain)

And he is lead, with dreadful inevitability, to a closing meditation on that great commonplace, the vanity of human wishes.

Thus, shall Man's proudest, noblest projects fade,
And, with their founder, in the dust be laid;
Th'imperial palace and the lowly cot
Alike must share this universal lot,
And bow before th'all conquering scythe of Time—
Such was proud Ilion's fate and such (alas!) is thine!

As with Robinson and Wentworth, the conventions adopted and the allusions invoked are not those of English poetry alone, but also of that longer tradition of 'universal' poetry and history, which had its source in Homer singing of the fall of 'Ilion', and which Australian poets were now joining.

Today the most highly esteemed of later colonial poets is Charles Harpur, rather than Henry Kendall or Adam Lindsay Gordon, who were more highly regarded in their lifetimes and well into this century; yet most of Harpur's considerable output of verse, and some of his miscellaneous prose, have only become available because of the recent attention of scholars—a telling example of how literary history is continually in the process of being constructed, or reconstructed.[9] The son of convict parents, Harpur began writing in the 1830s. He was aware of the English romantics, as well as their illustrious predecessors back to Homer (some of whose passages he 'translated'). His political

9 Current recognition of Harpur as a major writer of the colonial period is indicated by the following: the chapter on him in Judith Wright, *Preoccupations in Australian Poetry* (Oxford University Press, Melbourne, 1965); Adrian Mitchell, ed., *Charles Harpur* (Sun Books, Melbourne, 1973); Leonie Kramer, 'Imitation and Originality in Australian Colonial Poetry: The Case of Charles Harpur', *Yearbook of English Studies* 13 (1983), 116–32; Elizabeth Perkins, ed., *The Poetical Works of Charles Harpur* (Angus and Robertson, Sydney, 1984); Michael Ackland, ed., *Charles Harpur: Selected Poetry and Prose* (Penguin, Ringwood, 1986); Paul Kane, 'Charles Harpur and the Myth of Origins', *Australian Literary Studies* (13 October, 1987), 146–60. Perkins's edition of the complete poems runs to over one thousand pages.

interests as a republican and a democrat led him to publish satires and lampoons, formal public verses and parodies: and in longer, philosophically ambitious poems he donned the prophetic mantle of the native bard. Some of these like 'The Bush Fire' and 'A Kangaroo Hunt' employ 'local colour' subjects common to colonial poets and painters.

The longer poem which has received most attention since it first appeared in the *Sydney Weekly Register* in 1845 (in a shorter version; like most of his work it was constantly revised) was 'The Creek of the Four Graves'. This 'settler's tale of olden times', as the first line announces it to be, is about a party of five who set forth in search of 'new streams and wilder pastures'. Attempting to cross 'barrier mountains', presumably the Blue Mountains, they are attacked by Aborigines in the night and only the leader, Egremont, escapes to tell the tale. From its opening the poem invokes a mélange of styles through Egremont's chivalric name, the Chaucerian or Malorian way in which his party is described as 'meetly equipt', the echoing from Milton's 'Lycidas' of 'fresh fields and pastures new'. For his contemporaries, as much as for later readers, such heavily allusive diction could appear awkward and pretentious. But if aesthetic judgement is postponed sufficiently to consider the intentions behind Harpur's self-conscious literariness, these, like those of earlier colonial poets, prove revealing for the uses he was trying to make of the received tradition.

As Egremont's party makes its way westward (so following the 'course of empire'), they discover a creek lying between them and the 'new Appenines'—a naming that suggests the possibility of a coming civilisation. Whereas Robinson's, Wentworth's or Tompson's generic descriptions do not seek to number the streaks of the wattle, Harpur presents the creek with a particularity that is more romantic. It

> ... ran, shaded up
> With boughs of the wild willow, hanging mixed
> From either bank, or duskily befringed
> With upward tapering, feathery swamp-oaks—
> The sylvan eyelash always of remote
> Australian waters ...

By this creek the party camps for the night, and as the sun set

O what words, what hues
Might paint the wild magnificence of view
That opened westward! Out, extending, lo,
The heights rose crowding, with their summits all
Dissolving, as it seemed, and partly lost
In the exceeding radiancy aloft:
And thus transfigured, for awhile they stood
Like a great company of Archeons, crowned
With burning diadems, and tented o'er
With canopies of purple and of gold!

A Miltonic magnificence apotheosises the local grazier and his hands who, in a memorable, Platonising conceit, seem at dusk

To hang like mighty pictures of themselves
In the still chambers of some vaster world.

Set close to the beginnings of civilisation in Australia, before the pastoral fringe of society had extended beyond the Blue Mountains, the poem implies, by allusion, that it is also set at a phase of development that corresponds to the universal origins of 'civil society'. In the passage quoted above, 'Archeons' conflates the root of 'ancient' with the term for an early form of classical Greek government (it also has Hermetic associations). Elsewhere, Homeric epithets and periphrases abound—Egremont has his 'death-dealing tube' to pit against the Aborigines' 'heavy clubbed nulla-nullas'—and local customs and diction are assimilated to epic convention: the party's heroic feast of broiled rashers is served on 'quadrants from an ample damper cut', and washed down with 'cannikins' of tea. While invoking the English literary tradition from Chaucer on, but drawing (most heavily from Milton) on those elements that related this tradition in turn to 'universal poetry, Harpur is not attempting to see Australian landscape through 'English spectacles'—as later critics assumed colonial poets were—but to embrace that wider conception of poetry that, since Aristotle, has seen the poet as superior to both the historian and the philosopher, and the epic as the ultimate form, the foundation of any national literature.

Harpur engages with his lofty poetic purpose in meditative passages. Egremont, on watch in this sublime landscape, contemplating the transfiguring effects of moonlight (the romantic elements are accumulating), considers the 'subtle interfusion' of human nature with

> … all serene and beautiful and bright
> And lasting things of Nature.

This transcendentalist, and all but explicitly Wordsworthian, apprehension of a correspondence between man's higher nature and permanent natural forms is disturbed by the attack of the Aborigines, after which the poet himself reflects on how

> … this lovely world hath been
> Accursed for ever by the bloody deeds
> Of its prime Creature-Man. Erring or wise,
> Savage or civilised, still hath he made
> This glorious residence, the Earth, a Hell …

A traditionally Christian, and Miltonic, awareness of the problem of evil is here in conflict with romantic 'natural supernaturalism'. Regardless of Harpur's ultimate success, or not, in resolving such opposed metaphysics, his poetic engagement with them provides a fascinating instance of his endeavour to adapt a complicated set of influences to his own familiar landscape. In the poem's historical setting this becomes another lost Eden, the site for re-enacting the primal fratricide of Cain and Abel. Through the encounter between settlers and Aborigines, the creek finds its name, and the Muse a habitation in New South Wales. The site passes into the record of history: 'for many changeful years' travellers would come across the four graves covered with leaves

> from the old trees which there
> Moaned the same leafy dirges that had caught
> The heed of dying Ages …

In its opposing of Wordsworthian to Miltonic elements, 'The Creek of the Four Graves' represents a more general transition from the neo-classical influences on earlier figures, like Robinson and Tompson, to the romantic and Victorian influences on Kendall, Gordon and others in the second half of the century. The poem's explicit concern with the

Adamic process of naming, of assimilating a new world to the language of 'universal' literature and history, also makes it typical of most other colonial poetry; indeed most other colonial writing, including the journals of the explorers. In 1839, Ralph Waldo Emerson had written: 'What shall be the substance of my shrift? Adam in the garden. I am to new name all the beasts in the field and gods in the sky'.[10] Yet in Australia, as in Emerson's United States, new naming had been mainly old naming when it came to identifying settlements and topographical features.

Poetic contemplation of Australia as another possible Eden or Arcady repeated tropes that had already been employed in that other new world. Awareness of the United States as a model for Australia's cultural maturation, its social progress and even its political development was widespread among the colonial intelligentsia and reading public. From the 1820s on, American writers, pre-eminently Washington Irving, Fenimore Cooper ('the American Scott') and William Cullen Bryant, were becoming internationally recognised and their works passed into circulation here. Increasingly, American writers and the idea of an American literature were to provide an alternative set of influences; these may ultimately have derived from Europe (through a European settlement more diverse in its origins than Australia's), but they had already been assimilated and modified to an extent that could be seen by those so disposed as anticipating similar developments in the Antipodes.

Arguments for the necessity of a distinctive national literature had intensified in the United States following Sydney Smith's imperious question in the *Edinburgh Review* (which, like other British quarterlies, was read here) in 1818: 'But why should Americans write books, when a six week passage brings them, in their own tongue, our sense, science and genius?'. In the early nineteenth century, America's lack of romantic 'associations'—the complete dearth of ruined castles was most often instanced—seemed to exclude it as a fitting scene for literature. But following E. T. Channing, who had lectured Emerson, Thoreau and Oliver Wendell Holmes at Harvard, it could be claimed for American

10 Ralph Waldo Emerson, *Journals*, entry for 18 October, 1839, reprinted in Stephen E. Whicher, ed., *Selections from Ralph Waldo Emerson* (Houghton Mifflin, Boston, 1957), p.139.

literature that 'Its charm is its nativeness', and that the lack of the traditional, but also feudal and decadent, properties of romance testified to the republic's social and moral superiority.[11] This classical defence could also accommodate a native romanticism: while it enjoyed the lack of feudal 'associations', the United States had natural literary 'resources' of its own that put Europe's to shame.

W. H. Gardiner wrote in the *North American Review* in 1822

> ... we are not ambitious that scenes so purely imaginary should be located on this side of the Atlantic ... we have no particular longing after this species of American castle building ... The truth is there never was a nation whose history, studied with that view, affords better or more abundant matter of romantic interest than ours.[12]

Or, as Samuel L. Knapp put the second point more forcefully in his *Lectures on American Literature* in 1829: 'What are the Tibers and the Scamanders measured by the Missouri and the Andes?'[13] These rhetorical stances were commonplaces before they received their most memorable form in Emerson's *The American Scholar* (1837)

> I ask not for the great, the remote, the romantic, what is doing in Italy or Arabia; what is Greek art or Provencal minstrelsy; I embrace the common, I sit at the feet of the familiar, the low.... We have listened too long to the courtly muses of Europe.[14]

and in *The Poet* in (1844)

> America is a poem in our eyes; its ample geography dazzles the imagination, and it will not wait long for metres.[15]

Such assertions, echoed in Whitman's *Leaves of Grass* (1855), itself a

11 Edward Tyrrell Channing, from *The North American Review* (1816), reprinted in Richard Ruland, ed., *The Native Muse: Theories of American Literature: Volume I* (Dutton, New York, 1976), pp.89–90.
12 W. H. Gardiner, from *The North American Review* (1822), in Ruland, p.189.
13 Samuel A. Knapp, *Lectures on American Literature* (1829), in Ruland, p.171.
14 Emerson, in Whicher, p.79.
15 Emerson, in Whicher, p.238.

potent influence on some Australian poets (especially Bernard O'Dowd later in the century), re-echoed in Australia, where awareness of American writing has been documented from quite early in the century. In 1838, that great admirer of the United States as a political model, John Dunmore Lang, reprinted William Ellery Channing's lecture calling for an American declaration of literary independence, *The Importance and Means of a National Literature* (1830), in his Sydney paper the *Colonist.* Harpur addressed two sonnets to Emerson, and grappled with the ideas of the New England transcendentalists, as well as with those of their romantic European predecessors—a perhaps significant difference between these being that, to European eyes, the Americans' 'Nature', like the Australian bush, was a wilderness. The direct influence of Poe on Kendall and Gordon, and of Hawthorne's historical romances on Marcus Clarke, have been pointed out, and such examples could be multiplied.[16] But more important than American influences on individual writers in Australia was a widely-held (though not uncontested) view that the United States had developed a literature which, while it was still in the same language, was distinctively its own. This could be seen as the prototype of what eventually, but inevitably, would evolve here.

### Romance and Realism

The earliest sustained critical assessment of a body of local writing is Frederick Sinnett's 'The Fiction Fields of Australia' which appeared in the *Journal of Australasia* in 1856. Writing after the gold rushes, which had intensified and diversified cultural contacts with the northern hemisphere, Sinnett opens with a playful consideration of the view that Australia's lack of romantic 'associations' prevents writers from finding indigenous subjects appropriate for literature. Like American critics before him, and Henry James after him, Sinnett mockingly laments this lack of 'associations' before proclaiming the romance of Australia itself as a fitting subject for fiction. Australia has ample local colour'; the challenge for writers was to subordinate it to a 'picture of universal life

16 On poetic influences generally, see Vivian Smith, 'Poetry', in Leonie Kramer, ed., *The Oxford History of Australian Literature* (Oxford University Press, Melbourne, 1981), pp.271–426; on American influences, especially Hawthorne's on Clarke, see Michael Wilding, ed., *Marcus Clarke* (University of Queensland Press, St Lucia, 1976), pp.xv–xvi; xxiv

... modified by Australian externals', instead of producing 'books of travel in disguise'. Sinnett's judicious balancing of universal and local criteria in engaging with the troublesome issue of the relationship between a new national literature and the linguistic parent culture was clearly informed by American precedents. But while the declarations of American cultural independence had been made in the predominantly romantic first half of the nineteenth century, the comparable calls in Australia came in a period of reaction against romanticism, or 'romance' as Sinnett lightly disparages it, after the middle of the century. While an admirer of Scott, Sinnett sees the literary imagination's fascination with distant times and exotic places as a phase that has been superseded by the realism of Dickens and Thackeray. Among colonial fictions he prefers Catherine Helen Spence's *Clara Morison.* for its imaginative depiction of human nature in an unobtrusively detailed South Australian setting.[17]

The very year Sinnett's essay appeared, George Eliot, in the *Westminster Review*, extended Ruskin's term 'realism' (in *Modern Painters*, also 1856) to the discussion of literature and Emerson used it of Swift's style. Realism, or a range of 'realisms', predominantly in fiction, characterised the new (and for many disturbing) literary developments in Europe, the United States and, by the last decades of the century when a generation of predominantly native-born writers emerged, Australia. Realism was not a simple, single movement, as the names of some of the major, influential figures identified with it (and often, confusingly, associated simultaneously with naturalism) will suggest: Flaubert and Zola, Turgenev and Dostoievsky, George Eliot and Henry James, Ibsen and Verga... Nor was it a sudden, unprecedented departure from preceding conventions, not at any rate for writing in English. Such 'colonial romancers' as Marcus Clarke, Rolf Boldrewood, Ada Cambridge and Rosa Praed frequently shared settings and styles with writers committed to unillusioned representations of contemporary Australian reality. Romance and realism co-existed, often even in the work of the same writer who, with a change of mood, could vary documentary reportage with melodramatic improbabilities or sentimental

17 Cecil Hadgraft, ed., *The Fiction Fields of Australia* (University of Queensland Press, St Lucia, 1966); reprinted in John Barnes, ed., *The Writer in Australia: A Collection of Literary Documents: 1856 to 1964* (Oxford University Press, Melbourne, 1969).

evasions. The realism that reacted against what the Sydney *Bulletin* in 1881 called 'romantic ideality' itself provoked reactions against its own presumed amorality and fascination with the sordid. The decades of reaction against romance were also the decades of aestheticism, of French symbolism, the Celtic Twilight, and the popular 'new romances' of Ouida, Rider Haggard and Robert Louis Stevenson. These international movements and controversies were reflected locally and entered tendentiously into different views of Australian literature as the colonies moved towards Federation.

In 1898, Macmillan of London published the substantial *Dictionary of Austral English* by E. E. Morris, Professor of Modern Languages and Literatures at the University of Melbourne. Conscious that his fellow-Englishmen might imagine that the title could refer only to slang, Morris wrote in his introduction that

> The phrase Australian English includes something much wider than slang. Those who, speaking the language of Shakespeare, of Milton, and of Dr Johnson, came to various parts of Australasia, found a Flora and Fauna waiting to be named in English ... Since the days when 'Adam gave names to all the cattle and to the fowl of the air and to every beast of the field' ... never were so many names called for ... Much of Australian nomenclature is due to 'the man in the bush'—more precise address not recorded.[18]

Morris related the Adamic process inherent in much earlier writing (and of which Harpur's 'The Creek of the Four Graves' has already provided an example) to a theory of semantic change. English, as well as receiving additions from Aboriginal and Maori words, took on different meanings in Australasia because of the different referents. As with French in Canada, or Spanish and Portuguese in Latin America, the mother tongue effectively became another language. Because of the totally different environment this semantic shift was even more pronounced with English in Australasia than in North America; as an example, Morris gave the even by then hoary instance of what Christmas connotes in the Antipodes.

The stimulus for Morris's lexicographical labours had come from

18 Edward A. Morris, *A Dictionary of Austral English* (1898; facsimile edn, Sydney University Press, 1972), p.xii.

James Murray's request for Australasian entries for the *Oxford English Dictionary*. Like Murray's, Morris' work was compiled on historical principles and he drew on literature in its older and wider sense: books of natural history, explorers' journals, and newspapers of the day, as well as belles lettres. Boldrewood, Clarke, Gordon, Kendall—most of the representatives of the national literature as perceived from Melbourne, or London—provided Morris with sources, but he also drew on Henry Lawson, whose first separate collections of verse and prose appeared only two years previously. Sensitivity to his audience's presumed prejudice that 'Austral' English could comprise only slang perhaps led Morris to give disproportionate attention to botanical and zoological terms, at the expense of the colloquialisms that were being exploited by contemporary 'local colour' realists.

Morris, President of Melbourne's Shakespeare Society (which, with nearly five hundred members, boasted of being the largest in the world),[19] was also literary editor of the *Australasian Critic* (1890–91), a general review edited by Professors T. G. Tucker and Baldwin Spencer of the University of Melbourne. An unsigned article on 'The Characteristics of Australian Literature' in the November 1890 issue has been attributed to him. Taking issue with Clarke's claim that the beginnings of a national school of poetry had been made by Gordon, the writer of the article queried whether a 'too conscious attempt to be Australian' is likely to be productive because, all too often, authors 'are not content to let the country and the nation be the setting in which the subject is framed' but want to make them the subject. In the December issue of the *Critic*, another unsigned article attributed to T. G. Tucker, Professor of Classical and Comparative Philology at the University, appeared on 'Australian Short Stories'. The writer found their 'Australianity' obtrusive and feared that English readers would form the impression that

> big cities are unknown in Australia; that the population consists of squatters, diggers, stock-riders, shepherds, and bushrangers; that the superior residences are weatherboard homesteads with wide verandahs, while the inferior ones are huts and tents.

19 Ken Stewart, 'The Colonial Literati in Sydney and Melbourne', *New Literature Review* 6 (n.d.), 8–19.

The writer's embarrassment at the impressions English readers of Australian short stories might form of the country are best appreciated if we note that this was written in 'Marvellous Melbourne'.

Whatever the strictures of the Melbourne literati against 'too conscious nationalism', and their misgivings about unrepresentative images of the national life drawn from the bush and the past, they contributed greatly to institutionalising the idea of a national literature. Predominantly Englishmen who had come to the colony in their youth, they were committed to the belief of the morally elevating and socially improving role of literature which is now synonymous with the name of Matthew Arnold. They had replicated the societies, the reviews, even the bohemia of their idealised literary metropolis, London, and had granted local writing a place on their map of English literature. Indeed, they had canonised writers like Clarke and Gordon through their biographical, critical and literary historical studies (including Morris's *Dictionary*) but as Anglo-Australians still drawing on and contributing to the mother culture. Apart from Patchett Martin, they could not muster any enthusiasm for Banjo Paterson (not while, as Professor Tucker wrote, Homer waited on the shelf), Henry Lawson and the new school of Sydney *Bulletin* balladists and sketch writers: nor, for that matter, could James Smith as critic for the *Argus* muster enthusiasm for the '9 x 5' sketches of the Heidelberg school of painters.

The perception of Australian literature from pre-Federation Melbourne was not necessarily shared by the other colonies or by a later and native-born generation. The Sydney *Bulletin*, which has been central to accounts of the literary nationalism of the 1880s and 1890s, provides the chief example of a different set of cultural attitudes in the same period. Associated with the paper was a majority of the better-known, and mostly native-born, writers who have subsequently been seen, and who saw themselves, as establishing a literature that was not Anglo-Australian, like that promoted by Melbourne's literati, but aggressively national and distinct, a new beginning. By now the subject of numerous interpretations and revisions, the *Bulletin* as a weekly intended for, and largely written by, a national audience was necessarily eclectic. Any generalisation about its character is open to exception. It was radical, republican and democratic, but also racist, misogynistic and chauvinistic; it fostered a popular literature, especially in the ballad and short story, yet also published much that was conventionally literary, and even imported. Such eclecticism makes the *Bulletin* of the period fascinating for its apparently contradictory roles of being the most nationalistic of late colonial papers and also a conduit for contemporary European and American culture. The nature of this transmission though was not a passive reception of overseas influences, but a considered selection of those thought to be most pertinent to local circumstances.

The editor most responsible for determining the policies of the paper and setting its characteristic tone was J. F. Archibald, ardent republican and rabid Anglophobe, who discovered and encouraged Lawson, Paterson, Price Warung and a host of others. Archibald was not only a nationalist appalled by British Philistine 'cant' in the colonies, but also so ardent a Francophile that he changed his given names, John Feltham, to Jean François and concocted a more appropriate lineage for himself. Editorially, he enthused over Zola, Maupassant and other contemporary French writers, while deploring the decadence of metropolitan English culture. Translations of Maupassant stories appeared regularly during the early years of his editorship, as one of the kinds of models it offered aspiring contributors. With another Francophile, A. G. Stephens, who joined the paper in 1894 and became its literary editor, Archibald encouraged readers to take an interest in the most stimulating current thought and writing overseas, not merely in England.[20] In the mid-1890s, the Bulletin Book Exchange, a service to readers, listed titles by Dostoievsky and Tolstoi, George Eliot, Mark Twain and W. D. Howells, Olive Schreiner, Engels, Lombroso and Nordau, and C. H. Pearson's *National Life and Character.* Tolstoi, Twain and Howells were represented by a dozen titles each (though Ouida scored highest with twenty-seven, and Henry Kingsley was respectably represented also).[21] From the late 1890s, Christopher Brennan, under Stephens's encouragement, began contributing articles

20 Douglas Jarvis, 'The Development of an Egalitarian Poetics in the *Bulletin*, 1880–1890', *Australian Literary Studies* 10 (May 1931), 22–34; 'Lawson, the *Bulletin* and the Short Story', *Australian Literary Studies* 11 (May 1983), 58–66.

21 Grace Diana Ailwood-Keel, 'Homespun Exotic: Australian Literature 1880–1910: A Study of Writing in Australia in the 'Nationalist Period', with Particular Emphasis on Overseas Influence', PhD thesis, University of Sydney, 1978.

on classical writers, the French symbolists and German romantics. Although contributions on such topics from the least nationalistic, and most erudite, of Australian poets of the time do not sit easily with the simple stereotype of the *Bulletin* as 'the bushman's Bible', they indicate its editors' commitment to widening that awareness beyond the colonial inheritance of English culture.

Since the mid-century gold rushes on both sides of the Pacific, direct cultural contact with the United States had increased enormously. American books, magazines, newspapers (some in special 'steamer' editions for the Pacific area), entertainers and, as they were seen by some, political agitators had followed the miners from California. In the decades following the rushes, the vernacular 'local colour' realism and dialect humour of American writers, Bret Harte, Mark Twain, and Joaquin Miller especially, were reprinted and imitated in the Australian press. In 1879, the year before the Sydney *Bulletin* was founded, the San Francisco *Evening Bulletin* observed that

> It is an interesting study to notice the phases of English literature as they have developed outside Great Britain. The modes and habits of thought are different. Writers of all grades are insensibly influenced by their environment. The American novelist treats his subject from a different standpoint to the English author. He sees men, women and life under other aspects. Let any person also take up a work of fiction from the pen of an Australian and he will be struck with its distinctive features. Still stronger do these appear with journalism, as one of the fields of English literature is considered. The English newspaper appears dry and heavy to the average American. The American treats its topics with too much levity for the genuine John Bull. The Australian journalist is a cross between the two, but his writing is marked by a flavour peculiar to the conditions by which he is surrounded.

The Sydney *Bulletin*'s editorial tone, and its policy of fostering vernacular sketches, stories and ballads, had much in common with the 'new journalism' of the United States, especially that of the West Coast. Archibald had originally modelled much of the paper's format on American practice. According to Stephens, he had taken the name from the San Francisco *Evening Bulletin* and ideas from other papers in that city: the *News-Letter*, the *Argonaut*, and Ambrose Bierce's *Illustrated Wasp*. Archibald also admired Dana's New York *Sun*, and from that city Livingston Hopkins was enticed to become the *Bulletin*'s most celebrated cartoonist, 'Hop'. Features to be inextricably associated in local readers' minds with the Sydney paper, such as the miscellaneous observations of the typical Australian contributed as 'pars', or its blunt, often insulting 'Answers to correspondents', can be found in earlier West Coast papers.

After the turn of the century, on his way to England or shortly after his arrival there, Henry Lawson wrote a sketch entitled 'The Sydney *Bulletin*' which was intended for English readers. In it, he has Archibald advising a potential contributor, the archangel Gabriel: 'Every man has at least one story in him... Write as simply as you can ... Don't strain after effect ... Write carefully and write only when you have something to tell the people ...'.[22] As a policy for fostering a national literature (as distinct from observing, as Melbourne's literati were, an Anglo-Australian evolutionary step towards it), Archibald's advice joined with manifestos and movements in Europe and the United States that preferred 'fidelity' and 'verisimilitude' in subject and language to what was seen as literary 'artificiality'. But the tensions between realism and romance were found not only in the editorialising of Archibald, Stephens and others, or in such controversies as those that attended the 1884 prosecution of a Sydney bookseller for stocking Zola's *Nana*, or the 1889 Melbourne production of Ibsen's *A Doll's House* (a few months after the London premiere of the English translation).[23] These tensions can be found also in the writing of the period, and within the work of the two writers often later perceived as the single most important contributors to a distinctive national literature, Henry Lawson and Joseph Furphy.[24]

22 Henry Lawson, 'The Sydney "Bulletin" ', in *Henry Lawson: Complete Works*, compiled and edited by Leonard Cronin with introductions by Brian Kiernan, 2 vols (Lansdowne, Sydney, 1984), I, pp.872–73.

23 Douglas Jarvis, 'Francis Adams: Australia's Champion of Realism', *New Literature Review* 12 (n.d.), 25–32; Harold Love, ed., *The Australian Stage: A Documentary History*, (University of New South Wales Press, Kensington, 1984), pp.107–08.

24 As tensions between realism and romance in Lawson's work are discussed extensively in the next essay, some paragraphs have been omitted here.

While Lawson was no great reader beyond his adolescence, Furphy, who had received no more formal schooling in the rural area of Victoria where he grew up, acquired an awesome reputation as an autodidact and as the epitome of the literarily encyclopaedic culture of the Mechanics Institutes: he once composed a hundred lines of verse by taking single lines from the poems of English and American writers, many of them now forgotten. When he finished his *magnum opus*, *Such is Life*, he sent it, on Archibald's advice, to A. G. Stephens. After revisions, exclusions, and delays, it was published in book form by the *Bulletin* in 1903.

Because of its self-conscious literary play, *Such is Life* is finally unclassifiable by genre. Is it a 'picaresque novel *à la* Fielding-Richardson' (one of Furphy's descriptions), a philosophical novel, a precursor of modern metafiction, or an antinovel?—all claims which have been advanced. At first it was not taken to be fiction at all, but at face value, as the reminiscences of a former Riverina bullock-driver, which at least acknowledged one of the kinds of realism it embraces, the documentary and the didactic. One way of perceiving it is as an extended, ironic dramatisation of the tensions between realism and romance, truth and fiction, pragmatism and idealism. Tom Collins, its narrator and Furphy's literary alter ego (the pseudonym was a colloquialism for rumour-monger), begins by offering to present a 'fair picture' of Riverina life by writing up his diary entries for a week in 1883. Having embarked on this plan, Tom then finds that it would oblige him to include the bad language of some sheep drovers, so he changes the basis of the selection to consecutive months. But another unsavoury occurrence he has not anticipated (the 'lambing down' of two fencers by a shanty-keeper; a situation given many permutations in Lawson's stories) forces him to select extracts on yet another principle, one which, unsuspected by Tom, invests his faithful chronicle with a novelettish romantic plot. This despite Tom's vow to forsake 'the flowery bye-ways of the romancer' for the realist's slice of life.

Romance in general, including the 'new romance' of Ouida, Rider Haggard and Robert Louis Stevenson is scoffed at, but a special scorn is reserved for Henry Kingsley's *The Recollections of Geoffry Hamlyn*. This classic Anglo-Australian station romance is replete with the stock properties of colonial fiction that Tom has avowed to eschew: 'The outlawed bushrangers; the lurking black-fellows; the squatter's lovely daughter, awaiting the well-bred greenhorn ...'.[25] Collins continues the story of Kingsley's dashing Major Buckley beyond the closing pages of *Geoffry Hamlyn* (in which, having made his fortune in the colony, he returns to England and reclaims his ancestral seat) by telling us, with evident satisfaction, how he ended his days as the notorious 'Hungry' Buckley of Baroona station.

*Such is Life* is the most extended example of the 'local colour' realism of the period. It is crammed with examples of dialect humour; it presents the life of a region in a detail that invites comparison with the numerous late nineteenth century European and American novels that present 'scenes of provincial life'; and Tom, with his incessant curiosity and determination, is a parody of the 'scientific' or naturalistic novelist. Always seeking the universal behind the particular to explain 'the ageless enigma of Life', Tom frequently misses the obvious beneath his nose and is a figure of fun to others. Because he is preoccupied with his own pedantry, he even fails to notice that the boundary rider Nosey Alf is a woman. An exchange between them reveals obliquely Furphy's consciousness of the vexed issue, as it seemed, of whether the artist's first obligation was to truth or morality. They are exchanging 'swapping books' of the kind available through the *Bulletin* Book Exchange. Tom's is a Zola novel, Nosey Alf's is *Elsie Venner* (1861), an early 'scientific' novel by Oliver Wendell Holmes.

> 'I don't think it does a person any good to read Zola', remarked the boundary man gravely.
>
> 'Not the slightest, Alf—that is, in the works by which he is represented amongst us. But do you think it does a person any good to read Holmes? Zola has several phases; one of them, I admit, blue as heaven's own tinct; but Holmes has only one phase, namely, pharisaism ... Zola is all honest; he never calls evil, good; whilst Holmes is spurious all through.'[26]

Whether Furphy is presenting a view of life through Tom Collins—whether he is demonstrating a philosophical and moral viewpoint or

25 [Joseph Furphy], *Such is Life: Being Certain Extracts from the Diary of Tom Collins* (Bulletin, Sydney, 1903), p.271.

26 *Such is Life*, p.245.

adopting an unillusioned but comic perspective—has been a keen critical issue, and is likely to remain so, given Furphy's playfulness. Equally engaging is his parodic play with literature from Shakespeare to contemporary romancers. *The Buln-Buln and the Brolga*—originally a chapter excised from a typescript of *Such is Life* but not published until 1948—is an extended play (an appropriate word, as most of it is in dialogue) with the issue of the truth of fiction. Tom Collins is in Echuca, and an old school friend, Freddy Falkland-Pritchard, comes up from Melbourne with his family to visit him. At the same time Barefoot Bob, an acquaintance from 'up country', is passing through. Fred and Bob compete for the attention of Mrs Falkland-Pritchard by swapping stories of their exploits. The attractive Mrs Falkland-Pritchard writes occasionally for the *Bulletin* and the *Australasian* and is interested in philology. Fascinated by the antique associations of Aboriginal names, she approves of the town being called Echuca, for 'the map of this young land is already defaced by ugly and incongruous names transplanted from the other side of the world'. This hints at the nature of the contest that is to take place: the most plausible lie (for Freddy Falkland-Pritchard is an inveterate liar) will be the one most apparently authentic in its diction and manner.

The city-slicker Fred's tales are couched in the clichés of romance: how he rode at breakneck speed through enemy lines at Sedan to deliver a message to Louis Napoleon; how he fended off an attack by pirates single-handedly; how (*à la* Rolf Boldrewood) he hunted the bushrangers he had wounded down to their lair. In contrast to Fred's thrillingly paced, yet so modestly climaxed tales, Bob's yarns meander, gathering apparently extraneous details and observations as he reminisces about the hazards of exploring the unknown interior in search of water, or of 'dispersing' the savage blacks. Bob and his mate Bat arrive at one station just in time to rescue the squatter and his wife, who has been pinned to the wall by a spear through her frock. On another occasion, after 'dispersing' some cannibal blacks, Bob chivalrously decides to return and despatch the blacks' intended feast, a lubra whose back they have broken ('Please yourself' says Bat).

Laconically delivered in the vernacular, with an often painful attention to *les petits faits vrais* ('Curious thing about the Martini-Henry—you can hardly poke a finger through the hole where the bullet goes, but you could shove your fist in the place where she comes out.'), Bob's yarns have the ring of authenticity.[27] Only a reader, acquainted with the 'local colour' clichés of colonial fiction, of the kind that Tom Collins explicitly eschews in *Such is Life*, or Lawson in 'The Union Buries Its Dead', would recognise they are as much confections, and as conventional in their own anti-literary way, as Fred's more obviously second-hand fantasies. As with the contrasting in *Huckleberry Finn* of those two other great liars, Huck and Tom Sawyer, Furphy (and like Lawson and Steele Rudd he was a great admirer of Twain) is setting in opposition the romantic and the realistic modes, the debased literary and the anti-literary, or illiterate, the written fiction and the dialect yarn, to the confusion of listeners, and readers, as to what is true and what is merely romance. As in much of Lawson, the internationally current opposition of realism to romance finds a local immediacy.

Although he contributed some poems to the *Bulletin*, as well as articles and reviews, Christopher Brennan's reputation stands at the opposite extreme to that of Lawson, Furphy and the ballad-makers most strongly associated with that paper. Nevertheless, it was a reputation for commanding a wide-ranging set of interests in European literature, ancient and modern, that A. G. Stephens wanted to represent in its pages. Born in Sydney, Brennan had distinguished himself at its university which, like Melbourne's, had been established mid-century, more on the Scottish than the Oxford or Cambridge model. In 1892 a scholarship took him to Berlin for a couple of years, after which he returned to his native city and, eventually, to his alma mater as a teacher of German and Comparative Literature. As poet, critic and scholar—and bohemian who scandalised the wowsers—Brennan was admired by those who yearned after the cosmopolitanism embodied in his writings and his formidable presence. He gave the impression of an engagement with culture in its highest and widest senses. It was not for Brennan to celebrate 'our national literature', addressed to 'mythical individuals called Bill and Jim' and telling of 'imported fauna, such as the horse and the jackeroo' (as he wrote in *Hermes*, the University of Sydney magazine, in 1902), nor was it to celebrate the natural beauties of Sydney, as did such minor aesthetes as Arthur Adams and Victor Daley.

27 Joseph Furphy, *The Buln-Buln and the Brolga and Other Stories* (Rigby, Adelaide, 1971), p.71.

His concern was with that ideal Beauty, that paradisal state that poets down the ages had apprehended in an imperfect world and aspired to express.

Brennan wrote most of the contents of *Poems [1913]* before the turn of the century, and the cycle was effectively the culmination of his quest to rediscover the sources of essential Life (rather than mundane existence), the well-springs of which arose in such moments as the innocent, open perceptiveness of childhood, the experience of love, human or sacred, and in response to myth, to poetry itself. In the 1897 Prelude to the first selection, 'Towards the Source', the poet recalls 'Sweet days of breaking light' when he first read of 'The northern kingdom's dream' and when

by her well Romance
waiting the fabled chance
dream'd all the forest-scene
a shifting green.

The myths of literature present a succession of lost, ideal pasts: pagan Arcady and the Golden Age, the Biblical Eden, the heroic ages of ancient epic and the romances of chivalry, the romantic poet's own lost world of heightened sensibility in remembered innocence. These are evoked throughout the cycle by an allusive and decidedly literary diction and with metrical variety, to be contrasted with modes which recognise the drabness of existence.

If, for example, as in poem 38 of 'The Forest of the Night' section, the poet is exulted

The banners of the king unfold
to tend me on my evening way:
my trumpets flood the air with gold:
my pride uplifts the vanquish'd day

we remember the contrasting mood in the previous section

The grand cortège of glory and youth is gone
flaunt standards, and the flood of brazen tone:
I alone linger, a regretful guest,

here where the hostelry has crumbled down,
emptied of warmth and life, and the little town
lies cold and ruin'd, all its bravery done,
wind-blown, wind-blown, where not even dust may
rest.

The romantic irony, the recognition that absolute states cannot be attained in mere existence, or even states of exultation sustained, emerges through such juxtapositions of mood. The poetic persona assumes contrary attitudes which are as traditional as the diction in which they are cast; and a conflict of styles ensues, one that brings a full-blown romanticism into opposition with a disillusioned modernism, or anticipation of modernism, such as we find in the urban 'nocturnes'.

Deliberately more specific in setting and personal in tone is the concluding poem 'The droning tram swings westward', written in 1913. It is also more discursive, a summary of the themes of the whole cycle presented as the poet travels one evening through Sydney towards the university. He has descended from his 'tower of hermetic thought' and as his tram passes through town he attempts to establish some identification with, or sympathy for, what Lawson called (in a phrase to be echoed throughout Patrick White's second novel) 'the faces in the street'. Brennan's high romantic quest for transcendence, influenced by the French symbolists but also by the poetic tradition he perceived since Homer, ends in philosophical realism.

While Brennan was engaging with tensions between realism and romanticism at a much more rarefied level than Lawson and Furphy were with their rejections of the conventions of Anglo-Australian romance, he was still contributing to the same literary culture, a culture preoccupied by its continuity with, or its departure from, European influences. *Poems [1913]* assumes that the poet in Australia is heir to traditions as old as Homer and the Bible. Brennan was not alone in this belief. Although he wrote in 1927 that 'Australian poetry grew up long ago and claims treatment as an adult',[28] he has the reputation of

28 Christopher Brennan, 'Some Makers of Australia', *Cerise and Blue, St Joseph's College Old Boys Annual*, 1927, reprinted in T. L. Sturm, ed., *Christopher Brennan* (University of Queensland Press, St Lucia, 1984), p.381. In this address Brennan, with ambivalence apparent, outlines the German romantic view of a 'national literature'.

being the least nationalist poet of the period, and Bernard O'Dowd of aspiring to be the most. Yet both contributed to the *Bulletin*, and O'Dowd also had a classical education, was well versed in the French symbolists (though he rejected their influence), and drew on a similarly wide range of allusions in his writing: Biblical, and Cabbalistic, Scandinavian and Celtic, as well as English. His long poem *The Bush* (1912) muses on whether 'Troy tales of Old Australia' might not be gestating in the womb of 'Mother Bush' and Homers be 'waiting in the gum trees now'.

For Troy hath been, and Homer sang
Its younger story for a lodgings fee,
While o'er Scamander settlers' axes rang
Amid the Bush where Illium was to be.

*The Bush* idealises Australia as 'a temple we are to build', 'a prophecy to be fulfilled', and speculatively, playfully, yet optimistically, anticipates an Antipodean renaissance. From 'Melbourne mob and Sydney push' O'Dowd compiles a catalogue of heroic figures who have contributed already: fellow poets from Kendall on, the dramatist Louis Esson, Archibald and 'Rhadamanthine' Stephens, representatives of the fine arts and sciences. All history and literature will contribute to this next phase of universal cultural evolution, for

Who fenced the nymphs in European vales?
And Pan tabooed from all by Oxford dreams?
Warned Shakespeare off from foreign Plutarch's tales?
Or tethered Virgil to Italian themes?
And when the body sailed from your control
Think ye we left behind in bond the soul?
Whate'er was yours is ours in equal measure,
Altho' 'tis ours to grace the common treasure
With Lares and Pentes of our own!

Nationalist as he was, O'Dowd still, like Brennan, saw literature in Australia as being in continuity with European traditions.

Another view was that Australian literature was not an extension of English literature, nor a continuance of the European literary tradition since antiquity, but something new and of its own kind. Although

Lawson's sketch of the *Bulletin* for English readers was not published in his lifetime, it summed up a widely shared view that Archibald's paper 'proved to the people of Australia that they had artists and writers and materials for a distinct literature'. The *Bulletin*, he continued, brought about 'the birth of Australian Nationality, Letters and Art', which was followed by Angus and Robertson issuing 'the first purely Australian series of books' (his own and Paterson's being amongst the first in this series). In 1905, Paterson published his collection of *Old Bush Songs*. He opened it with two Aboriginal chants, because he was not concerned with transmitted literary forms but with 'the rough songs and ballads' that had emerged at successive stages of settlement and the social conflict. While the influence of Irish ballads in particular was admitted, Paterson was interested in tracing the origins of an indigenous literature. His introduction begins by quoting Macaulay's definition of ballad poetry as 'a species of composition which scarcely ever fails to spring up and flourish in every society at a certain point in the progress towards refinement', and as Paterson observes: 'So far as materials for ballads go, the first sixty or seventy years of our history are equal to about three hundred years of the life of an old and settled nation'. Rough as they are admitted to be, the old songs are found to have 'quite a character of their own'.[29]

By Federation, longstanding expectations (themselves imported) of the eventual emergence of a national literature seemed to the patriotic to be well in the process of fulfilment. The critical task was to identify what was distinctively Australian in the writings of Lawson, Paterson and the *Bulletin* school generally; the creative task to build on their achievements. Others, such as Melbourne's Professor Tucker in his *Cultivation of Literature in Australia* (1902), saw such claims as premature and 'self-conscious' nationalism as an impediment to progress. The prevailingly evolutionist habits of mind could lead equally to the 'cultivation' of literature being seen in gradualist Lamarckian terms (whether the new growth was seen as a transplanted cutting, or as a branch continuing to draw its sap from the parent tree), or in conflictive Darwinian terms. Such romantic, organicist analogies continued to

29 A. B. Paterson, ed., *The Old Bush Songs: Composed and Sung in the Bushranging, Digging and Overlanding Days* (Angus and Robertson, Sydney, 1905), pp.ix–x; p.xiv.

proliferate and become entangled with each other in this century, as different perceptions of the origins, the distinguishing characteristics, and the development of literature in Australia, and different perceptions of relationships to literature elsewhere were advanced.

## Realism and Modernism

For most of this century, the 1890s—usually extended from the beginning of the 1880s to the end of World War 1, and perceived as the 'nationalist period'—have provided historians and critics with a focus for advancing different views of cultural development. Yet, however they have constructed 'Australian literature' and perceived its origins, characteristics, and autonomy, and whatever role they have accorded writers of the 1890s, the period itself could not be said to have ushered in a new age in the 'development' of a national literature. In *Australia* (1930), a contribution to a series on different countries in the Empire, W. K. Hancock observed of readers and theatre-goers in Melbourne and Sydney that: 'Nowhere in the world is there so large a mass of people content to live so much of its life at second hand'.[30] Overwhelmingly, books and magazines were imported from the United Kingdom, and local writing remained the pursuit or interest of a minority within a predominantly English literary culture.

Among contemporary writers Hancock mentioned—as novelists 'who have at last understood the significance of Australian history as a transplanting of stocks and the sending down of roots in a new soil'—were Martin Mills [Boyd], Henry Handel Richardson, Vance Palmer and Katharine Susannah Prichard (p.261). Boyd and Richardson were both expatriates, the themes of their major works Anglo-Australian. As with a generation of American writers between the wars, expatriation would eventually prove an influential form of cultural transmission (at the time Hancock was writing, Christina Stead had left Australia, while Patrick White was jackarooing before returning to England to complete his education at Cambridge). Boyd's civilised comedies of manners, drawn from the history of his family which over generations had moved between Melbourne and England, provided elegant departures from the sagas of pioneering that were the more usual form of tracing 'the sending

30 Hancock, p.262.

down of roots in a new soil'. Richardson had been deeply influenced by later nineteenth century, particularly French and Scandinavian realism, and related Australian themes and settings to this major movement in her trilogy *The Fortunes of Richard Mahony*, published in its entirety in England and the United States in 1930.

Vance Palmer and his wife Nettie worked as freelance writers and reviewed widely in the Australian press. Nettie promoted Richardson's work strongly once she became aware of it (for there was little cultural transmission within Australia itself, a situation the Palmers set out to remedy), and Vance was committed to winning wider recognition for Furphy. Both were interested in American literature, and criticism such as that of Van Wyck Brooks (whose 1918 essay on creating a 'useable past' was so pertinent to their own interests).[31] Nettie's fluency in a number of languages was reflected in the wide range of her reviewing, which included Spanish-American writing, another possible analogue for Australia's hoped-for renaissance. Her monograph *Modern Australian Literature* (1924) discerned a new, post-colonial stage in the country's literary development. As a tireless correspondent, she communicated her views on this to others, including Hancock and the American Hartley Grattan, who published a pamphlet on Australian literature in the United States, with a preface by her, in 1929.[32]

From his 1905 article in *Steele Rudd's Magazine* until after World War II, when his revisionary *Legend of the Nineties* (1954) appeared, Palmer expounded the bush 'legend' or the 'Lawson-Furphy' tradition. As various studies have shown, the Palmers were much more sophisticated and cosmopolitan than many who dismissed their 'literary nationalism'. They travelled overseas frequently and extensively. Vance had worked on Orage's *New Age* in London before World War I, and was acquainted with English intellectual circles remarkably different from the cultural establishment idealised by Anglophiles in Australia. In Russia, Scandinavia, and (closer to 'Home') Ireland, he had observed the quickenings of national culture, most conspicuously in the theatre, that he hoped would be emulated in his own country.

31 Van Wyck Books, 'On Creating a Useable Past', *The Dial* (1918), in Richard Ruland, *A Storied Land: Theories of American Literature: Volume II* (Dutton, New York, 1976), pp.381–87.

32 C. Hartley Grattan, *Australian Literature* (University of Washington Press, Seattle, 1929).

From 1922–26, the Palmers were closely associated with Louis and Hilda Esson and others in Melbourne who were attempting to establish a 'national theatre', the Pioneer Players. Esson, who had spent a few months as a youthful dandy on the boulevards of Paris, was well aware of 'little theatre' movements overseas. He had met with Yeats and Synge, and been encouraged by them to write about his own country. Some of his pieces, like the Players' first production *The Battler*, were modelled on Yeats's or Lady Gregory's 'country comedies'. During World War 1, Esson had seen the Washington Square Players, and some of his stark, realist one-acters, like *The Drovers*—with the laconic precision of an early Lawson sketch—invite comparison with the early realist plays of Eugene O'Neill then being produced in American little theatres. The Pioneer Players had been influenced by Lawson (Palmer had adapted 'Telling Mrs Baker' for the stage), but at the same time they could be seen as being in line with international movements.[33]

Among others associated with the Players was Katharine Susannah Prichard. In her writing, she was reacting against the drabness of Lawson's settings and exploiting the variety of 'local colour' Australia had to offer. Hancock noted the influence of D. H. Lawrence on her novels, and this was detectable also in her best play, *Brumby Innes*, which, although it won a prize the year after the Players had folded, remained unperformed until the early 1970s because of its controversial subject of race relations in the far north. Prichard was a founding member of the Communist party of Australia and the most prominent figure identified with the 'social realist' school. In its ideology, the school was both internationalist, seeing itself in the mainstream of 'progressive' writing throughout the world, and also nationalist in its conscious efforts to build on the tradition of the 1890s. The political commitments of other writers who were broadly on the Left in the fight against Fascism (the Palmers, for example, supported the Republican cause in the Spanish Civil War) meant that many who were often regarded as narrow 'literary nationalists' often had closer acquaintance with aspects of contemporary European culture than their conservative detractors. The nationalists' shared conviction that Australian culture, which they saw

33 For the Palmers and their circle see Vivian Smith, *Vance and Nettie Palmer* (Twayne, New York, 1975) and David Walker, *Dream and Disillusion: A Search for Australian Cultural Identity* (Australian National University Press, Canberra, 1976).

as essentially democratic, should be part of culture more widely and not merely a colonial off-shoot of British culture, was best expressed through the quarterly *Meanjin* (Brisbane 1940–44, Melbourne 1945–). This included European and American contributions and its nearest equivalent was the American left-liberal *Partisan Review*.

Though writers and readers were well aware of the waves of formal and stylistic experimentation in Europe and America between the wars, most Australian prose remained predominantly realist, most verse late romantic or Georgian. One could note clear exceptions, such as Chester Cobb's Virginia Woolfish stream-of-consciousness novels or Bertram Higgins's Eliotesque verse, but their marginality only proves the rule. While awareness of modernist experimentation is apparent in the work of conscious contributors to the 'national literature', as that literature was (in Vance Palmer's phrase) for 'the common man', anything smacking of elitism, and likely to estrange an already perilously small audience, was to be avoided. Besides, unlike modernists in Europe, the consciously Australian writers were trying to build on a tradition, not overturn one, and for the doctrinaire social realists among them, modernism represented decadence and a retreat into subjectivity. The majority culture was even more conservative, as academic scorn for T. S. Eliot and 'free verse', and the banning of *Ulysses* and other modernist works for indecency, indicated.

Others again reacted against both the majority, and English-oriented, literary culture and the minority claims for a national literary tradition. An early example was the magazine *Vision* (Sydney, 1923), edited and mainly written by Jack Lindsay and Kenneth Slessor, with Frank C. Johnson. Lindsay's editorial for the first of the magazine's four issues scorned 'verse about shearers and horses'. Like their mentor Norman Lindsay, with his *fin de siècle* Nietzschean aesthetic, the *Vision* poets modelled themselves on the great figures in their idealised European tradition, a tradition they felt had collapsed into modernist chaos in Europe itself (but might find a further renaissance in Australia?). Later in the 1920s, Jack Lindsay and fellow Queenslander P. R. Stephensen established the *London Aphrodite* to retransmit to Europe the ideas that Norman Lindsay had synthesised in the bush at Springwood, and to outrage equally 'the modernist and the reactionary'. Stephensen returned to Australia and in 1935 published the first part of his essay 'The Foundations of Culture in Australia' as the editorial to the first (and last) issue of his own mythologically titled 'national literary magazine', the *Australian Mercury.* The occasion for the essay was an article in the *Age* earlier in the same year in which the Professor of English at the University of Melbourne had written that 'literary culture is not indigenous, like a gum tree, but is from a European source'. Stephensen's retort was that 'a gum tree is not a branch of an oak', but he also disparaged the *Bulletin*'s 'larrikin' influence and urged that 'imported culture' be used to build up the indigenous.[34] By this time, though, any precise and absolute distinction between what had been imported and what was 'indigenous' would have been difficult to establish.

Stephensen's call for Australians to absorb and learn from European culture provoked Rex Ingamells in Adelaide to issue his Jindyworobak manifesto *Conditional Culture* (1938). Ingamells saw transplanted literary forms and diction as preventing local writers from expressing their own responses to their environment: 'Pseudo-Europeanism clogs the mind of most Australians preventing a free appreciation of nature'.[35] Instead of following foreign models, writers seeking to develop more appropriate techniques should study the culture of Aborigines. Such an extreme call, as it seemed then, to cultivate the indigenous conflicted with the cosmopolitan interests of another group emerging in Adelaide, those associated with the magazine *Angry Penguins* (Melbourne, 1940–46). This was destined to become the best remembered avant garde little magazine of the first half of the century when James McAuley and Harold Stewart sprang their 'Ern Malley' hoax to ridicule the 'NeoApocalyptic' surrealism of Max Harris and his associates. The resulting prosecution of the editors for obscenity, and A. D. Hope's mocking reviews of Harris's surrealist novel and the Jindyworobaks' poetics, were indications of the official and academic resistance that 'literary nationalism' and modernism alike encountered.

The two decades following World War II saw the culmination of efforts to win recognition of a national literature with the publication of, especially, Vance Palmer's *Legend of the Nineties* (1954), Russel Ward's *Australian Legend* (1958), A. A. Phillips's *Australian Tradition* (1958) and H. M. Green's *History of Australian Literature* (1961). The

34 Reprinted in Barnes, pp.204–44; Stephensen quotes Cowling, p.210.

35 Barnes, pp.245–65.

appearance of such works coincided with, and helped stimulate, the introduction of courses in Australian history and literature in universities and schools. With the rapid expansion and democratisation of secondary and tertiary education in the post-war decades, the universities which had been the main conduit of European (overwhelmingly English) culture began, however reluctantly in some cases, to take Australian culture into consideration. A. G. Mitchell, for example, in *The Pronunciation of English in Australia* (1946) maintained that Australian English was not a degenerate colonial form of the mother tongue, but a language shared by a national community. The 'discovery' of a local social and literary tradition (or questioning of such findings) in the writings of Palmer and others indicated broad parallels with the post-war expansion of American studies in the United States. But although American models provided some stimulus for local cultural historians, for example, F. J. Turner's frontier thesis for Ward's *Australian Legend* and H. L. Mencken's *The American Language* for Sidney J. Baker's *The Australian Language* (1945), the parallels were less the result of direct American influence than of a response to similar circumstances in both countries which, with consciousness of their democratic institutions heightened by the war, were undergoing social reconstruction.

The claims made for Australia's national literature followed broadly, if unconsciously, those made from the Renaissance onwards for English and other vernacular literatures. Indeed, it was a commonplace assumption of literary history that a renaissance was a necessary stage in the establishment of a national literature: as Stephensen, who reveals the pervasive influence of Taine, wrote in his 'Foundations of Culture', 'Literature and culture blossom at their best during a period of national expansion, as in England during the reign of Queen Elizabeth, and again in England during the reign of Victoria'.[36] Yet, following a late nineteenth- century, and particularly Nietzschean, revival of classicism within Europe,[37] the connotations of 'renaissance' in Australia could be either nationalistic and democratic or, as with Norman Lindsay and his followers, anti-nationalistic and elitist. Poets as different in their attitudes towards nationalism as O'Dowd and Hugh McCrae—or the young Slessor

36 Barnes, p.229.

37 Noel Macainsh, 'The Renaissance—Revival in Early Modern Australian Poetry', *Quadrant* 21 (July 1987), 65–73.

—thought that the desired renaissance could be inaugurated by inviting the whole pantheon of Greco-Roman mythology to assume a local habitation. For others, though, indulging in such exotic fancies was worse than irrelevant to the forging of a distinctively national tradition.

If a Shakespeare, a Dante or a Goethe had provided the vernacular literatures of Europe with their equivalents of Homer and Virgil, and ensured their 'universality', then similar father figures would be required for Australian literature. The mid-nineteenth-century American 'renaissance', so conscious of the Elizabethan model, had Emerson and Whitman among its founding fathers; perhaps Lawson, Furphy and Paterson had assumed such roles for Australian literature during the 'renaissance' of the 1890s? In romantic theory, the national literature represented the 'characteristics' and values of the people. For Australian, as for American literature, the distinguishing trait was its democratic spirit; perhaps, however, what differentiated Australians from Americans was their ethic of mateship (rather than individualism) and a certain sardonic scepticism towards ideals? In *Introducing Australia* (1942)—a book that was reprinted a number of times both in the United States and Australia, and revised after the war—the American Hartley Grattan, who had been in constant contact with the Palmers and who was responsible for the 1948 American edition of *Such is Life*, 'the greatest book yet produced in Australia', discerned 'the basic Australian literary tradition' as 'a compound of sound learning, rebellious, ardent faith in the common man, and an even more ardent faith in the Australian future', in other words as having more in common with American than with European literatures.[38]

The term 'tradition' had acquired from T. S. Eliot and others a prominent, if problematical, place in the lexicon of the 'new criticism' that had developed in English and American universities between the wars. This criticism was proving very influential in the rapidly expanding universities here, which were beginning to teach Australian literature. Was it not, though, premature to talk about a local tradition and a canon of literature? If one were to do so, which tradition should be taught, the nationalists' canon of predominantly realist texts, or an alternative constructed according to the Anglo-American criteria of

38 C. Hartley Grattan, *Introducing Australia* (John Day, New York, 1942), p.168; p.174.

'literary' rather than socio-historical value? (The alternative still might contain many of the same elements though, as the 'true' value of, say, Lawson's and Furphy's texts could be disputed.) Prominent antagonists of those claiming that Australia had a democratic national literary tradition were McAuley and Hope, both Professors of English, leading poets, and influential critics whose aesthetic preferences were for the neo-classicism prevailing at the time Australia was settled. While the concepts and constructs at issue in the often partisan discussions of Australian literature could be seen as local responses to current English and American critical models, they had the effect of moving 'Australian literature' (however this was constructed) closer to the centre of literary cultural interest, whereas previously it had been marginal to the concept of literature institutionalised through teaching, book distribution and literary journalism. The publication of Australian books—histories, anthologies, and social commentaries, as well as novels and collections of poetry—increased markedly from the late 1950s on, in response to the expanding educational market, and the interests of a larger and more affluent population.

Actual cases of cultural transmission proved more complicated than the stereotypes of two opposed lines of influence, local and European, assumed. The best example is the reception of Patrick White following the publication, in England and the United States, of his novels *The Tree of Man* (1955) and *Voss* (1957). White's 'establishment' education at an English public school and Cambridge, his long expatriation before and during World War II, and his preoccupation with themes of spiritual isolation rather than with shared adversity seemed to proponents of social realism to align him with the earlier Anglo-Australian tradition. For opponents of 'literary nationalism' White's metaphysical concerns could be welcomed as universal (and epic), though his techniques could be disturbingly idiosyncratic and discomfortingly modern.

White proved especially significant in transmitting the modernism which had been resisted both by those who saw themselves as continuing the 'Lawson-Furphy' tradition and those who were, selectively, preserving the great tradition of European literature. His first novel, *Happy Valley*, set in the Monaro showed the influences of Joyce, Eliot, Woolf, Lawrence and Hemingway. Published in London in 1939, it had won the Australian Literature Society's Gold Medal, but this fact, like the author's second novel, *The Living and the Dead* (1941), and even his name, had slipped from most minds after the war. His third and most experimental novel, with its Homeric (and Joycean) motifs, *The Aunt's Story* appeared in 1948, the year White returned to Australia, but attracted little notice. In the mid-1950s, *The Tree of Man* and *Voss* appeared to critical acclaim in the United Kingdom and United States. They were both modernist—or post-modernist, in the literal sense that their author had absorbed the wave of post World War I experimentation —and also traditional, in a local as well as universal way. *The Tree of Man* was a variation on the pioneering saga, *Voss* on the journey of exploration, both staples of the predominantly realist Australian fiction between the wars.

These novels were followed in the 1960s by *Riders in the Chariot* and *The Solid Mandala*, short stories and plays. While White continued to engage with 'universal' themes, he was also satirising contemporary Australian suburbia in highly observant detail and mimicking its speech, so recentring Australian literature in the contemporary city rather than the bush. As well, his long expatriate phase enriched his work with European, especially Greek, settings. White had absorbed much European culture at first hand, as he had much European literature, and could relate both to writing about contemporary Australia. His novels, short stories and plays both contained and transcended the apparent conflicts between imported and idealised high literary culture and a less rarefied indigenous literature for, and about, the common man. They were both modern and traditional, local and 'universal', realist and symbolic, 'European' and Australian. His winning of the Nobel Prize in 1973 finally domesticated Literature, perhaps by many still thought of almost exclusively as something imported, with guarantees and testimonials attached. His success in being simultaneously both an international figure and undeniably Australian in many of his subjects and settings helped to produce a climate in which other, and particularly younger, writers felt encouraged to experiment formally and stylistically.

This is most apparent with the way that White's plays of the early 1960s anticipated the emergence towards the end of that decade of an experimental Australian drama. Following the success of Ray Lawler's *Summer of the Seventeenth Doll* in 1955, it became possible to speak of a 'renaissance' of Australian drama. In the nineteenth century, the popular theatrical forms of melodrama and vaudeville (as well as high drama, especially Shakespeare) had been exported quite literally to the colonies, and had been adapted readily to Australian subjects and settings (while the poets in their closets wrote five act, blank verse tragedies about bushrangers). But attempts like those of the Pioneer Players to found a national drama had been continually frustrated. Lawler's part celebration, part critique of the bush legend, written in a realist mode reminiscent of Tennessee Williams (the Americans Williams and Arthur Miller were the most prominent dramatists in English at the time) had been followed by other realist studies of local myths and mores. White's plays, influenced by German expressionism were committedly anti-naturalistic and decidedly satiric in presenting local mores. They employed, seemingly, every technique to be found in the work of the 'New Wave' playwrights a few years later, especially a comic and satiric exploitation of the vernacular and, although White was not necessarily a direct influence on their reactions against 'bourgeois naturalism', he again helped to establish a climate more receptive to innovation.

'Bourgeois naturalism' for younger playwrights, most notably Alex Buzo, Jack Hibberd, John Romeril and David Williamson, was encapsulated by *The Doll*. They were reacting against the formal restrictions of its realist conventions and at the same time attacking the stereotype of the 'typical' Australian as the bushman, or at least as retaining rural-communal, egalitarian values. (At a time when this stereotype was being attacked more widely—by historians and social commentators as well as poets, novelists, and dramatists—for being a sentimental evasion of the reality that most of the population lived in the suburbs.) Their early plays, such as Hibberd's *White With Wire Wheels* (1967), Buzo's *Rooted* (1969), and Williamson's *Stork* (1970), satirised the mateship ethos—and the male chauvinism (a term just coming into currency then)—of the junior executive inheritors of the bush legend. It was an intensely indigenous movement, exploiting Australian speech (which had been held by some to be inherently unsuited to drama because of its characteristic laconicism) in a variety of individual ways; yet it was also a movement conscious of being in line with contemporary theatrical developments in Europe and the United States.

The most commonly identified starting point for the 'New Wave' has been 1967, when Betty Burstall opened her La Mama coffee-shop theatre in Melbourne's Carlton. This she named after one of the Off-

off-Broadway theatres she had been attending in New York the year before, and plays the La Mama groups first wanted to emulate, in local terms, were those by Megan Terry, Sam Shepard and other new American writers then being performed in London as well as North America. The influences selected from overseas models operated simultaneously at various levels, on the writing, on the style of directing and acting, and on the organisation of companies. Alex Buzo's *Norm and Ahmed* (1968), which brought the movement to broad public attention after prosecutions for obscenity in two states, bore strong structural similarities to Edward Albee's *Zoo Story*, one of the early American absurdist plays. The ideas of the English director Peter Brook, that assimilated both Shakespeare and Brecht into anti-bourgeois 'rough theatre', influenced the policies and style of the Australian Performing Group, which grew out of the La Mama experiment. In its organisation, also, the APG was responsive to ideas from overseas, and replicated the Portable Theatre set up by David Hare in England to play to factories and schools. Considered as a movement (though it was more an overlapping set of spontaneous responses to circumstances at home and influences from overseas), the 'alternative' theatre of the late 1960s and the earlier 1970s presented some paradoxes. It deplored the cultural cringeing that had filled the bourgeois theatres for generations with hits and stars from the West End and Broadway, yet it was fascinated by Brecht, Beckett and the European absurdists. Sceptical of national legends, it was nostalgic for a lost popular Australian theatre of melodrama and vaudeville; and the first big success of indigenous 'rough theatre' was *The Legend of King O'Malley* (1970), which was quickly followed by other historical burlesques. It claimed, justifiably, to be uniquely, indeed idiosyncratically Australian, yet at each point it was in line with similar developments elsewhere.

What, in retrospect, might seem contradictions between nationalist and internationalist tendencies had been their own consistency for those involved. During the later years of the Vietnam War, the dominant cultural influences on younger generations in Australia, as in Western Europe, became those of the American counter culture. The adversary culture of the United States—the opposition of blacks, radicals, feminists, gays to the establishment—was readily adaptable to local circumstances. Alternatives to the perceived establishment culture in Australia followed models provided by this international, but heavily United States-inspired, counter culture. The 'New Wave' in the alternative theatre was followed shortly after by a not unrelated development in local filmmaking. There was a new poetry, stimulated by New York, Black Mountain and West Coast experimentation. A 'new' fiction drew on American models, including some that had already responded to Latin American and contemporary European influences. There was a 'new' journalism, again influenced by American practices, which observed a 'new nationalism' in the early 1970s. New developments in print technology facilitated a whole range of alternative publications—weekly papers, magazines and books. There was also a 'new' criticism, or set of adversary criticisms, drawing stimulus from diverse models: New Left political radicalism, feminism, and, from Europe, epistemological scepticism. Whatever the particular influences they responded to, the new critics agreed on the need to interrogate such 'ideological constructs' as literature; and previous conceptualisations of Australian literature were seen to have marginalised women, Aborigines, migrants and the politically committed 'social realists'.[39] As well as suppressing these social differences, perceptions of a national literature were also seen to have denied significant regional differences.[40]

Assumptions about cultural transmission—both transmission from Europe, predominantly, and transmission within Australia itself—have underlain many of the historical differences between critics: between (and an attempt to sort the polemics into chronological sequence follows) 'localists and universalists', 'democratic populists and Anglophile elitists'—or ' "Abos" and "Pommies" ' as A. A. Phillips once suggested—'nationalists and internationalists', 'post-colonials and Eurocentrics'. Most often, their different assumptions have been couched in the

39 A lively, engaged account of recent critical differences is provided by John Docker, *In a Critical Condition: Reading Australian Literature* (Penguin, Ringwood, 1984). On migrant writing see 'Ethnic Writing Not Australian Yet?', transcripts of a 1986 Warana Writers Week symposium in *Outrider* 3 (December 1986), 60–110. For examples of feminist readings, and re-readings, see Carole Ferrier, ed., *Gender, Politics and Fiction: Twentieth Century Women's Novels* (University of Queensland Press, St Lucia, 1985).

40 Extended considerations of regional differences are found in John Docker, *Australian Cultural Elites: Intellectual Traditions in Sydney and Melbourne* (Angus and Robertson, Sydney, 1974); and Bruce Bennett, *Place, Region and Community* (Foundation for Australian Literary Studies, Townsville, 1985).

evolutionary metaphors of transplantation, adaptation and modification, hybridisation, or the rejection of exotic varieties and the spontaneous emergence of new indigenous growth. Such metaphors seem endemic to discussions of culture, and are themselves part of the conceptualising discourses about literature that have been continually transmitted to Australia—as originally were the very notions of universal poetry and a national literature, with all their potential for conflict. But while such metaphors promise an explanation of the processes of transmission at a quasi-scientific level of generality, they can, at the same time, obscure the immediate and ever-changing influences operating in every period, and ultimately on every writer, who has always had to make an individual, selective, and imaginative response to diverse sets of stimuli, both local and international.

# 'From Mudgee Hills to London Town': A Critical Biography of Henry Lawson

On 23 April 1900, at his studio in New Zealand Chambers, Collins Street, Melbourne, John Longstaff began another commissioned portrait. Since his return from Europe in the mid-1890s, when he had found his native Victoria suffering a severe depression, such commissions had provided him with the mainstay to support his young family.

While abroad he had studied in the same Parisian atelier as Toulouse-Lautrec and a younger Australian, Charles Conder. He had acquired an interest in the new 'plein air' impressionism from another Australian, Charles Russell, and he had been hung regularly in the Salon and also in the British Academy. Yet the successful career and stimulating opportunities Longstaff could have assumed if he had remained in Europe eluded him on his return to his own country. At first he had moved out to Heidelberg, but the famous figures of the local 'plein air' school, like Tom Roberts and Arthur Streeton, had been drawn to Sydney during the depression. Longstaff now lived at respectable Brighton, and while he had painted some canvases that caught the texture and tonality of Australian life—most memorably his study of the bushfires in Gippsland in 1893—local dignitaries were his more usual subjects.

This commission, though, was unusual. It had come from J. F. Archibald, editor of the not fully respectable Sydney weekly, the *Bulletin,* and it was to paint not another Lord Mayor or Chief Justice,

---

First published as the introduction to Brian Kiernan, ed., *The Essential Henry Lawson* (Currey O'Neil, Kew, Vic., 1982). This selection included previously unpublished material among the Lothian Papers in the La Trobe Library, Melbourne. The footnotes within square brackets refer to some significant studies which have appeared since the essay was first published.

but a writer of verses, stories and sketches named Henry Lawson. Although he was only thirty-three (the age Longstaff had been on his return) Lawson was already admired and popular throughout Australasia, and was now off to try his luck in the literary metropolis of London.

Lawson with his young family was en route from Sydney when he received the telegram from Archibald asking him to sit for Longstaff while his ship was in Melbourne. In Lawson's mind, this was a voyage he had started much earlier when, as the eldest son of a selector on a worn-out goldfield, he had yearned 'for something better—something higher'.[1] Now, at last, he was going 'from Mudgee Hills to London Town'[2] and, he hoped, to wider fame, or at least financial security.

Painter and sitter might have found much to talk about, if time had not been so short, and the writer so hard of hearing, for many threads of personal and cultural history crossed with their meeting. Both had been born on the goldfields, had grown up on farms, and remembered the days of the bullock drays and Cobb and Co. coaches. The previous year, in the *Bulletin,* Lawson musing on the theme 'If I Could Paint' had mentioned first of all Longstaff's 'Breaking the News', the canvas —based on an incident remembered from the painter's childhood in the goldmining town of Clunes—that had won Longstaff his scholarship to Paris in 1887, the same year that Lawson first had verses accepted by the *Bulletin.*

The owner of the *Bulletin* had purchased the painting, and later his paper carried some of the trade advertisements that Longstaff, in difficult times, had designed. And Lawson's writings, which emphasised the 'weird melancholy' of the bush, had their correspondences with paintings: with the '9 x 5' sketches by the 'plein air' impressionists of the Heidelberg school which captured what was characteristic of Australian life and landscape, and also with Longstaff's more academic paintings, which so much appealed to the writer. Writing of Longstaff, Bernard Smith sees 'a curious survival of the melancholy interpretation of Australian life and nature' that had characterised earlier periods in

1 'A Fragment of Autobiography' (MS. 1903–06), in *Henry Lawson: Complete Works*, compiled and edited by Leonard Cronin with introductions by Brian Kiernan, 2 vols (Lansdowne, Sydney, 1984), I, p.30. Subsequent volume and page references included in the text in parentheses refer to this edition.

2 The title of a manuscript (1913) continuing Lawson's autobiography, in *Complete Works*, II, pp.945–51.

local art. For Longstaff, as for Lawson, 'Australia was a land of flood, fire, and famine'.[3]

They could have talked about the difficulties they had experienced as fellow artists in Australia; and how, although a new century had just opened and Federation was approaching (with the first Parliament to meet in Melbourne early the next year) they could share no optimism about fulfilling their ambitions in their own country.

Lawson's prolific output of verses, stories and sketches about the people and the ways of life he had known in the pioneering days and the present, in the country and the city, had been taken to heart by the public across Australia and in New Zealand. Almost every week, for over a decade, a new ballad or lyric or radical song, a story or sketch or article had appeared in the papers: the *Town and Country Journal,* the *Boomerang,* the Sydney *Worker, Truth,* or the *Bulletin.* And there were his books published by Angus and Robertson which had sold well, verse in *In the Days When the World Was Wide,* prose in *While the Billy Boils,* and new collections of verse and prose were appearing around the time of his departure. His send-off from Sydney had been momentous, attended by the best-known literati associated with the bohemian Dawn and Dusk Club and the *Bulletin,* including its literary editor A. G. Stephens who, once again, hailed Lawson as the country's most 'representative' writer.

Yet, though he had been extraordinarily successful by the measures of popularity and fame (and had received a number of interested enquiries from English publishers) Lawson had not been able to live by, and devote himself exclusively to, writing in Australia. Now, with the assistance of Earl Beauchamp, the Governor of New South Wales, David Scott Mitchell, the wealthy bibliophile, and George Robertson, his publisher, he was going to London, where he hoped this might be possible.

Longstaff also craved the success and wider recognition that Lawson was seeking. The following year, the commission to paint his grandly gloomy 'Burke and Wills' was to take him to London (because the donor, assuming no colonial would be capable of filling the commission, had

3 Bernard Smith, *Australian Painting* (Oxford University Press, Melbourne, 1962), pp.139–40; Nina Murdoch, *Portrait in Youth of Sir John Longstaff 1861–1941* (Angus and Robertson, Sydney, 1948).

stipulated it be painted there), where he began a successful career as a fashionable portraitist, and eventually attained a knighthood. His very success prevented his celebrating in paint the Australian landscape he extolled on a later, brief return. But on his departure in 1901, the same Earl Beauchamp, his term as Governor over, commissioned a portrait of Edward VII as a gift to the State's National Gallery. This and a companion portrait of Queen Alexandria were hung together with those of Lawson and the painter's wife. Lawson had seen his still wet the morning after his sitting, and again in the Gallery after his return from London:

> O Scotty, have you visited the Picture Gallery,
> And did you see the portraits of the King and Queen and me?
> The portraits made by Longstaff, and the pictures done by Jack
> Of the King and Queen and Lawson and the lady all in black?

'Perhaps', he wrote long after, 'the reason why I have never seen it since is that it is, in a way, connected with the tragedy of my life.'[4]

A studio photograph, taken in Sydney in 1902, soon after Lawson's return from London, shows him as alert, purposeful, his eyes magnetic. Yet Longstaff's painting expresses the personality we know from Lawson's writing more tellingly than the camera. The painter posed his subject conventionally, and somewhat stiffly, so that sitting upright in ready-made suit and uncomfortably high collar (though Longstaff omitted the starched cuffs), with his pipe constrained to his lap, Lawson gives the impression of awkwardness, a sense that he is not in his natural attire or attitude.

The earthy colours suggest textures other than those associated with the complacently bourgeois civilisation Longstaff's commissioned subjects usually represented. Instead of a confident, prosperous, smiling public face, we see a private, withdrawn, vulnerable man, handsome but haggard for someone in the traditional prime of his life. The expression of the mouth is masked by a full moustache, which accentuates the deep, soft brown eyes that everyone remembered

4 'The King and Queen and I' (*Bulletin*, 1905) and 'The Longstaff Portrait', (MS. 1910), *Complete Works*, II, p.236; p.927.

Lawson by, eyes which look not outward, as might have been expected of someone of Lawson's early achievement now on his way to London, but inwardly, as though on the past, and on another Australia than the country he was leaving on the eve of Federation.

His earliest memories, as he wrote in the autobiography commissioned by George Robertson after his return from England, were of the tent he had been born in on the Grenfell goldfields—though he only remembered it from the age of three when the tent (or hut, because it had been extended in bark) was the temporary family home at New Pipeclay, outside Mudgee. Gold had been discovered there in the 1860s, at Golden Gully, and gold, or the hope of it, had affected his family's fortunes and movements in Henry's early childhood.

His father, Nils Hertzberg Larsen, a Norwegian ship's officer, had jumped ship to join the earlier rushes in Victoria. Eventually he had made his way to Golden Gully, where he met Louisa, one of the daughters of Henry Albury, proprietor of a public house on nearby Sapling and Gully field. They married in Mudgee in 1866, when Louisa was nineteen, and Nils thirty-five, and joined the rush to Grenfell. Their first child was born there on 17 June 1867 and named Henry Lawson, not Larsen. Nils, or Peter as he was called in Australia, and Louisa returned to New Pipeclay with the infant shortly after.

Louisa's family had settled in the Mudgee area before her birth in 1848. Both her parents had been emigrants from England. Henry Albury had arrived with his farm labourer parents from Kent in 1838, and in 1845 he had married Harriet Winn, born at Norwich. Louisa, the second of their seven children, was born at Guntawang station near Mudgee, where her father was then working.

Henry Albury, the writer's grandfather, was not susceptible to gold fever like his Norwegian son-in-law, and his way of sharing in the prosperity that followed the rushes was to buy the good will of a public house. It was to this 'shanty', the Albury home, that the Larsens, now Lawsons, returned from Grenfell. Peter re-erected the tent on a two-acre paddock adjoining the house, and after the birth of a second child, Charles, in 1869 he built a hardwood cottage. He worked with his father-in-law around the district until in 1871 he finally persuaded his wife to join the rush to Gulgong, some miles to the north, that had broken out the preceding year. Then four, young Henry could remember the excitement of packing and moving to Gulgong, the film-set frontier town that is preserved today, and the trip to Sydney after his father struck gold. In 1873, the family returned to New Pipeclay (soon to be returned to its Aboriginal name of Eurunderee) and Peter took up a selection under the Robertson Acts—forty acres adjoining the two they had previously occupied—and a third son, Peter, was born. The following year, ironically, the rush to neighbouring Log Paddock brought prospectors to dig up the land that Louisa had hoped her digger husband would settle down to farm.

Having been born on the goldfields, and thus historically linked to Eureka and the 'roaring days', was an important part of the romance in the imaginative young Henry's mind—part of the family romance he grew up with—like being descended from mysterious Gipsy and heroic Viking forbears. But such reveries could not compensate for the unromantic reality of his childhood. The predominant note in his memories is of inner desolation, as though in response to the abandoned diggings all around.

For the visitor today, Mudgee on the winding Cudgegong River is a pleasant and prosperous country centre with wide streets of broad-verandahed homes, stately old hotels and shops. Approached through Sofala, Hill End and other picturesque mining townships, including Gulgong, 'the town on the ten dollar bill', it is the hub of a region rich in historical associations, chiefly Lawsonian. And although only the chimney of the Lawson house at Eurunderee still stands, it is surrounded by lush varied countryside, with cattle grazing on the river flats, vineyards on the slopes, and, in the distance, the enclosing blue hills. It is an archetypal Australian landscape of the kind that generations of artists have brought us to appreciate as painterly.

But for Lawson as a child it was, as he recalls it in his autobiography, 'a miserable little hell', and he returns repetitively, as though still haunted by their pathos, to memories of his father returning home after dark, and a full day's work elsewhere, to labour on the selection (with the ground so hard that in desperation he tried breaking it up with blasting powder)—and the constant, bitter quarrels between his parents.

The father was always working and away from home on contracting jobs for increasingly extended periods; and the mother, as well as having the strain of bringing up the children alone and running the selection, tried to supplement their meagre income by dressmaking. From the age of eight their eldest son had a heavy round of chores before and after school. At eleven he was taken out of school for a time—to help his father build the new schoolhouse at Eurunderee.

As well as disruptions to his education, and the dubious benefit of learning from Irish National Readers under Mr Tierney, the boy was suffering from deafness, and when he was sent to school in Mudgee was regarded as 'barmy' by the others. In 1877, when Henry was ten, the twins Gertrude and Henrietta were born, further increasing the strain on Louisa's and the family's resources. Henrietta died the next year, Louisa published a poem in the local paper, which spurred Henry's first attempts at verse. At the age of thirteen, Henry left school to help his father with contracts in the Mudgee area. Around this time he made a visit to Sydney to consult a doctor about his deafness and then worked with his father on building contracts in the Blue Mountains. In 1883 Louisa leased the selection, moved to Sydney, and sent for Henry who was apprenticed as a carriage hand with Hudson Brothers at Clyde.

These are the bare, familiar facts of Henry Lawson's early life and family background. The popularity of his writings—in which he provided many versions, direct and indirect, of these early years—and the fact that he has been the subject of more biographical studies than any other Australian writer mean that his formative years are the most familiar. From his directly autobiographical writings, and the personal elements in his fiction and verse, as well as from the records provided by members of his family, biographers have constructed their interpretations of his personality: what it must have been like to have been Henry Lawson, to have been born on the goldfields, grown up on a selection, had a few broken years of schooling made miserable by deafness, then the abrupt transition to the grinding poverty of the city.

Such experiences have A. G. Stephens's 'representative' quality, in terms of their typicality for thousands of others, who responded to his writings when they appeared, and who had themselves observed the transition from a predominantly rural to an urban-industrial Australia. But these factors alone do not explain Lawson's emergence as a writer—why this boy, unlike those thousands of others, should have become the imaginative historian of these experiences and these changes.

All who have attempted to explain this are agreed on Louisa's commanding influence during the future writer's formative years. Peter, who Henry describes in the autobiography as 'the kindest, hardest working man' he had ever met, is a benign though often absent figure in his memories of childhood. In Louisa's own accounts, and those of her daughter Gertrude, which echo her mother's, she decided to take up the selection after the return from Gulgong, at first running it and finally leasing it to start a new life for herself and the children in the city. Whereas Gertrude's sympathies are with Louisa, Henry's are with his father, and in the autobiography Louisa is most often referred to detachedly as 'the mother'.

Henry had been ten when Gertrude was born. This gap between them, combined with the itinerant pattern of Henry's life in his later teens meant that she would not have known him well. But as Brian Matthews has pointed out, her rambling and repetitious accounts in manuscript in the Mitchell Library, although frequently misleading about her brother's life, provide a strong impression of her mother's personality. Indeed, their vagueness and repetitiveness are their value, because behind Gertrude the reader can sense Louisa *talking*.[5]

Ostensibly, some of Gertrude's accounts are of Henry and the rest of the family, but all are dominated by the figure of Louisa, and all agree in their details and phrasing when recounting some common incidents, as though Gertrude is setting down from memory what she had heard over and over from her mother. How she had to have the selection put in her husband's name because there was no Married Women's Property Act then. How she kept Peter working on the farm by the sheer strength of her will. How she organised the establishment of the provisional school for the neighbourhood; and how she decided after her second child that there would be no more until they found a better way of life in the city.

Although there are factual inconsistencies between Henry's and Gertrude's accounts, and within Gertrude's own, hers have their value in the version of the family romance they convey. Every family has its romance and each child locates itself in the family's history in its terms: 'When your grandfather was still a young man ...', 'When I was a girl ...', 'When your father and I first met ...', 'When you were

5 Brian Matthews, 'Louisa and Henry and Gertie and the Drover's Wife', *Australian Literary Studies* (May 1980), pp.286–97. [See also his *Louisa* (McPhee Gribble, Melbourne, 1987).]

still just a baby …'. A romance not because it is untrue, necessarily, or exaggerated, but because the details of time and place, often vague and confused in the telling, are less important than the imaginative significance the story holds for teller and listener.[6]

From the stories Louisa told Gertrude—who records them with all the time-worn embellishments that look tawdrily novelettish when set down on the page—we can readily imagine how Louisa perceived herself and wanted others to see her. As the sensitive, solitary adolescent who found solace meditating and declaiming her poetry in the bush, where she had her sacred place. When this was invaded by a black snake, which she dubbed Judas, she killed it and carried it away to burn so that it would not defile her shrine. As the strongly independent daughter, too proud to go into service (the only employment available), who walked out of chapel in protest at a bigoted sermon. As the tall, slender bush girl, the darling of the diggers at her father's shanty, who wanted to get up a subscription so that she could have the voice that so delighted them trained in London, but whose mother refused because she had a horror of her children 'going public'. How Peter Larsen won her hand, to his rivals' surprise, when he came upon her sitting on a log and weeping over her lot in this tiny rural community—though Henry preferred a more stirring version involving a disturbance at the Alburys' shanty with the plucky little Norwegian sailor to the rescue.

As well as being gifted with her voice, and poetic temperament, she was also a splendid horsewoman who took command of a runaway team of horses pulling the local coach. And there was also the story which must have been told many times, and eventually written and published as a short story by Louisa herself in 1915 (long after her son's 'The Drover's Wife' had appeared) about how, when her husband was away one evening, there was a suspicious noise and the glimpse of a gloved hand at the window; and how, taking a batten from the sofa and the dog in the other hand, she confronted the prowler, sending him off, but then huddled with the children in the same bed all night with the

6 'Family Romance' is not used here in any psychoanalytic sense. For a Freudian interpretation of Lawson's life and work, see Xavier Pons, 'Henry Lawson's Literary Vocation', *Meanjin* 2 (1980), 237–48. [See also his *Out of Eden: Henry Lawson's Life and Works—A Psychoanalytical View* (Angus and Robertson, Sydney, 1984).]

dog on guard at its foot.[7]

These were some of the stories we can assume the children grew up on and heard often—so often that Gertrude knew them by heart. The family romance about the earlier lives of parents, relatives and neighbours mingled with the children's own immediate memories, and so extended itself into their generation. For example, Henry's reminiscences about his grandfather incorporate Louisa's stories about how her father would bring home presents for herself and his other children and then hide them. Such stories mingled with his own memories of Harry Albury, as his memories of the drovers down on the river flat who put 'whisker-seed' on his younger brother Charlie, or of the Gulgong rush, mingled with the previous generation's lore about 'the roaring days' before his birth, providing him with the 'visitable past' that he entered so often in his writings.

Convinced (as Gertrude wrote) that she was 'born to better things', Louisa was the dominant, indeed domineering parent—the 'Chieftainess' as Lawson referred to her in later life. Yet she was also given to 'strange fits of abstraction' when, according to her daughter, she would retire and 'vegetate' for days, before rousing herself and driving everyone before her again. From all accounts and interpretations, it would seem clear that Louisa was a 'good' mother to Henry, in the ironic psychological sense of imbuing her first-born with her own dissatisfactions and aspirations 'for something better—something higher' (I, p.30), especially her literary aspirations. He attributes the initial encouragement he had to write to his mother, and she is remembered most fondly as reading *Robinson Crusoe,* Poe, Gordon, and *For the Term of His Natural Life* to the young boys. Dickens, Cervantes, Bret Harte and Twain are other authors referred to in the autobiography.

Gertrude also remembers an edition of the *Encyclopaedia Britannica,* which reinforces the impression that Lawson was not as culturally deprived as many others who also grew up on selections and had only a few, broken years of formal education. As well as Adam Lindsay Gordon (probably with Marcus Clarke's preface and its phrase 'weird

7 'The Senior Sergeant: A True Incident at Eurundee Farm 1822', *Woman's Budget*, 8 July 1915. A clipping of this story is in the Louisa Lawson Scrapbooks, Mitchell Library (ML) A 1895; beneath it Gertrude has written, 'A true incident on the farm. I was five years old but remember it distinctly'.

melancholy' to describe the bush, which was to echo throughout Lawson's writings), we could also expect there had been lots of Henry Kendall. Louisa had become fascinated by the native-born poet and his struggle for recognition. She dreamed of communing with him about poetry—her poetry which she had been writing since she was a girl. The move to Sydney took place in the year of Kendall's death, and in one version Gertrude tells of Louisa being called to the city by the spirit of the poet. In his fragment of autobiography, Henry refers to there once having been another 'Barmy Harry' in Sydney (Kendall), which suggests something of a family cult of the 'misunderstood' identifying themselves with the poet.

Shortly after her arrival in the city, Louisa set about organising a campaign to have a memorial erected over Kendall's grave—at a time when she was having great difficulty in establishing herself and her young family. Within five years, through slaving at dressmaking, she had acquired a small news-sheet for Henry to be the nominal editor of, the *Republican,* and founded a paper for women, the *Dawn*. Despite all the economic difficulties, the forceful personality, that could not find its outlets in the country, assertively found itself in the city, especially in the cause of women's suffrage. It also made its demands on her eldest son.

When the parents had first separated, Henry had stayed with his father, working first in the Mudgee area then at Mount Victoria in the Blue Mountains. The relationship between Louisa and her husband remains a matter for conjecture, with conflicting impressions having been given by contemporary and later commentators. But what is clear is that his mother's sending for Henry to join the rest of the family in the city proved crucial to his development, by exposing him to a productively confusing set of stimuli.

When Louisa moved to the centre of Sydney, having first of all attempted to start a boarding house at Marrickville, Henry's wages as an apprentice carriage hand paid only the rent. Yet Louisa's aspirations for her family persevered. After rising before dawn, walking some miles to the train, working all day and making his way home again, Henry was enrolled in night school to better himself—paying his fees through overtime. 'My tribe wanted a gentleman, or the appearance of a gentleman, in the family, but they wanted every penny I could earn also', he remarks bitterly in the autobiography (I, p.33). The shy, sensitive, awkward bush lad, as he later looked back on himself in those days, had swapped the drudgery of the selection for that of the city.

However, on moving to Sydney, Louisa had also, initially through the Progressive Spiritualist Lyceum, brought the family into contact with an intellectual milieu that only the city could offer. Her home in Phillip Street became in these years a meeting place for radicals of many persuasions—spiritualism and secularism, socialism, republicanism, and the feminism which became Louisa's, and for a time Henry's, preferred cause in the nationalistic Utopian mood that was rising in response to economic difficulties and the moves towards Federation.

For Henry, these were unsettled years of moving back and forth between Sydney and the Blue Mountains, where his father remained, and also working for brief periods in Newcastle and Melbourne—where he went to have treatment for his deafness. Although he twice failed the examinations to qualify for the Public Service or university entry, Louisa had succeeded in imbuing him with her aspirations for something higher, and he described himself as always hanging around the School of Arts library.

He was also writing, and his first success came when the *Bulletin* accepted 'A Song of the Republic' and 'Golden Gully' in 1887. At the age of twenty, the 'Bush boy who was skinny city work-boy in patched pants and blucher boots struggling on the edge of the unemployment gulf' (I, p.34) had been published, and in the *Bulletin,* the most national among the plethora of radical papers that appeared in the 1880s and 1890s to propagate a wide range of causes. Lawson was later to write for a number of these: as editor, for the *Republican* (which became the *Nationalist* before folding), the *Boomerang* and the *Worker* in Brisbane, the Sydney *Worker,* as well as for mass circulation papers such as *The Town and Country Journal* or *Truth.*

Many of the young poet's contemporaries found such poems as 'A Song of the Republic' and, in the *Bulletin* the following year, 'Faces in the Street' and 'The Army of the Rear' memorable expressions of widely shared radical sentiments. When, much later in his life, Lawson recalled writing them, he deplored their 'deadly-in-earnest ring' and 'thunderous resignation' (II, p.945). Today we might agree with his mature judgement, while still valuing these oft-quoted protest verses for their encapsulation of a past ethos; but the equally familiar bush ballad he wrote around the same time, like 'Andy's Gone with Cattle' (*Town and Country Journal*, 1888) retain their simple appeal. Varied as his early verses were, they would have struck a common chord for readers then —that of expectations fulfilled, now the long-awaited native Australian literature was emerging with the verses of 'Banjo' Paterson, Victor Daley, Barcroft Boake, E. J. Brady and other writers for the *Bulletin* whose ranks Lawson had joined.

The rush of verses that followed his first publication in the *Bulletin* showed Lawson responding to a range of traditional and contemporary popular models. Kipling, Moore, Burns, Tennyson, Hood, Poe and Bret Harte were among those noticed when his first collection appeared. Other detectable influences are the poets his mother was fond of: traditional Irish and Scots ballads, which by this time had been adapted to produce the 'bush ballad' frequently found in the *Bulletin* and other papers; the declamatory protest verse found in radical papers; and the sentimentally 'concerned' popular verse of the kind exemplified by G. R. Sims's 'Christmas Day in the Workhouse'. Instead of settling into one measure or manner Lawson wrote across the wide range of popular models.[8]

However, even his first reviewers regarded Lawson more highly as a prose writer. Whereas his verse is most often conventional, his prose writings, since their first appearance, have been valued for their freshness and individuality, their direct, 'artless' realism and (what some intended by this seemingly unflattering epithet) his break with literary conventions prevailing in a late Victorian colonial culture.

His first published story, which he said was also his first attempt at prose of any description (though his recollections of his own work were not always accurate) was 'His Father's Mate'. This displays a conflict between the conventionally 'literary', through the stilted gentility of the style in its opening and a melodramatic development, and the 'realistic' in terms of the more direct, dramatic representation of life

8 For contemporary reviews, see Colin Roderick (ed.), *Henry Lawson: Criticism* (Angus and Robertson, Sydney, 1972). For accounts of popular verse and influences on Lawson see Edgar Waters, 'Ballads and Popular Verse' in G. Dutton (ed.), *The Literature of Australia* (Penguin, Ringwood, revised edition 1976), pp.293–306; Colin Roderick, 'Lawson the Poet' in Leon Cantrell, ed., *Bards, Bohemians and Bushmen* (University of Queensland Press, St Lucia, 1976), pp.203–17; Graeme Davison, 'Sydney and the Bush: An Urban Context for the Australian Legend', *Historical Studies* 71 (1978), 191–209.

in Golden Gully. The opening, with its heavily narrational manner, ponderous personification ('poor tortured earth') and dragged-in classical allusion to Timon, suggests that the young author is trying to write up to some fine, if dull, literary models.

This conventionality reveals his awareness of the literary beyond what we might have imagined from knowledge of his limited formal education. Like his other early pieces in prose, this first story disposes of assumptions that his minimal, broken schooling may have been a benefit, allowing him to remain an untutored and unspoilt natural. Instead, the melodramatic shaping through the concealed relationship of the brothers, the return (but just too late) of the prodigal son, and the Victorian pathos of the child's death—a subject that continued to appeal to Lawson, partly one suspects because it licensed self-pity for his own childhood—show how literary he was, in prose as well as verse, at the start.

In other early pieces he can be seen as casting around among various models and influences for the technical means and authorial voice to express his concerns. Although he said that his first 'real, living character' was Peter M'Kenzie of 'Payable Gold'[9]—the story of an old digger on Log Paddock written a couple of years later—the Isley of 'His Father's Mate' with his 'old fashioned face' is reminiscent of Lawson's descriptions of himself as a child elsewhere. Another very early story, 'Malachi', in which the 'barmy' youth, butt of all, ennobles himself and confounds his persecutors by his sacrificial death, has some markedly autobiographical correspondences. 'The Third Murder', a tale about sleeping in a haunted house, in which the narrator thinks he must have imagined voices in the night, but then later discovers from a newspaper that a murder was being committed, seems with its heavy reliance on 'documentation' to be a variation on Poe, to whom Louisa had introduced the children. 'A Narrow Escape' is a parody of journals of exploration in the perilous hinterland. 'We Called Him "Ally" for Short', with its Twain-like description of the dog's 'chewing-up apparatus that an alligator might have envied', might well have reminded contemporaries of the Western frontier humorists' tall stories and vernacular humour (and Alligator in 'The Drover's Wife' has an even more Western 'chawing-up' apparatus).

9 Lawson's comments on his early stories in 'From Mudgee Hills to London Town', *Complete Works*, II, pp.947–48.

While today, with hindsight, we would appreciate 'His Father's Mate' most for what it reveals about his first efforts, contemporaries were impressed by it. When J. F. Archibald brought out his selection from the *Bulletin*'s first decade in 1890, *The Golden Shanty,* he included it together with 'A Song of the Republic'—a clear indication that the young Lawson was accepted immediately, even eagerly, as one who was making literature from Australian life, performing the miraculous synthesis that had been anticipated for so long.

Compared with his writing of a few years later, 'His Father's Mate' seems now to reveal the conflicts for Lawson between literary artifice and realistic observation. What is most 'Lawsonian' and memorable about it, is the terse, dramatised description of the preparations for Isley's funeral: the improvised shroud and coffin, the gin cases for the women to sit on in the 'hearse'. These coalesce into an image of the outward poverty but essential, inner humanity of these bush people, who are so much on the margin of civilisation that even their 'town' is put thus, in quotes, to suggest that it is not really a town at all, in the genteel reader's sense—merely the characters' necessary delusion that they still live within society.

These details, rather than the lavishly literary evocation of 'the predominant note of the scene' in the story's opening, provide the authenticating 'local colour'. This phrase from the criticism of the time, conveyed the imaginative presentation of details to capture a way of life that lay outside what traditionally had been shown in literature. The 'local colourists' of the American West had made the language and customs of new communities there the subject of a new and ostensibly anti-literary literature, and provided one potent model for the writer in colonial Australia.

For all the literariness in Lawson's first story, especially with the subject of the death of a child, the apparently objective itemisation of the funeral 'defamiliarises' the conventional, presenting the customs observed as bordering on the eccentric, even bizarre. The details which seem so real, so authentic are composed to imply some unspecified revelation or significance. This power of suggestion was to be at the heart of Lawson's mature work.

In 1890, unemployed in Sydney, Henry met Mary Cameron, a young schoolteacher from the country, whom later generations were to know as Dame Mary Gilmore. Sharing literary and political enthusiasms, they became close friends, though whether there was any romantic attraction between them remains uncertain. In some accounts, Louisa packed Henry off to Albany, W.A., because of his interest in Mary Cameron; in others, because he had tested his appeal to the opposite sex by proposing to one of his mother's boarders, and had been accepted. Whatever the reason, and seeking employment was no doubt a part of it, he went with his younger brother Peter, to find Western Australia economically depressed and offering no opportunities beyond the writing of some articles for the *Albany Observer.* He returned to find eastern Australia in the turmoil of the Maritime Strike. Early the next year, 1891, he certainly developed a romantic interest during a visit to Eurunderee where at the old family home he met another schoolteacher, Bridget Lambert, a niece of the tenant. His poem, 'A Free Selector's Daughter' followed, which, like the early stories 'The Third Murder' and (under a different title) 'We Called Him "Ally" for Short', he contributed to the Brisbane *Boomerang.* In March he was invited to join its staff. As opportunities for employment, which in Lawson's case had never been good, were worsening, he accepted—and took his first, and as it was to turn out, his only full-time writing job.

The *Boomerang* had been founded by William Lane, the socialist leader and publicist, who was now editing his own paper, *The Worker,* in Brisbane, and later would organise the establishment of New Australia, the Utopian community in Paraguay that Mary Cameron was to join. Lawson also wrote for the *Worker,* notably 'Freedom on the Wallaby' during the Shearers' Strike. But under *Boomerang* editor Gresley Lukin his regular job was to select snippets from the country newspapers and cast them into rhyme.

A. G. Stephens, who was to become editor of the *Bulletin's* literary 'Red Page'. and Lawson's most demanding critic, was also on the staff of the *Boomerang* and remembered him as 'a tall, dark, wiry young man with large luminous brown eyes' who was responsible for the 'Country Crumbs' columns 'From nine to five daily Lawson was at the office, usually walking up and down the room allotted to him, making verse painfully and persistently. For months I listened to him pounding out his rhymes, often aloud, as he paced to and fro:

> Four horses in the pound
> —Bound, crowned, drowned, sound—
> Four horses in the pound
> —Warwick pound, Warwick found—
> Two horses better drowned.'[10]

As always, Lawson was prolific in verse during his time on the *Boomerang,* and his contributions to it, other than the 'Country Crumbs' columns, included not only militant songs like 'As Ireland Wore the Green', or the hectic 'Triumph of the People' ('Lo, the gods of Vice and Mammon from their pinnacles are hurled'), but also the fey, *fin de siècle* 'The Water-lily' originally published in Louisa's *Dawn.* Among contributions to the *Bulletin* that appeared while he was in Brisbane was 'The Fire at Ross's Farm'.

The worsening economic situation in Queensland during the period of the Shearers' Strike led to Lawson and others being retrenched from the *Boomerang.* Returning to Sydney in 1892, he lived either in cheap boarding houses or, relations with Louisa having become strained, at the home of his Aunt Emma at Dawes Point, and freelanced for the *Bulletin,* the Catholic *Freeman's Journal,* and John Norton's *Truth* at the proverbial penny-a-line. From this time, following his removal from his mother's direct influence and his experience of being a self-supporting man of letters in Brisbane, he began to become the bohemian writer, dossing in cheap lodging houses, such as 221 1/2 Castlereagh Street for five shillings a week, when flush, or in the Domain when not, making a circle of literary and political acquaintances as his reputation brought him more confidence. One of Lawson's favourite haunts was McNamara's bookshop in Castlereagh Street, to which he would return whenever in Sydney and where he met enthusiasts for all radical causes, including Billy Hughes, W. A. Holman, and his future brother-in-law Jack Lang. After his return from Brisbane, Lawson also became friends with E. J. Brady, bush balladist and, editor of the *Australian Workman,* and 'Banjo' Paterson, with whom he cooked up a verse debate in the *Bulletin* over the 'issue' of the country versus the city to make some ready cash.

10 A. G. Stephens, 'Henry Lawson', an obituary in *Art in Australia,* November 1922, reprinted in Roderick, *Criticism,* pp.220–21.

While he was still only in his mid-twenties, he had been writing prolifically, chiefly in verse, for over five years. Imaginatively, however, his increasing artistic confidence and maturity were being expressed in his prose. 'A Day on a Selection', 'The Drover's Wife', 'The Bush Undertaker', stories which drew on his memories of past life in the country, and which still remain among the most highly regarded of his works, were written at this time. 'Stories' though is not perhaps the word with the most appropriate connotations for the context in which Lawson was then writing.

Thinking broadly of the publishing opportunities available to him, we could see him as having two opposed models for fiction. One was the conventionally 'literary' magazine story, heavily narrated and contrived to achieve a pointed resolution, whether melodramatic or humorous. Its opposite was the sketch, not ostensibly a fiction at all but a quick impression of a typical character, scene or incident, drawn from life 'photographically'—for critics were inclined to consider its effectiveness by comparison with the graphic arts. Lawson's prose began appearing in an age of realism and, in the English-speaking world particularly, one of controversy over this movement and its anti-romantic engagement with contemporary life. Maupassant, even Zola, Bret Harte and Mark Twain were among those Lawson was likened to by contemporaries when his major prose collections appeared. But, to locate the context in which his writing appeared, we need not go to Walter Besant, Edmund Gosse, W. D. Howells, Henry James, Robert Louis Stevenson and others engaged in debate over realism on both sides of the Atlantic around this time (a debate into which Lawson was enlisted by Edward Garnett in his 1902 *Academy and Literature* article). Nor need we consider the emergence of vernacular, 'anti-literary' realist literatures elsewhere, in places as remote as Russia or Italy. The same context of romance and realism was provided by the *Bulletin* and other magazines Lawson read and wrote for. Although the conventionally well-told, fully rounded story predominated in those A. G. Stephens selected for the *Bulletin Story Book* in 1900, the magazine was famous for its 'pars'—the brief realistic sketches and vernacular anecdotes that revealed the typical, albeit through the eccentric.

Sketches from 'low' life were long established in colonial

Australian journalism. Marcus Clarke and the 'Vagabond' (John Stanley James) were earlier examples from Melbourne, though their sketches of urban life affected a patronising attitude towards their subjects, a conscious rakishness that winked a reminder to the gentle reader that the writer was really one of them. As the *Bulletin* was in large part, through its 'pars', written by its readers, this literary smugness hardly obtained. The style was briskly and economically factual, something like this:

> The scene is a small New South Wales Western selection, the holder whereof is native-English. His wife is native-Irish. Time Sunday, about 8 a.m.
>
> ('A Day on a Selection', *Bulletin* 1892; I, p.224)

> Bush all round—bush with no horizon, for the country is flat. No range in the distance. The bush consists of stunted rotten native apple trees. No undergrowth. Nothing to relieve the eye save the darker green of a few she-oaks which are sighing above the narrow, almost waterless creek. Nineteen miles to the nearest sign of civilization—a shanty on the main road.
>
> ('The Drover's Wife', *Bulletin* 1892; I, p.238)

In its 'stylelessness' this is anti-literary realism that aligns itself with the terse, factual 'par' rather than with the displays of fine literary writing we find in the opening of the conventional story of the day, or in 'His Father's Mate'. Instead of 'literary' description, the feeling is more of stage directions (and Lawson felt that the theatre had been an important stimulus to his writing).[11] However, in both these pieces the 'literary' is also there to contrast ironically with the sketched reality: with references to the works of Edward Bellamy, Henry George and Ignatius Donnelly in 'A Day on a Selection' and to the *Ladies' Journal* in 'The Drover's Wife'. One way, as here, of establishing one's credentials as a realist rather than a romancer was to disparage

11 'Family History of the Lawsons', manuscript by Gertrude O'Connor (née Lawson), ML A1898, includes an unpublished holograph note by Henry which states, 'First idea of writing at the age of 12 or 13, came from the theatre probably'. Elsewhere, he frequently recalls his youthful fondness for the theatre.

literature as fanciful and artificial, to heighten the illusion that *this* by comparison was real, as Twain had done in *Huckleberry Finn* (and Lawson claimed to have read all of Twain).

In these early but fully-achieved sketch stories, Lawson can be seen drawing on his memories of selection life (which he would have shared with thousands of his readers), on stories that Louisa and others had told, and on remembered local characters, such as his grandfather for 'The Bush Undertaker'. The manner of the paragraph sketch which records such lore is extended towards the length of a story, though without the conventional contrivances of the plot.

With 'The Drover's Wife', within the dramatic framework of the killing of the snake, Lawson presents an archetypal figure who suffers fire, flood and drought through a succession of sketches written in the past tense. But the realistic details, such as the finger poked through the corner of the handkerchief, make her individually, and revealingly, 'typical' in the manner of the observant 'par', as well as familiarly representative. Although these early pieces are heavily narrated, and Lawson's development was to be in the direction of fuller dramatic presentation, they have that apparent 'artlessness' which contemporary commentators appreciated. 'The Drover's Wife' does not seem like 'literature', something made up, worked over, but the 'real' thing (so subliminal are the Biblical associations of the snake and the plagues inflicted on this mythic mother).

In comparison 'The Bush Undertaker'—which presents a weird individual and a macabre train of events to typify, rather than represent, how the bush acts as 'the nurse and tutor of eccentric minds'—is more conventionally a story in its development and more formal narrative manner. And if 'A Day on a Selection' is more a sketch than 'The Drover's Wife', and that less formally a story than 'The Bush Undertaker', this suggests how Lawson was perceiving two opposed models for fiction and experimenting with blending them in varying combinations.

Looking back in later life to this time when he was a new contributor to the *Bulletin,* and to the editor's preferences, Lawson wrote that:

> Archibald in those days, preferred the short story to the short sketch. I thought the short story was a lazy man's game, second to 'free' verse, compared with the sketch. The sketch, to be really

> good, must be good in every line. But the sketch story is best of all.[12]

At the same time that Lawson was experimenting with the apparently opposed forms of the realistic sketch and the literary story—to shape his memories of country life into fictions that would ring true to his experience—he was also writing about life in the city. While there was a set of local conventions for presenting bush life (some of which, as an anti-literary realist he was to enumerate in 'The Union Buries Its Dead'), the city was a challenge to the writer's imagination. Its 'types' had not been established as had those of the bush, with the squatters and selectors, sundowners and New Chum jackaroos, the drovers and bush heroines of fiction and the stage. Even for contemporaries, there was the apparent paradox that local writing seemed to be preoccupied with the life of the countryside, when by this time, the early 1890s, Australia was among the most urbanised of nations.

In the early 'Arvie Aspinall' sequence of stories about apprentices at 'Grinder Brothers', Lawson drew on his own experiences of a few years before as a carriage hand at Hudson Brothers to express his sympathy with the new class of young urban manual workers—or 'larrikins' as they appeared to the middle-class press. These stories (which began appearing in the *Bulletin* in 1892, before 'The Drover's Wife') are generally, and rightly, held to be sentimental, showing the worst of Dickens's influence on Lawson. (And their Dickensian notes seem to be reinforced by the larrikins' dialogue, which looks like an imitation of how 'low-life' characters 'spoke' in English fiction; though perhaps this should be seen as Lawson's realism asserting itself, for in his autobiography he recalls that most of the apprentices at Hudson Brothers were from Birmingham and the North Country.) But succeeding pieces set in the city capture the typical through apparently quick and detached sketches from life, frequently of lonely men in boarding houses.

While, outwardly, Lawson's life continued the pattern of moves away

12 'Three or Four Archibalds and the Writer' (MS. 1919), *Complete Works*, II, p.987.

from Sydney in search of employment and returns to freelance journalism and, increasingly, bohemian company, an imaginative development was rapidly taking place. A decisive stimulus and source of experience, for him as a writer—like his earlier years in the country and then his marriage—was the journey he took to Bourke, 'the metropolis of the Great Scrubs' in north-western New South Wales near the Queensland border, from September 1892 to June 1893. He arrived during the worst drought ever recorded, and, although Lawson had affected scorn at Paterson's romantic idealisations of the bush during their verse 'debate', he was unprepared for what he found 'right up country'. As he wrote to his Aunt Emma from Hungerford on the Queensland border in January: 'Once in Bourke I'll find the means of getting back to Sydney—never to face the bush again ... You can have no idea of the horrors of the country out here. Men tramp and beg and live like dogs'.[13]

In Bourke he stayed at the Carriers' Arms hotel, 'Watty's', where he met many of the models for his characters, like the Oracle and the Giraffe, in the stories that were to follow over a decade. The immediate imaginative outcome, however, was some of his most memorable sketches: 'In a Dry Season' (the journey up), the Twain-like 'Darling River', 'Hungerford', 'In a Wet Season' (the journey back) and the contrast between city and bush in 'Dossing Out and Camping'. These read as straight sketches, reportage, though imaginative reportage full of suggestive detail.

The early Mitchell pieces—'Enter Mitchell', 'Mitchell a Character Sketch', 'On the Edge of the Plain'—are sketch stories, vernacular vignettes that present the typical with dramatic directness, and without a sense of the author as a genteel intermediary presenting us with a representative instance of 'low' life. The often delicate distinction between fictions such as these, with their origins in the *Bulletin* 'par' (as some first appeared), and more conventionally shaped stories can be seen from the two versions of '"Rats"', which was first published in the *Bulletin* in 1893. When Lawson included this in his first collection, *Short Stories in Prose and Verse,* he added a concluding paragraph which turned the sketch of meeting an old hatter fighting with his swag and fishing in the dust, into the story of how the hatter had been taking in,

13 Letter to Emma Brooks (1903) in Colin Roderick, ed., *Henry Lawson: Letters 1890–1922* (Angus and Robertson, Sydney, 1973), p.53; reprinted in Brian Kiernan, *Henry Lawson*, Portable Australian Authors (University of Queensland Press, St Lucia, 1976), p.120.

and taking down, his audience. This ending makes it another of the many stories about practical jokes and confidence tricks that Lawson was writing around this time and later. In his form it loses the disturbing implications—that the hatter is in some unstated way revealingly typical of existence in the bush—which were regained when the final paragraph was dropped for *While the Billy Boils*.

For an editor, this story poses the problems of whether Lawson's apparent preference for the version with the twist at the end should be respected. To a critic, the two versions can suggest an artistic uncertainty and opposed resolutions of it: whether to turn a story neatly, with an ironic twist to its ending, and limit its possible significance for readers, or to leave it 'unfinished', as more a sketch than a well-made story, to reverberate in the reader's mind.

One of the great early stories and a crucial one in marking the development of his characteristically dramatic method and colloquial manner, is 'The Union Buries Its Dead'. Significantly subtitled 'A Sketch from Life' when it first appeared as 'A Bushman's Funeral' in *Truth* in 1893, while Lawson was still 'up country', this is a sketch story, with the sharp observations of the sketch extended to fill the whole frame of the action, yet with its significance left implicit, and indefinite. The narrator's voice is flat, yarning, laconic. The details he provides and his own observations contribute—most often with terse directness, though at times with seeming digressiveness—to the story's enigmatic 'point': his attitude towards life and death.

Through him, we see men on the margin of existence, so much so that their values are definable only by contrast with the absolute negative of death. 'It didn't matter much, nothing does' is, ostensibly, the nihilistic attitude that pervades this story. This might remind us of the Bush Undertaker ('it's all over now; nothing matters now—nothin' didn't ever matter, nor, nor don't') and of what might have might been the ending point of his story, not an apprehension of transcendent mysteries but a return to mundane and meaningless existence: 'He sat down on a log near by and passed his hand wearily over his forehead—but only as one who was tired and felt the heat ...' (I, p.248). As in this earlier story, the emphasis in 'The Union Buries Its Dead' falls on the grim comedy of life rather than on the possible consolations of death.

Approached as an imaginative expression of Lawson's encounter with the realities of mateship and unionism in the heartland, 'The Union

Buries Its Dead' might seem sardonically disillusioned. 'Trades unionism is a new and grand religion', Lawson had written in the *Albany Observer* in 1890.[14] For the narrator here, 'unionism is stronger than creed' but 'drink, however, is stronger than unionism'. The bushman who looks like a drover just returned from a big trip, and could be Paterson's Clancy, is easily inveigled into the hotel. Life goes on—but what distinguishes these men from the dogs (like which, in Lawson's letter to his aunt, they live and die) is their ritual acknowledgement of their common fate. In this funeral, the universal traditional pieties attached to death are 'defamiliarised' and seen—like the Bush Undertaker's burial of Brummy, or even the Sunday promenade of the Drover's Wife—as defences against absolute nullity, as the final vestiges of civilised humanity that these characters cling to for their salvation in this world.

The story is not only a register of Lawson's view of how the fraternal ideals of unionism were realised in Bourke while he was there. Its language is both specific and general, so that it can also imply the universal function of rituals through which mortals face together their own ultimately lonely and absurd fates.

The title by which we now know the story arouses expectations of solemn public piety, the mourning of a hero. The details, particularly the fact that the deceased is unknown, make this ironic. Yet what transpires lends some precarious sense of dignity and meaning to the lives of those who attend the ritual. Just before the end, the narrator steps out of the fictional frame to allude to local literary conventions that he assumes his readers would expect a story, as distinct from 'a sketch from life', to observe. His references to the absences of wattle, a tearful mate, and 'the sad Australian sunset' proclaim him to be an anti-literary realist; and this paragraph, which might seem excrescent, is part of the whole defamiliarising process the story follows in departing from literary as well as social stereotypes and expectations.

14 'The New Religion', *Albany Observer*, July 5 1890, in *Complete Works*, I, p.112. This was part of a series of articles headed 'Straight Talk' which appeared under the name of 'Joe Swallow', a pseudonym Lawson frequently used around this time, for verse as well as prose. 'Jack Cornstalk', also the name of a character, was another pseudonym he favoured.

In June 1893, Lawson returned to Sydney, 'never to face the bush again', as he had vowed in the letter to his Aunt Emma, but clearly, from the writing that followed, his imagination was filled with memories of the Great Scrubs and the men he had met up country. He renewed contact with the radical and political figures who gathered at McNamara's bookshop, and had hopes of being appointed editor of the Sydney *Worker*. When these were disappointed he crossed to New Zealand in November (his letter to Emma Brooks from Hungerford had mentioned the offer of the editorship of a New Zealand paper). New Zealand was then regarded as one of the Australasian colonies, a prospective member of the proposed federation: 'I think the most pleasant days of my life were spent on an old telegraph line in New Zealand. Am inclined to prefer New Zealand of all the colonies', he wrote in an autobiographical note bound into Gertrude's 'The Lawson Family' manuscript in the Mitchell Library.

He arrived penniless in Wellington and was preparing to 'doss out' in the park when Tom Mills, then foreman compositor of the *New Zealand Times* sought him out and offered hospitality. This story, which Mills told in *Henry Lawson by His Mates* suggests (like all those other stories of the local press greeting Lawson and carrying him off to fete him wherever he berthed) the appeal his writing had for his generation all over Australasia. Mills knew Lawson only by his writings, but had already been lecturing on these to sympathetic gatherings. The days on the telegraph line, which Lawson remembered happily, were spent as a member of the gang laying a cable between Picton and Dunedin. 'Stiffner and Jim', 'His Country After All' and the 'Steelman' stories have their origins in his experiences during this time.

Late in July 1894 he returned to Sydney, expecting to take up a position on the *Daily Worker*, only to find it was on the point of folding. Once again he was disappointed in his hopes of finding regular, congenial employment as a writer, and returned to casual penny-a-line journalism for the weekly *Worker* and other papers, staying with his Aunt Emma or in cheap lodgings, still a Castlereagh and Pitt Street hack, a *lumpen-littérateur*.

Even so, this was a productive period. He continued to produce verse and fiction, as well as articles, prolifically; and he was reappraising his attitudes. His time on the *Boomerang* in Brisbane had set him free from his mother and her causes, and the Shearers' Strike had forced him to consider the distance, even conflict, between the ideals he had held abstractly and the realities he encountered, as also had the times spent around Bourke in the heartland of the Australian legend.

In *Henry Lawson by His Mates,* John Le Gay Brereton remembers first meeting the poet he admired so much at Mary Cameron's in 1895: 'You can take it from me, Jack, the Australian, workman is a brute' were Lawson's first words when they left together. In the pieces he contributed to the *Worker* he deunbunked the bush legend. Immediately after his return from Bourke he wrote:

> The average Australian bushman is too selfish, narrow-minded, and fond of booze to liberate his country. The average shearer thinks that he is the only wronged individual, and that the squatter is the only tyrant on the face of the earth. Also, the shearer is often a god-almighty in his own estimation; and it would be good for him to know that Australia might worry along if there wasn't a sheep in all the land.
>
> ('Our Countrymen', *Worker,* 1893; I, pp.308–09)

He criticised the shearers for claiming a monopoly of wrongs, and for asserting these selfishly and divisively against the interests of workers throughout the whole economy:

> Get rid of the idea that the shearers are the only wronged men on earth and the squatters are the only tyrants. Remember that the hardship of bush life at its worst is not a circumstance compared with what thousands of poor women in cities have to go through. Remember that there are bitterer struggles and grander battles fought by the poor of cities than ever in the country.
>
> ('A Word in Season', *Worker,* 1894; I, p.400)

At the same time, Lawson was a critical observer of 'mateship':

> The egoistic word 'mateship'—which was born of New Australian imagination, and gushed about to a sickening extent—implied a state of things which never existed any more than the glorious old unionism which was going to bear us on to freedom on one wave. The one was altogether too glorious, and the other too angelic to

exist amongst mortals.
('The Cant and Dirt of Labour Literature', *Worker,* 1894; I, p.399)

Here the 'New Australian' imagination refers specifically to William Lane's campaign to establish his socialist community, his ideal Australia, in Paraguay. But, more generally, Lawson was critical of 'mateship' in practice as both the traducing of a humanitarian ideal to sectional class interests, and as a creed more honoured in the breach than in the observance among its presumed adherents. The stories that followed his trip to Bourke do not unambiguously celebrate a 'collectivist, egalitarian' ethos any more than do these journalistic comments just quoted.[15]

'Baldy Thompson: A Sketch of A Squatter', based on the station owner who helped Lawson and his mate get back to Bourke, appeared in the same issue of the *Worker* as 'The Cant and Dirt of Labour Literature'. It revealed 'mateship' operating across the rural class divisions and aroused considerable indignation because of this. By contrast, a number of sketches and stories about the 'nomadic tribe' of bush workers elaborate the situation in 'A Typical Bush Yarn', which first appeared as a *Bulletin* 'par' in 1893:

> They were two chaps named Gory and Blanky. They were tramping from Nevermineware to Smotherplace. Gory was a bad egg, and Blanky knew it; but they'd fallen in with each other on the track and agreed to travel together for the sake of company. Blanky had £25, which fact was known to Gory, who was stumped.
>
> Every night Gory tried to get the money, which fact was known to Blanky, who never slept with more than one eye shut. When their tracks divided, Gory said to Blanky:
>
> 'Look a-here! Where the deuce do you keep that stuff of yourn? I've been tryin' to get holt on it every night when you was asleep'.

15 Russel Ward, comparing the Australian and American 'frontiersmen' writes of 'our collectivist, egalitarian bias' in *The Australian Legend* (Oxford University Press, Melbourne, 1958), p.258. [For a different reading see Michael Wilding, 'Henry Lawson's Socialist Vision' in *Studies in Classic Australian Fiction* (Sydney Studies 16, Sydney Association for Studies in Society and Culture, Sydney, 1998), pp.32–75.]

'I know you have,' said Blanky.
'Well, where the blazes did you put it?'
'Under your head!'
'The —, you did!'
They grinned, shook hands, and parted; and Gory scratched his head very hard and very often as he tramped along the track.[16]

The variations on the relationship between these mates, Brummy and Swampy as they became in later versions, can be seen as Lawson's critical appraisal of 'mateship' in practice. It is reflected in his work immediately after the Bourke experience with an unillusioned, sometimes sardonic realism. There is no idealisation of the bush as a moral alternative to the city. Also in the *Bulletin* in 1893 was his enumeration of 'Some Popular Australian Mistakes' which concluded: 'We wish to Heaven that Australian writers would leave off trying to make a paradise out of the Out Back Hell ... What's the good of making a heaven of a hell when by describing it as it really is we might do some good for the poor lost souls there?' (I, p.275).

Some years later he described his typical bushmen as themselves the victims of blinding 'literary' preconceptions about the Out Back:

> Bill and Jim do not see the bush as it is; and if they write verses about it—as they frequently do in camp—they put in shining rivers and grassy plains, and western hills, and dawn and morn and eve and gloaming; and forest boles of gigantic size—everything, in fact, which is not and never was in bush scenery or language; and the more the drought bakes them the more inspired they seem to become. Perhaps they unconsciously see the bush as it should be, and their literature is the result of craving for the ideal.
>
> ('The Bush and the Ideal', *Bulletin,* 1897; I, p.522)

At the end of 1894, just before Christmas, Louisa brought out Lawson's first book, *Short Stories in Prose and Verse,* on her *Dawn* press. Although it contained some of his finest early stories, including 'The Drover's

16 Lawson reworked this anecdote in 1894 and incorporated it within 'Two Sundowners', *Complete Works*, I, pp.394–95.

Wife' and 'The Bush Undertaker', it was poorly printed and produced. In his preface, its author expressed his glumness when he first saw it:

> This pamphlet—I can scarcely call it a volume—contains some of my earliest efforts, and they are sufficiently crude and faulty. They have been collected and printed hurriedly, with an eye to Christmas, and without experienced editorial assistance, which last, I begin to think, was sadly necessary. (I, p.427)

But he put up a brave front by opening with the assertion that:

> This is an attempt to publish, in Australia, a collection of sketches and stories at a time when everything Australian, in the shape of a book, must bear the imprint of a London publishing firm, before our critics will condescend to notice it, and before the 'reading public' will think it worth its while to buy nearly so many copies as will pay for the cost of presenting a suitable volume. (I, p.426)

Today, when the 'literary nationalism' of the past is often deplored, we need to remember the economic realities of the colonial literary culture, which Lawson knew so well by this time. Although there was a flourishing periodical press, Lawson who wrote prolifically for newspapers and magazines could not live by his writing in Sydney and was forced to seek painting and labouring jobs elsewhere. Book publication, which promised the chance of financial independence and a wider reputation, was still dominated by London and Edinburgh. But in 1895 Brereton introduced Lawson to George Robertson who had accepted the 'Banjo's' *The Man from Snowy River,* and Robertson agreed to publish a volume of verse and another of prose. Both appeared the following year: *In the Days When the World was Wide* and *While the Billy Boils.*

Much of what today we would think of as the essential Lawson appeared in *While the Billy Boils.* Essential not only because the collection as a whole displays those nationally 'representative' characteristics that A. G. Stephens was concerned with (as were many others after him), but also because it contained a good proportion of his best-known pieces: 'The Bush Undertaker', 'The Drover's Wife', '"Rats"', 'The Union Buries Its Dead', the early Mitchell sketches and Steelman stories, the travel sketches based on the trip to Bourke.

Although the four 'Joe Wilson' stories and at least 'The Loaded Dog' would need to be added, a short-list of the most popular and critically favoured pieces of Lawson's prose could almost be drawn from this volume alone. The fact that it collects pieces written before he was thirty suggests that his writing did not develop. This is true of his verse. The poems most fondly remembered today were amongst his earliest and were collected in *In the Days When the World Was Wide*. Nevertheless, a pattern of development, in technique if not always in quality, is discernible in, or behind, the fifty-two pieces that make up the prose collection; and it is a pattern that was to continue.

This pattern is most elusive in *While the Billy Boils* because the arrangement is not chronological. For example, 'His Father's Mate', his first story, appears half-way through the volume. Establishing the date of composition for other pieces is rarely so straight-forward: even though most had been published previously in periodicals, the dates of their appearances did not necessarily approximate to the dates of composition. Editors would hold contributions over for special issues, particularly their Christmas numbers, so that this, like Lawson's later prose collections, does not directly record his artistic development nor, fully, realise his intentions in composing a volume.

Stung by A. G. Stephens's criticism of the lack of organisation in *While the Billy Boils,* Lawson defended himself by saying there were pieces he wanted to include but the *Bulletin* would not release them. Later commentators, reacting quite properly against Stephens's conventional demands for 'a single plotted, climaxed story'[17] have emphasised the originality and modernity of Lawson's narrative discontinuities and have perceived underlying thematic relationships. While it is true, as they have argued, that the characters, events and settings that Lawson drew from his experience were unified in his imagination, this is not particularly observable with *While the Billy Boils.* (Logically, such an assertion, perhaps a truism with any writer, works against claims for the particular unity of a specific collection, because the assertion is ultimately directed beyond it, to the writer's complete corpus.) Although Stephens was unsympathetic to Lawson's imaginativeness, he was right in discerning the generic and qualitative

17 A. G. Stephens, 'Lawson's Prose', *Bulletin*, 29 August 1896, in Roderick, *Criticism*, p.51.

differences within this collection: some pieces *are* better than others and of a different imaginative order, even though we may not agree with Stephens's examples.

*While The Billy Boils* shows Lawson developing different techniques, working simultaneously in a number of genres (which is why 'development' becomes a difficult term after his earliest stories and sketches), sometimes observing, sometimes confusing expectations of what 'fiction' and 'journalism' should separately be. It shows him writing freely across a range of possibilities for imaginative prose and revealing opposed tendencies: towards melodrama, sentimentality, and moralising on the one hand, and on the other towards an austere realism that can generate symbolic suggestions of the absurd and the tragic, the ambiguously disturbing rather than the consolingly resolved. These extremes can be found in *While the Billy Boils* because it contains, for example, the early (and awful) 'When the Sun Went Down' as well as the unsentimentalised early stories that remain among his finest. This manifest variety in genre and quality is more revealing about Lawson as a writer in a specific literary culture and market than the postulated ultimate unity of all his work.

The collection displays a wide range of possibilities for imaginative prose and fiction, from the ostensibly factual Bourke sketches, through sketch stories like 'Going Blind', to a conventionally structured magazine story like 'The Geological Spieler'. To identify this as a magazine story is not to disparage it. Like 'The Iron Bark Chip' and 'The Loaded Dog' it is a good magazine story, with some morally unconventional or worrying overtones left to reverberate. Rather, it is to emphasise its distance from the sketch, and so the variety in the pieces Lawson was writing around the same time. This variety reflects the literary culture and the models he was responding to, as a freelance trying to live by his writing. Perhaps, if his markets and models had been different, he might have produced more of the open-ended sketch stories that modern critics prefer. But perhaps not. Late in his life, recalling Archibald as editor of the *Bulletin,* Lawson wrote that he had difficulty in persuading him 'to let me leave tragedy (as in 'His Father's Mate' or 'The Drover's Wife') for (alleged) humour'.[18]

The opposed tendencies within Lawson's writing from its beginnings

18 'Three or Four Archibalds and the Writer', *Complete Works,* II, p.987.

are symptomatic not only of his artistic personality but also of his circumstances as a penurious professional trying to judge advantageously the literary market in which he was working. Only by a ruthless selection from his prolific and varied journalism in the 1890s can we perceive him as a Chekhov, Joyce or Hemingway, an artistic purist. He could be that—as his close and continual revisions reveal. But he was also living from day to day by penny-a-line journalism and at the same time exploring how he could extend those apparently casual and 'authentic' sketches from life into the greater length and dramatic complexity of the magazine story—which paid more.

One of the last written and artistically mature of the stories in *While the Billy Boils* is 'Going Blind', which appeared in the *Worker* in 1895. It suggests the technical and imaginative developments that were taking place together within Lawson's fiction at this time, and within the outward confusion of his life. In 'Going Blind', the narrator, down on his luck, is boarding in the Full-and-Plenty Dining Rooms in Sydney. There he sympathetically befriends an older man who has come down from the country to seek treatment for his failing eyesight. They talk about the bush they both come from and about the old days. As the bushman's condition worsens, and it seems he has nowhere to return to nor any means of supporting himself in the city, the narrator attempts to help him, only to realise his own precarious situation. Then the bushman's brother, a drover, turns up unexpectedly to take him back up country.

From the narrator's nonchalant manner we might presume that this is an anecdotal sketch: that Lawson is writing up an encounter he has recently had in a boarding house on that 'urban frontier' between threadbare respectability and hopeless penury that he knew so intimately in these years. We have the same sense that he is writing up, as distinct from making up in 'Board and Residence' (also in *While the Billy Boils)* which is clearly an autobiographical sketch about city boarding house life; and in 'Mr Smellingscheck', which appeared in the *Bulletin* in 1897, and gives the impression of being a character sketch based on an actual encounter. But while 'Going Blind' has in its narrative manner and details the same sense of 'authenticity' as these sketches, it is clearly a *story* in the fullness of its dramatic development and its manipulation of the narrator's point of view, so that he becomes an observed, not merely an observing, character who extends the implications of the story to a complex extent.

The note of 'authenticity' in the presentation of the Full-and-Plenty Dining Rooms, the image of contemporary urban reality against which the memories and ideal of country life are to be tested, is achieved by literary means. There are the rhetorical repetitions in 'greasy little table', 'greasy little corner', 'greasy little dining room', 'greasy little kitchen'; the personalising of the impersonal with the 'roast beef one' or 'corn beef and cabbage one', and the comic grotesquerie of the waiter seen as a living skeleton in miniature.

These elements, which seem to be contrasting the realistic setting against which memories of the bush as an ideal alternative can be contrasted, are heavily literary. In a word they are 'Dickensian', amusing the reader and distancing him from the 'low' life which they present in all its quaintness. But they are not drawing on the Dickens model for conventional sentiment, as the earlier Arvie Aspinall stories were. Here they are employed dramatically by Lawson, on behalf of the narrator, who provides the setting in a jocularly depreciatory, embarrassed way, as though to suggest that if you looked on the funny side, if you could see their 'bohemian' character, the Full-and-Plenty Dining Rooms were really colourful. He poses, that is, as an amused, detached but knowing observer of the seamier side of life. Then he meets the bushman who has come from one of the old Selection Districts, like Lawson himself, and from the past:

> We talked about grubbing and fencing and digging and droving and shearing—all about the bush—and it all came back to me as we talked. 'I can see it all now', he said once, in an abstracted tone, seeming to fix his helpless eyes on the wall opposite. But he didn't see the dirty blind wall, nor the dingy window, nor the skimpy little bed, nor the greasy wash-stand: he saw the dark blue ridges in the sunlight, the grassy sidings and flats, the creek with the clumps of she-oak here and there, the course of the willow-fringed river below, the distant peaks and ranges fading away into a lighter azure, the granite ridge in the middle distance, and the rocky rises, the stringy-bark and the apple-tree flats, the scrubs, and the sunlit plains—and all I could see it, too—plainer than ever I did. (I, p.455)

Of course, the man who is going blind cannot 'see it all'. His vision is formed by homesickness and nostalgia for the past of his youth. It is the narrator who does the seeing for him—as he does more literally elsewhere in the story—but the narrator too 'sees' the vision plainer than ever he did. But what reality has this vision compared with the dirty, dingy, greasy reality in which they actually are? It also is a literary description—a cadenced, composed, romantic landscape with echoes of the 'Banjo's' 'sunlit plains extended'.

Instead of a simple disjunction between a literary ideal of the bush and contemporary urban reality, we have the literary versions of both thrown into question. The vision of the old life of the country is that of memory and imagination; and the jauntiness of the narrator's opening sketch of the Full-and-Plenty Dining Rooms is quickly undercut. The man who is going blind runs out of money, he is forced out of his room, and hopes to survive as 'a street musician', that is, a beggar.

This development and his desire to assist, force the narrator to a realisation of his own marginal position in society. The opening description of the Full-and-Plenty Dining Rooms, we now realise, was sentimentalised by the narrator remembering when he was 'a respectable single man'—which has ambiguous implications for what he is at the time of telling this story. The appearance of Jack Gunther's brother, who arrives unexpectedly to take him back to the world within those dark blue ridges, threatens a clumsy resolution. It could provide a dramatic confirmation that the moral alternative to the city is there to return to in fact, not only in memory and imagination.

But the story does not fall into sentimentality. The focus on the brother's protectiveness towards Jack puts the emphasis on the present, and the uncertain future, rather than on the past. The quiet closing line, 'I felt their grips on my hand for five minutes after we parted', leaves the story open, and the narrator alone in the now unfriendly environment Jack has been rescued from, with only the memory of the contact he had established with the brothers, and no suggestion that he will have anyone else to turn to, to assist him in maintaining his amusement with 'low' city life.

'Going Blind' is a story which brings together many of Lawson's preoccupations: 'Sydney or the Bush'; 'mateship' or the brotherhood of those enduring together the adversity of life; the temptation to engage in nostalgic reverie for a lost, simpler past, which, like the temptation to escape into drink that comes into the end of the story, Lawson knew so well himself. These cultural and personal preoccupations are brought together delicately yet, for all the story's casually colloquial manner of narration, in a fully dramatised way that opens up implications rather than enforces a point. These implications are that our purchases on 'reality' are as uncertain as our fortunes—or our health. 'Reality' is an image we form subjectively and imaginatively to invest life with some meaning. The contemporary cultural contraries, Sydney or the Bush, become subsumed under a wider set of dramatically reconciled contraries—the real and the ideal, the 'actual' and the 'literary'. While it is necessary to attempt to apprehend the world as it is, without succumbing to drink, delusion or despair, one needs also to retain those ideals and imaginative qualities which can sustain one in adversity and sympathetic rapport with others.

We cannot say that Lawson 'sees' the idealised image of the Bush which the narrator of the story does, but we could say that Lawson implies some ideal is necessary in a reality that would otherwise be unendurably bleak. It is then, to use A. A. Phillips's important distinction, an 'unashamedly sentimental' story in being a moving account of the sympathetic but momentary contact between transients, but through its wealth of implication, its thematic complexity, it avoids 'sentimentality', the neat, simple resolution.[19]

In 1896, the same year as *While the Billy Boils* and *In the Days When the World Was Wide* appeared, Lawson married Bertha Bredt, a nineteen-year-old trainee nurse from Melbourne. He had met her the previous year when she visited Sydney to see her mother, who had married W. H. T. McNamara, the proprietor of the Castlereagh Street bookshop. Lawson cut short a second visit to New Zealand to court Bertha.

With the favourable reception of two books and marriage in the same year, Lawson might have seemed to have established himself securely and at last to be starting on a stable career. Financially this was not to be so, for while he continued to write prolifically, his income remained uncertain, and all the more inadequate now he was married. In fact, he had to borrow ten pounds to marry and soon after the newlyweds left

19 A. A. Phillips, 'The Craftsmanship of Lawson', *Meanjin* 2 (1948); *The Australian Tradition* (Cheshire, Melbourne, 1958), p.12.

for Perth in search of employment during the boom there—only to find that they had to live in a tent while Henry returned to his old trade of house-painting. It is possible that Bertha wanted to take her husband out of Sydney, away from his drinking companions, for the once shy, awkward bush lad now regularly found conviviality and confidence through drink.

From the beginning of the marriage, there was conflict between the bohemian city habits that Henry had formed, at least since his return from Bourke, and the domesticity that Bertha could reasonably have expected marriage to bring. Like all Lawson's past and future attempts to resolve his difficulties by going elsewhere, their stay in Western Australia was short-lived. After their return, Bertha's concern may have been increased by talk of her husband's interest in Hannah Thornburn, a young woman who modelled occasionally for one of his artist friends. While the nature of the relationship between Henry and Hannah is uncertain, she later grew in his imagination into a romanticised, compensating figure: one who, like his dead sister Nettie, became the focus for his wistful, wounded broodings over what might have been. In any case, Bertha was anxious to remove him from the company he was keeping in Sydney and persuaded him to look again for work in New Zealand.

They arrived in Wellington in April 1897 with a reference from Archibald that, with Lawson's reputation as a writer and the co-operation of politicians and officials, secured him a post as the teacher of a Maori school at Mangamaunu. The best part of six months was spent here, in what at first appealed as idyllic isolation, but which soon became a wearisome and stressful confinement. Bertha provides the chief sources on this period, through her contribution to *Henry Lawson by His Mates,* and the later *My Henry Lawson* 'ghosted' by her de facto Will Lawson (who was no relation). But she has been shown to have been inaccurate about many of the details she recalled, more than thirty and forty years later (especially details relating to the Joe Wilson stories), and unrevealing about this testing time in their marriage.

The Lawsons' stay at Mangamaunu has been closely reconstructed by W. H. Pearson in his *Henry Lawson Among Maoris* (1968). He argues from the literary evidence that the experience, which was intended to result in freshly inspired writing, induced instead an 'artistic crisis' when Lawson, confronted by cultural values he could not sympathise with, withdrew to 'a recognition of the limitations in time and place in which his talents could operate'.[20] This crisis anticipated what was to happen in London, and later in Sydney, following his return to a very different Australia from the one he had come to artistic consciousness in.

Bertha's pregnancy provided the excuse to return to Wellington from Mangamaunu in October 1897. It was there that Bland Hold commissioned a playscript, 'Pinter's Son Jim', which ended up as the story (rather than the announced novel), 'The Hero of Redclay'. From Wellington Lawson wrote a letter to his old friend 'Jack' Le Gay Brereton, suggesting that he was feeling some conflict in adjusting to the responsibilities of marriage after the careless days of 'knocking around' with his mates. A similar sentiment is expressed in the poem 'Written Afterwards', dedicated to Brereton, which appeared in the *Bulletin* early in 1898. In February that year, his son 'Jim' was born and the family returned to Sydney the following month.

Again, as in New Zealand, a tradition of state patronage assisted the writer of growing reputation, and family, but without any steady means of support. A sinecure was found for him in the Government Statistician's Office. Lawson, however, was cavalier about the minimal obligations of signing on and off entailed (perhaps because he found them demeaning) and it was revoked. Archibald, the most generous of editors, responded to constant requests for advances and loans, and George Robertson, the most generous of publishers, protected Lawson against his willingness to dispose of his copyright. But still colonial Australian society could not provide a writer it esteemed with a market he could live by. In New Zealand, Lawson had decided that his best hope of making a career from writing full-time lay in London. He had been encouraged by interested enquiries from Blackwood, Chambers and Methuen. He began preparing stories with which to break into the metropolitan market, and wrote to Angus and Robertson that he did not intend to 'sacrifice any more *prose* work in Australia'.

Back in Sydney again, however, he found himself among the old difficulties, and old friends. These were the years celebrated in George Taylor's *Those Were the Days,* Arthur Jose's *The Romantic Nineties*

20 W. H. Pearson, *Henry Lawson Among Maoris* (Australian National University Press, Canberra, 1968), p.155.

and Randolph Bedford's *Naught to Thirty-Three,* of Sydney bohemia and the Dawn and Dusk Club—though from these accounts by contemporaries, 'bohemia' seems to have meant mainly beer, some cheap red wine with food, lots of talk and then home to the family by the last ferry or tram. For Lawson, with his low tolerance of alcohol, such distractions were injurious.

Towards the end of 1898, he entered a home for inebriates, and then began a more stable period while he revised *In the Days When the World Was Wide* for a new edition, to appear in 1900; put together a new collection of verse and another of prose for Angus and Robertson; and worked on material he was intending to try on the London market. When the new collections, *Verses Popular and Humorous, On The Track* and *Over the Sliprails* appeared in 1900, Lawson was finally on his way to London, having been obliged, as he wrote to Earl Beauchamp requesting assistance, to 'sacrifice two more books in Australia'.[21]

Like *While the Billy Boils* (and the prose collections that were to follow), *On the Track* and *Over the Sliprails* provide no clear guide to developments in Lawson's writing, as they include pieces written before his previous collection, such as 'The Darling River' and the Steelman stories inspired by his first visit to New Zealand. Their inclusion contributes heavily to the sense of formal variety in the two volumes (which were also combined in the same year). While the pieces known to have been written later show variety across a range of modes and moods ('The Iron Bark Chip', 'They Wait on the Wharf in Black', 'No Place for a Woman', 'The Hero of Redclay') they have, when considered together, the common characteristic of further extending the sketch or sketch story towards the length and shape of the magazine story. They are more fully rounded off, with amplification of settings and characters. They continue the process, discernible among the later stories in *While the Billy Boils,* and suggest that with the realisation that he could not live by his writings in Australia, Lawson was deliberately extending the sketch stories that had made him famous, but kept him penurious in Australia, to the length preferred by English publishers of books and magazines. The risk, inherent in his fiction from the beginning, was that, in departing

21 Letter to Hugh Maccallum, Angus and Robertson, 30 December, 1897 in Roderick, *Letters*, p.82; letter to Beauchamp, 19 January 1900, ibid., pp.112–14; and in Kiernan, pp.181–83.

from the austere realism of the sketch, he would succumb to his own worst 'literary' tendencies towards melodrama and sentimentality, tendencies he was better able to control in the sketch-based shorter fictions.

'The Hero of Redclay' epitomises this, as did Lawson's pursuit of success by experimenting with different popular forms. First announced as a novel (though Lawson in his letters to George Robertson soon changed his mind about his abilities to write one 'or something connected'),[22] it was attempted as a stage melodrama for Bland Holt, before receiving its final prose version as a story in *Over the Sliprails*. There was later also to be a verse version titled 'Ruth'.

The story enlists Mitchell as its narrator and the matter of Bourke for its setting to lend 'authenticity' to a contrived tale of noble self-sacrifice that, in its sentiments, is reminiscent of such apprentice pieces as 'The Tale of Malachi', and anticipates the sentimentalising of the 'Bush' that was soon to occur in London. Colin Roderick tells us that after the turn of the century Lawson insisted on the capital 'B' to 'designate the ideal inhabitants of his ideal commonwealth' and to distinguish this from any actual rural society. In the article 'Crime in the Bush' for the *Bulletin* in 1899 the lower case bush is remembered as a place of unnatural horrors—murders, arson, incest, feuds—bred out of isolation, hardship and ignorance. But in 'The Hero of Redclay' the idealised Bush—'the ideal social setting for unselfishness, mateship, nobility, and virtues of all kinds, but also the alien force that vitiated the heroism of these virtues'—is already apparent.[23]

In the *Bulletin* in 1899 also appeared ' "Pursuing Literature in Australia" ', a review of his career, which ended bitterly with his advice for the young Australian writer to somehow get to England, the United States, anywhere else—or shoot himself. A. G. Stephens's rejoinder to this in his own magazine, the *Bookfellow*, pointed out it was Lawson's own poor business sense in selling his copyright for immediate return that was responsible for the poor return from his books, not Australia which 'admires and loves and liberally encourages him'.[24] Stephens

22 Roderick, *Letters*, pp.63–64; Kiernan, pp.181–83.

23 Colin Roderick, 'Commentary' in *The Bush Undertaker and Other Stories* (Angus and Robertson, Sydney, 1970), p.264. See also his introduction to *Henry Lawson: Short Stories and Sketches* (Angus and Robertson, Sydney, 1972), p.xix.

was right but, even so, the Australia which had responded so warmly to Lawson could not support him adequately through advances and royalties.

When he wrote to Earl Beauchamp asking for assistance to get to London, Lawson enclosed a copy of ' "Pursuing Literature in Australia" ', and claimed, with exaggeration, that there was no market for purely Australian literature within Australia itself'. There was, as Lawson had shown, but he had also found that it was not large enough to support him fully as a self-employed writer. With the assistance from Beauchamp and others, he was able to sail with his family (which now included two-month old Bertha) to the literary metropolis, as he had been preparing himself to do since at least his stay at Mangamaunu. He also left with the intention of helping an aspiring young Australian writer, having arranged to have sent on to him in London the manuscript of Miles Franklin's *My Brilliant Career.*

Outwardly, at least, the move to England seemed to bring the success that Lawson had been seeking. After a couple of weeks in London on their arrival, the family settled in the village of Harpenden, Hertfordshire. As he recounts in ' "Succeeding": A Sequel to "Pursuing Literature" ', he engaged the pioneering literary agent James B. Pinker, who acted for some of the most prominent writers of the day, including Conrad, James, Wells, Kipling and Bennett, and was advised to concentrate on 'good work' rather than attempt to calculate what would suit the London market.[25]

He contributed to such prestigious literary magazines as *Blackwood's, Cassell's,* and *Chambers'*. William Blackwood proposed republication of *While the Billy Boils,* and a selection from this, together with a dozen stories from *On the Track* and *Over the Sliprails,* was published in 1901 as *The Country I Come From.* Also from the same publisher in the same

24 A. G. Stephens, 'Lawson and Literature', *Bookfellow,* 18 February 1899, in Roderick, *Criticism,* p.81.

25 A. G. Stephens extracted some passages from this sequel to 'Pursuing Literature', and published them as 'The Sweet Uses of London' in the *Bulletin,* October 1903. The remainder of the manuscript is among the Lothian paper in the La Trobe Library, Melbourne, together with that of 'Going on the Land' referred to below. They were first published in Brian Kiernan, ed., *The Essential Henry Lawson* (Currey O'Neil, Kew, Vic., 1982).

year appeared a new collection, *Joe Wilson and His Mates.* In 1902 Methuen brought out another new collection, *Children of the Bush.* With three books within two years, Lawson had made an impression in the literary metropolis, most notably on Edward Garnett, who wrote a laudatory appreciation of Lawson as a critical realist, the imaginative interpreter of Australian life.

The four Joe Wilson stories from the first of these new collections are generally regarded as the peak of Lawson's artistic development. In them, the move towards the more expansive form of the magazine story, while still retaining the 'authenticity', the austerity and edge, of the earlier sketch stories, reaches its fullest elaboration. So much so that the sequence as a whole has been taken to be another attempt, following the abortive 'The Hero of Redclay', at writing a novel and answering A. G. Stephens's criticisms of the lack of structure in *While the Billy Boils.* These had rankled with Lawson and, although he had recognised soon after that his talent was for short stories and sketches rather than 'a novel, or something connected', his correspondence while in England (and later referring back to that period) still mentions plans for a novel.

It is not clear, though, what Lawson understood by this term. Even Stephens's original remarks had been ambiguous: his demands for 'unity of ideas and treatment' could have been satisfied by a narratively-linked story cycle, such as the Joe Wilson sequence provides, or a more thematically and modally composed collection in the volume as a whole (such as Lawson claimed he had aimed at with *While the Billy Boils,* but was never to achieve). Lawson was most likely envisaging a number of formal possibilities when he wrote later of constructing a novel, 'a Bush strike novel' or 'an Australian novel' with 'A Child in the Dark and a Foreign Father' as the opening chapter.[26]

But the assumption he would have seen as underlying Stephens's use of the term, that a longer, continuous narrative is superior to short stories, would have been widely shared by publishers and readers. If false aesthetically, such a hierarchical view was sound commercially, as Lawson would have been well aware. Should the sequence of Joe Wilson stories be taken to indicate the form Lawson had in mind when

26 Letter to Edward Garnett, 27 (or 28) February 1902 (original in Humanities Research Centre, University of Texas; photocopy in Chaplin Lawson Collection, Rare Books, University of Sydney Library); letter to Thomas Lothian, 18 March 1907, in Lothian Papers, La Trobe Library.

he referred to his intentions of writing a novel? And does it fall within our understanding of what a novel may be, an understanding which is perhaps more accommodating today because of formal experimentation since the turn of the century?

Beginning the first (but last written) story, 'Joe Wilson's Courtship', the reader might initially be put off by the sentimental narrator with his reiterated advice to 'make the most of your courting days, you young chaps', and be reminded of Lawson himself at his self-pitying and moralising worst. Joe and Lawson are close: the sense we have from the tone that the narrator is a version of the author's self is reinforced by details, throughout the whole sequence, that are recognisably drawn from the family romance of Lawson's childhood. (The recently identified fragment of another Joe Wilson story, 'Going on the Land', is a fictionalised version of a neighbour's, Spencer's, death recorded in the autobiography—and also an indication of the loosely (auto)biographical structure Lawson later had in mind for an extended Joe Wilson series or 'novel'.)

Although Bertha claimed that she and Henry in Manamaunu were the models for Mary and Joe, Lawson was not drawing directly and exclusively on his own experience. While he set the stories in the area in which he had grown up, the time in which the events take place is vaguely that of an earlier generation; and Joe's courtship of May has echoes of Peter Larsen's courtship of Louisa and Henry Albury's of Harriet Winn in Lawson's, Louisa's and Gertrude's reminiscences. The rosebush, the grapevine, and the ivy that weave their elusively suggestive pattern in the first story might remind readers familiar with the total text of the family romance of Louisa's plantings at Eurunderee, but in their fictional context they take on an imaginative resonance to serve the story's theme—a classically literary one—of *carpe diem,* or 'Gather ye rosebuds while ye may'.

Instead of a single source in personal history being drawn on, Lawson's own, his parents', his grandparents' reminiscences and those of his Uncle Job and Aunt Gertrude Falconer at Lahey's Creek (she was also a model for 'The Drover's Wife')[27] are conflated, and relocated in the eternal Arcady of courtship. Those with an eye for autobiographical

27 Letter to Frank Beaumont Smith, n.d. (June 1916), in Roderick, *Letters*, pp.248–49.

correspondence will also detect aspects of the author distributed among the characters other than Joe Wilson: Joe's friend Jack, who is poetical and inclined to be sentimental about himself, and Romany, with the gipsy blood that Lawson was romantically inclined to claim for himself.

Despite the maundering tone of the opening, the interplay between the two ages—the golden age of youth that the garrulous older Joe remembers with nostalgia, and the actuality the younger Joe experiences—is controlled with assurance by the author behind the narrator to bring out the story's, and the story cycle's, theme of the precariousness and transience of all happiness. While this theme is dramatically pursued in the second (but first written) story, 'Brighten's Sister-in-law', with Joe fearing his young son (named Jim, like Lawson's own) will die in a convulsive fit, the tone and structure are quite different.

Again there is a conflation of personal experiences (Lawson's memories of himself as a child and a father) and again the literary element is marked, but this time with some unfortunate melodramatic effects when Joe sees the apparition of a woman above the trees and imagines the black horse racing beside him. In contrast with this literary inflation is the presentation of Brighten's shanty and his sister-in-law which has all the precision of detail in the earlier sketch stories and is like these in allowing the details (the black bottle, the polished tins, the old china) to suggest rather than explain the anomalies and enigmas met with in the bush.

'Water Them Geraniums', the key story (or stories, because 'A Lonely Track' and 'Past Carin' that comprise it were written separately and in reverse order) contains a succession of sketches: the Wilsons' selection, memories of Gulgong, the Spicer lad who arrives with the gift of meat on his remarkable horse ('Jack Cornstalk in His Teens', as he had appeared in another version in the *Australian Star* in 1899), the Spicer selection. If it seems *the* great Lawson story quintessentially, it would be because it contains so many of the subjects and themes found in his earlier writing. Mrs Spicer is his mature version of the Drover's Wife, with the same incongruous interest in fashion plates, the same ridiculous experience of putting her finger through a hole in her handkerchief; though, significantly, this incident is dramatised rather than directly narrated in this version, and it is Mary who insists on the civilising ritual of the Sunday promenade. Much other 'material' from earlier stories and sketches, in verse as well as prose, can be glimpsed in it, but we are not left with a sense of fragmentation because it all forms part of Joe's perception of Mrs Spicer, and of his own wife whom he has brought to what seems 'no place for a woman'.

To compare 'Water Them Geraniums' with the earlier sketches, say 'The Drover's Wife', is to appreciate the nature of Lawson's development during his most creative decade. The ability to present a succession of precise, authenticating details and leave them to suggest their deeper significance is the constant characteristic of his most imaginative writing over this time. Here, the geraniums especially have such a bedraggled particularity that one would not want to belabour their simultaneously metaphoric function in suggesting Mrs Spicer's hopes of 'something better—something higher'. At the same time, the whole story is much more fully dramatised than the earlier sketch stories: through the interaction of more characters, through dialogue, and through Joe's narration, which produces a distancing, a filtering of effect that might otherwise have been sentimentalising or defeatedly pessimistic.

To attempt to do justice to 'Water Them Geraniums', one falls back lamely on hackneyed and fulsome appeals to 'life', 'compassion' and 'the human condition'. Nothing in Australian writing looks further into the emptiness of life for the individual and yet finds some meaning in it, through Mrs Spicer's gruff love for her children and her hopes for their future, even though their lives seem as blighted as those geraniums. While its power is reinforced by its place in the sequence as a whole, with its recurrent theme of the bush as 'no place for a woman', and with drink, madness, or death as the only means of escape, it also stands completely achieved within itself.

'A Double Buggy at Lahey's Creek' rounds the sequence off in an open way by showing the Wilsons enjoying some prosperity and experiencing again some of the happiness of their courting days. It is, in a lighter, more simply sentimental vein, a variation on the sequence's theme of the evanescence of happiness within life's predominantly melancholy course which allows some happiness to be recaptured, at least momentarily. While self-contained, 'A Double Buggy' depends more than the preceding stories on its place in the sequence for it to achieve its full effect, and win the readers' interest in its characters and their domestic situation.

Internally, then, the cycle of four stories as it appeared in *Joe Wilson and His Mates* has its thematic interconnections, and a cumulative effect transcending that obtained when each part is read separately. But these are only some characteristics of the novel, whereas they are distinguishing attributes of the 'discontinuous' short story narrative. While having linking characters and concerns, such narratives need not be consistent in mode or characterisation, nor causally related, and so can present a different view of life, of the way things happen, than novels, or at least the paradigms of the novel Lawson would have known. Seeing the Joe Wilson sequence as significantly structured to express the discontinuous and discrete nature of the individual experience frees it of the imputation that it falls short of achieving another (and, it is assumed, superior) form.

But after these stories were published, Lawson wrote to William Blackwood and Edward Garnett that he was working towards a novel. Did he see the Joe Wilson cycle as such, or in embryo? This issue, as it has become in Lawson criticism, is not finally a matter of facts (though there is the indisputable fact that, whatever his intentions, Lawson was never to write a novel), but of interpretation—of what a novel is, and what Lawson meant by the term.

Little was known about Lawson's time in England until recently (and many personal details remain uncertain), and no certain chronology had been established for the composition of some of his most famous stories which appeared while he was there. This obviously presented any critical biographer with problems in interpreting the fullest body of evidence, the writings. Were the Joe Wilson stories written earlier at Mangamaunu (as Bertha claimed), and others, like 'The Loaded Dog' and 'Telling Mrs Baker', before Lawson left for London, so that his best late fictions were completed in anticipation of English publication?

In his postscript to the four Joe Wilson stories in the book, Lawson states that 'Brighten's Sister-in-law' was written first. Lawson is not always reliable on such details, but Colin Roderick has located Blackwood's letter accepting this story on 13 August 1900. The letter Blackwood wrote on 10 October 1900, enclosing proofs of 'your excellent sketch "Brighten's Sister-in-law"' and accepting 'A Double Buggy' would seem to be the letter Lawson recalls in ' "Succeeding" '. If this more recently discovered manuscript is accepted as reliable, it further suggests that 'Brighten's Sister-in-law' was 'the simple domestic little Bush story' that Lawson wrote after meeting Pinker, and that the Joe

Wilson series was begun in England.

Pinker's accounts to Lawson for typing (in the Chaplin Lawson Collection, Rare Books, University of Sydney Library) reinforce this by showing that 'Brighten's Sister-in-law' was typed in July 1900. It appeared in *Blackwood's Magazine* for November 1900, and was followed by 'A Double Buggy', "'Past Carin'", 'Joe Wilson's Courtship' and 'A Lonely Track'. While the correspondence with Blackwood establishes that Lawson was working to a plan for a Joe Wilson series, it was much more loosely conceived than the presentation of the four stories in *Joe Wilson and His Mates* would suggest, and included the Peter M'Laughlan stories in which Joe is either the narrator or a secondary character. Having been rejected by Blackwood, these stories were to appear in *Children of the Bush.*

Colin Roderick plausibly conjectures that a house editor or reader, possibly Edward Garnett, or Arthur Maquarie (the friend described in "'Succeeding'") proposed the arrangement of the stories for book publication. Roderick's reconstruction of Lawson's work while in England (which is confirmed by Pinker's accounts for typing) shows him continuing to write spasmodically in various modes and moods, rather than concentrating on a sustained project. Yet, and despite the letter he had written to George Robertson in January 1897, in which he had recognised he was not a novelist, Lawson's correspondence to Blackwood and Garnett shows he retained an ambition to write a 'novel', perhaps the 'single, plotted, climaxed story' A. G. Stephens had suggested, or some otherwise unified volume.[28]

(If Lawson had not conceived the Joe Wilson sequence as a 'novel', he came to consider the possibility of its becoming one. In 1907, on 18 March, he wrote to Thomas Lothian from the *Bulletin* office that "'A Child in the Dark" was commenced in England as an Australian novel,

28 Colin Roderick, 'Henry Lawson's *Joe Wilson:* Skeleton Novel or Short Story Sequence?', *Overland* 66 (1977), 35–47. See also, John Barnes, 'Henry Lawson in London', *Quadrant* (July 1979), 24–35. Both articles quote correspondence between Blackwood and Lawson, and Barnes the correspondence between Garnett and Lawson. Photocopies of the latter are in the Chaplin Lawson Collection, Rare Books, University of Sydney; for a description see Harry F. Chaplin, *Henry Lawson: His Books, Manuscripts, Autograph Letters and Association Copies,* Studies in Australian Bibliography (Wentworth Press, Surry Hills, N.S.W., 1974), pp.72–73.

but broken off and published as a leading Xmas *Bulletin* story. I have great hopes for a novel.' A scribbled note listing the proposed contents of *Triangles of Life,* which includes 'A Child in the Dark' and the later Joe Wilson stories 'Drifting Apart' and 'James and Maggie', has 'A Child in the Dark' struck out with the remark alongside, 'To complete Joe Wilson'. This, and the fragment 'Going on the Land', also among the Lothian Papers, suggest that Lawson saw his (auto)biographically related, but discontinuous sequence of stories as potentially the 'novel' he still hoped to write—though by this time he was having great difficulty in putting any kind of new collection together.)

While, as a collection, *Joe Wilson and His Mates* again fell short of Lawson's proclaimed ideal of a composed volume (to fill it out, he included some reworked material reaching as far back as 1894), it contained two other classic stories written in England which show him working in other modes and moods. 'The Loaded Dog' is not merely a splendid example of one kind of comic magazine tale, an Australian version of 'frontier humour', but it also has its dark and Promethean overtones—which might be why it is such a perennial favourite of children. The retribution that is visited blindly and excessively on the nasty yellow dog also wreaks its toll on the innocents among the canine population; they resignedly have to suffer with the guilty the effects of Andy Page's working in mysterious ways.

'Telling Mrs Baker' also has its resonances and unresolved implications. Critical opinion is divided (and is likely to remain so) whether this story's ending, with the girl from the city telling both narrators 'I like the Bushmen! They are grand men—they are noble' and kissing them, topples into sentimentality, or retains its precarious balance with the laconic nudge from the final line, 'I don't think it did either of us any harm'. But scholastic attempts to resolve the contrasting modulations Lawson is offering simultaneously might distract us from the story's revealing dramatisation of an artistic decision for its author. These are two versions of Baker's death, the true story which Jack tells us and the fiction his mate Andy invents to tell the widow. The difference is between a faithful sketch from life, which emerges as 'squalid' realism, or a fictional artifice which, while it runs the risk of seeming false or evasive, succeeds, with equal plausibility, to invert the truth, grant Baker some human worth, and impose some dignity on his death.

Regardless of how successful Lawson is seen in balancing realism and romance at the story's end, their opposition is central to its whole conception. To ask which is, artistically, the preferable version—Jack's 'true' but inherently nihilistic account, or Andy's false but consoling fiction—is to recognise Lawson's awareness, through *his story*, of problematical relationships between life and art. There are a number of references to art and artifice here—the reproduction of Wellington's heroic meeting with Blucher at Waterloo, with the dead heaped up 'a bit extra', the *Sydney Illustrated Journal,* the sister who has written for the *Bulletin.* But there is no suggestion that Andy's story is bad art, even though the sister suspects he has not told the truth. She approves of the way he has reshaped it to meet conventional expectations, to familiarise it, and to leave for his family some sense of meaning and value in his life.

This can be read as a paradigm of Lawson's own artistic development: he also had sought to be true to remembered experience, to sketch it accurately, yet to discover within it a value that would give some meaning to otherwise pointless, inhuman, or unendurable existence. Looking ahead to Lawson's next collection, *Children of the Bush,* 'Telling Mrs Baker' can be seen as hovering over a decisive brink: Lawson's artistic decision was to side with Mrs Baker's sister and her idolisation of the capitalised Bushmen, to prefer the consolations of the romantic (if still ostensibly realistic) version to the disturbing truth of remembered experience.

Technically, the stories in *Children of the Bush* (which was published by Methuen in 1902, after Lawson had departed for Australia) continue the pattern of extending the manner, and matter, of the earlier sketch stories into magazine stories. But a new development in Lawson's attitudes to the bush is obvious. 'Send Round the Hat', 'That Pretty Girl in the Army', 'Lord Douglas', 'Shall We Gather at the River?' 'His Brother's Keeper' would be the stories we would look to first of all for the enunciation of the creed of mateship and to find Lawson in the role of, as in H. P. Heseltine's ironic title, 'Saint Henry—Our Apostle of Mateship'. The verse epigraph to the collection, 'The Shearers', sums up the sentiments of the creed with a simple, moving eloquence, the colloquialisms checking any more fulsome and fervid tendencies. But this is not the view of the bushmen that Lawson had conveyed through his earlier writings. In them, although mateship could be sentimental, in the relations between parents and children, or even a man and his dog, it was more often problematical as a social code, seeming 'a combination of cruel practical joking, irresponsible behaviour, and, occasionally, even dishonesty'.[29]

The stories in *Children of the Bush* lack these incongruous elements found in the best of earlier pieces, even the humorous tales, when Lawson is presenting the relationships between men facing a hard world together. In being rounded out, such rough edges are smoothed away; a sense of community is discovered among social reprobates, warm hearts are found to beat beneath the roughest of exteriors, and one touch of kindness is shown to make the whole world kin.

We can enjoy the more novelistic narration of these stories, with their greater amplification of character and situation, while still recognising that they are magazine stories for which those comparisons with Bret Harte, that Lawson had so much resented earlier, are not inappropriate. Their conventions are not only those of heart-warming Victorian sentimental melodrama—already dated by the time they were written—but also Lawson's own, those he had created in his earlier work. His vernacular narrators and by now stereotyped 'typical' characters, the matter of Bourke and the matter of Eurunderee, are drawn on mechanically to win his audience's acceptance of them as familiar and 'authentic'. For example, 'Gentleman-Once' begins: 'Peter M'Laughlan, Bush missionary, Joe Wilson and his mate Jack Barnes, shearers for the present, and a casual swagman named Jack Mitchell, were camped at Cox's Crossing in a bend of Eurunderee Creek'.

Instead of being the beginning of an apparent 'sketch from life' that, like 'Going Blind' or 'Water Them Geraniums', develops into a sketch story of magazine length, this is the conventional opening to a magazine story which enlists these familiar characters, and this setting, in the hope of looking an 'authentic' Lawson story. From extending sketches towards the length of magazine stories, Lawson has come nearly full circle, to writing conventional stories that pretend to be sketched from life. Out of his memories of Bourke in '92 and '93, and out of the family romance, he is creating an ideal world that answers to his homesickness in England, his nostalgia for a simpler past, and his humanitarian

29 H. P. Heseltine, 'Saint Henry—Our Apostle of Mateship', *Quadrant* 1 (1960), in Roderick, *Criticism,* p.347.

sympathies, now detached from the political causes he had espoused in more youthful years.

'Send Round the Hat' presents itself as a sketch story, with its writer-narrator Harry, who is painting a hotel in Bourke (as Lawson himself had done), sketching from life the Giraffe and other typical locals and recounting a revealing incident. Essentially, though, it is preaching the social gospel in the homely terms of mateship, with the Giraffe as a simple saintly figure protecting the women taken in adultery. As part of this sketch's fuller fictionalisation, Mitchell is allowed his wry worldly observations, which contribute to the dramatisation of Harry as another simple decent character in the story. But innocence and instinctive charity win hands down over Mitchell's cynical realism when Harry, back in the squalid, selfish city, adds the final, framing paragraph.

This might well remind us of the sentiments at the end of Paterson's 'Clancy of the Overflow', but it is written almost a decade after the 'Sydney or the Bush' debate with the 'Banjo', and Lawson's return from Bourke vowing never to go bush again. 'Send Around the Hat' can be enjoyed as a sentimental and humorous homily, but it is not what could have been expected from the author of 'The Union Buries Its Dead' and the other earlier stories and sketches of Bourke. And its greater technical sophistication does not mark an artistic advance over even the earliest stories: 'The Drover's Wife', with that apparent 'artlessness' contemporary readers appreciated, remains more 'authentic' and imaginatively powerful than this story with its artful, fluent and varied narrative procedures.

Like 'Send Around the Hat', 'Lord Douglas' parables a tenet of practical Christianity—in its case 'Love thy enemies ...' In 'That Pretty Girl in the Army', we are told that the lovable reprobates of Bourke observe the social gospel by their deeds rather than by heeding the cant of institutionalised religion. But through its action this story has another subversive purpose—to assert the power of love to find its way despite the repressiveness of the self-righteous. It is a frontier variation on the traditional comic scenario of love confounding the puritans. Inserted into it are a variety of realistic elements: digressive passages on bush socialism and mateship, a speculation by the author on what he would be writing if this were fiction and not truth, brief sketches of Bourke and some of its notable characters in '92, the modelling of the Pretty Girl on Hannah Thornburn. But these flashes of 'local colour' only make it more reminiscent of Bret Harte (who, in the story itself, a sentimental shearer has been reading).

A sentimentalised 'realism' is also found in 'Shall We Gather By the River?', the first of the stories about the bush missionary, and explicit Christ figure, Peter M'Laughlan. When he translates the Sermon on the Mount into local terms for the Eurunderee congregation, every sentence seems to go straight to someone present:

> I believe he looked every soul in the eyes before he had done. Once he said something and caught my eye, and I felt a sudden lump in my throat. There was a boy there, a pale, thin, sensitive boy who was eating his heart out because of things he didn't understand. He was ambitious and longed for something different from this life; he'd written a story or two and some rhymes for the local paper; his companions considered him a 'bit ratty' and the grown-up people thought him a 'bit wrong in his head', idiotic, or at least 'queer'. And during his sermon Peter spoke of 'unsatisfied longings', of the hope of something better, and said that one had to suffer much and for long years before he could preach or write; and then he looked at that boy. I knew the boy very well; he has risen in the world since then. (II, p.24)

That such a self-indulgently sentimental story as this, or the other M'Laughlan and Bourke stories were written around the same time as the Joe Wilson sequence, 'The Loaded Dog' and 'Telling Mrs Baker' is revealing about Lawson's nature as a writer. While in England and at the peak of his career, he continued his habit of working simultaneously in a variety of modes and moods. Despite references in letters to his intentions, or ambitions, to write a novel, he was still writing hurriedly and anxiously to maintain his family. Financially and temperamentally, he was not able to forgo journalism and devote himself to consciously 'artistic' writing ('good work' in Pinker's phrase)—a distinction that was perhaps foreign to him after his years as a freelance in Australasia. It was not as though there were the Joe Wilson and other admired stories, and then the nostalgic and sentimental tales, so that we could enquire what went wrong, and when precisely, in the events of his life (his own unspecified illness he mentioned in letters and in 'Succeeding', Bertha's breakdown and the strains on their marriage) which might explain the marked inconsistency in the quality of the fiction written in England.

The pattern of conflicting tendencies in his writing observable from the beginning continued. He was still torn between a realistic and a romantic 'literary' impulse, still either resisting or succumbing to the temptations to sentimentalise, melodramatise, moralise. (A related pattern can be seen in the fluctuations between idealism and scepticism, even an embittered cynicism at times, in his social and political attitudes; shifts in these though are too complicated to attempt to discuss here.) The achievement of the Joe Wilson sequence can be seen, in personal artistic terms, as his holding in balance these conflicting tendencies.

While, in terms of publication and recognition, the visit to England seemed to bring at least the beginnings of the security he was seeking, these outward indications of success did not have their correspondences in his personal life. In May 1901, Bertha was admitted to Bethlem Royal Hospital, presumably suffering a nervous breakdown from trying to cope with two young children and an unstable husband in a strange environment. After her release in August, the Lawsons lived in the village of Charlton (where Henry had shared a cottage with Arthur Maquarie during Bertha's absence, the children having been boarded out in a neighbouring village) before moving back to London. There Mary Cameron, now Gilmore, and her husband stayed with them on their way home from Paraguay.

Bertha decided to return with the Gilmores, taking the children and leaving Henry to finish preparing *Children of the Bush* for the press. He followed the next month, May 1902, and through an accident to their ship overtook them in Colombo. In Adelaide, Henry left the ship and travelled by rail to Melbourne, presumably to see Hannah Thornburn —only to find that she had died the previous month. At the end of 1902, having returned to Sydney with his family, Lawson threw himself off a cliff near Manly, sustaining only minor injuries. The years of conspicuous decline, personal and artistic, had begun.

The apparent suddenness of Lawson's personal and artistic deterioration after his return from London would seem to call for explanation in psychological terms. A dependence on alcohol and a strained, then broken marriage (Bertha won a judicial separation in 1903) were the outward symptoms, and possible causes—though it is not hard to think of other writers for whom drink and emotional disturbance have acted as stimulants. For Lawson's biographers, to account for the collapse of his personality would be challenging enough, even if there were complete and reliable records of these years. (New evidence was uncovered in 1981, when a selection of the manuscripts and letters Lawson sold the Melbourne publisher Thomas Lothian was published; more may still come to light. A known source of possibly revealing information is the records of Bertha's admission to Bethlem Royal Hospital, which in the normal course will not become available this century.)[30]

The most substantial body of evidence the biographer has available is Lawson's own writings: three volumes of verse, two of prose, and one of letters in Colin Roderick's edition.[31] For even in his periods of adversity and the long years of physical and mental deterioration, Lawson remained a writer, translating experience into language, even if only fitfully into literature, after 1902. The course of his life only glancingly illuminates, and certainly does not explain, how he came to produce his best work. Close examinations of this though have suggested aspects of his artistic personality that knowledge of his life, especially his formal education and reading, would not lead us to expect; for example, his conscious literariness which manifests itself in such contradictory ways. Why he declined as an artist cannot be answered confidently by positing any single cause, but the complicated pattern of his development and the nature of the decline can be described, as it has been by A. A. Phillips, T. Inglis Moore and by Brian Matthews.[32]

In *The Receding Wave,* Matthews demonstrates from the writings how the artistic decline was not sudden, nor the consequence of the period in England, but that the seeds of it were there in Lawson's work

30 *La Trobe Library Journal,* Henry Lawson issue 7 (October, 1981); information from Russel Meares, Professor of Psychiatry, University of Sydney.

31 *Collected Verse*, 1967, 1968, 1969; *Letters*, 1970; *Short Stories and Sketches* and *Autobiographical and Other Writings*, both 1972 (all Angus and Robertson, Sydney).

32 A. A. Phillips, *Henry Lawson* (Twayne, New York, 1970); T. Inglis Moore, 'The Rise and Fall of Henry Lawson', *Meanjin* 4 (1957), in Roderick, *Criticism,* pp.316–28; Brian Matthews, *The Receding Wave* (Melbourne University Press, Melbourne, 1972).[Colin Roderick in *Henry Lawson: A Life* (Angus and Robertson, Sydney, 1991) argues persuasively that Lawson inherited a predisposition towards manic-depression.]

from much earlier (as were the propensities in him towards alcoholism and emotional instability). As we have seen, the conflicting tendencies in his fiction between the conventionally 'literary' and his individual, symbolically suggestive realism are apparent from his very first story. The subsequent course of his development does not describe a steady rise then fall, but constant fluctuations between these opposed tendencies until early this century.

To ask if drink and emotional disturbance caused the decline in the quality of his writing, or if instead it were waning imaginative powers and the exhaustion of the inspiration he had drawn from Eurunderee and Bourke, is to make an ultimately artificial distinction between the inner, artistic personality and the outer, social life which contained it. Although their interrelationship remains elusive, with Lawson's imaginative development continuing until 1902, despite the itinerant and unsettled course of his social life, the two proceeded together, as did the conflicting impulses in his fiction.

Critical preferences today (which should not necessarily be assumed to be at odds with those of Lawson's time) would exclude the melodramatically and sentimentally resolved in favour of stories seemingly uncontrived in their structures and ironic or comic in tone. These preferences, influenced by modernism, have led later critics to seek (and enjoy some conspicuous successes in finding) the modern artist within the late Victorian writer. Such discrimination which locates the artistic core within Lawson's prolific writings of all kinds is necessary, but, at the same time, too ruthless a selection according to these preferences can mask the persistent attraction towards melodrama and sentimentality throughout his work. Thus it can throw into false relief the issue of why he declined, suggesting a sudden and total artistic reversal during his time in England or immediately after.

To turn the question around, to ask instead how a late Victorian colonial with Lawson's disadvantages, working under constant pressure in the popular newspaper and magazine markets, and responding to a confusing conflict of models and influences, came to produce a substantial body of imaginative prose that still meets the severest critical demands, and commands an ever growing popularity, might be to put the question of his decline into more perspective.

After the return to Australia, he continued to draw on the same sources of inspiration, returning to the landscape of childhood for 'A Romance of Three Huts' and for another tale of heroic self-sacrifice with 'Roll Up at Talbragar'; to tall folk yarns and comic tales; and, increasingly, to personalised journalistic sketches like 'The Rising of the Court'. He was working all the old veins—characters, settings, modes and themes—with decreasing energy and imaginative return, trying to recapture, or at least exploit, his earlier successes. There was also the verse, reams of it as always. On this, it is virtually obligatory to quote Vance Palmer's reference to 'the primrose path to the eternal bonfire', which, in the main, is cruelly true because so much of it was written on the spot by a desperate man for the price of a drink.[33]

Some time after the judicial separation from Bertha in 1903, Lawson went to live with Mrs Isabel Byers, a woman in her mid-fifties who had worked in and kept a number of boarding houses. About the same age as Louisa, Mrs Byers became the 'Little Mother' to the poet she admired, and she was to care for him at a succession of addresses, mainly the North Sydney area, for most of his remaining twenty years.

Between 1905 and 1910, Lawson was imprisoned seven times for arrears of maintenance, and was admitted constantly to hospital for alcoholism. During these difficult years the managements of Angus and Robertson and the *Bulletin* showed great forbearance, and generosity, towards the increasingly spectral figure whose youthful writings they had been among the first to make so popular. But Lawson in his cups could be cantankerous and George Robertson had to ban him from his firm's premises in 1906 because of irresponsible behaviour.

Nevertheless Robertson brought out *Children of the Bush* as *Send Round the Hat* and *The Romance of the Swag* the following year, provided Bertha with a job and Mrs Byers with housekeeping money, and responded to Lawson's incessant battery of begging notes. A couple of years later, Lawson smashed some glass panels in the *Bulletin* office in one of his not infrequent fits of rage; and he paid for their replacement with his fee for the excerpts from his autobiography, then appearing in Archibald's *Lone Hand.*

Lawson was becoming the figure that Low captured in his cartoon

33 Vance Palmer, 'The Writer: Henry Lawson' in *National Portraits* (Melbourne University Press, Melbourne, 1940), p.166.

during the war years: the emaciated but genially grimacing 'character' with his Chaplinesque props of hat, stick and pipe, the trademark of his new identity as a living legend around town. The desperately sad, and at times unpleasant, personality behind this mask is glimpsed in the many letters begging money that he scribbled. But his mates who contributed to the 1931 memorial volume edited by Bertha and John Le Gay Brereton preferred to remember him not for his scrounging and intemperate outbursts but for his generosity (such as his habit of carrying small change to distribute among the North Sydney urchins) and the flashes of his old wit.

Even at his lowest, Lawson retained affection of his friends and the respect of admirers. Some formed a committee to assist him. Sister A. de V. McCallum of the Mental Hospital, a receiving house where Lawson often went to dry out, sought a Commonwealth pension for him, others a State stipend, both of which were eventually granted. In 1910 a number of friends, including Tom Mutch, twice N.S.W. Minister of Education, mounted a 'rescue operation' to get him out of the city and sent him for a holiday at Mallacoota with his old friend E. J. Brady. The same year, Angus and Robertson brought out his first new collection of prose since he had left London, *The Rising of the Court.*

In 1913, his 'Elder Man's Lane' series began appearing in the *Bulletin:* confabulatory and even maudlin as the embarrassing title suggests, these sketches, musings and stories project his personality at this time through the persona of 'John Lawrence'. Two other books appeared this year, verse in *For Australia* and prose (some of it dating back to the London period) in *Triangles of Life,* but from the Melbourne house of Lothian, as Angus and Robertson recognised that the quality was far below what they had published earlier.

The theme of the 'Elder Man's Lane' series—the loss of a more romantic past to the mechanised present—sums up Lawson's major preoccupations in his later writings, and reveals his Victorian consciousness, his inability to accept contemporary urban Australia. In *Children of the Bush* the evocation of the past had become nostalgic, an idealisation of those rural communities which previously he had presented with often sardonic realism. A similar process can be observed in his writing about Sydney after his return to Australia. The city is no longer presented as a succession of anonymous faces in the street and impersonal boarding houses; instead, as a defence against that sense of alientation captured in his earlier writings, it is decentred, made suburban, folksy, and personal.[34]

In 1914, Lawson revisited Eurunderee twice, and nostalgically. Another revival of the past came a couple of years later when he met again a mate from the days of Bourke and the tramp to Hungerford, Jim Gordon, who wrote himself under the name of 'Jim Grahame'. They met and renewed their friendship on the irrigation area at Leeton where Lawson, with Mrs Byers, had been accommodated, officially to publicise it through his writings, unofficially to keep him away from alcohol as it was a 'dry' area. Neither plan was successful. His last prose series about 'Previous Convictions' was set here, where during 1917 he worked on the proofs of his *Selected Poems.* When Lawson returned from Leeton it was to resume his familiar round of life in Sydney, which Denton Prout describes as 'poverty, cadging, ill-health, bickerings with landlords, futile broodings, and short-lived resolutions to "pull himself" together'.[35]

He was depressed by the deaths of friends, including Archibald, and of his mother. Her driving energies had finally dissipated themselves in efforts to win credit for her contribution to the women's movement, and recompense for an improved mailbag fastener she had invented. In 1921 Lawson suffered a cerebral haemorrhage and was hospitalised. On 2 September 1922 he died in the cottage at Abbotsford he had been sharing with Mrs Byers. Typically, he was writing up until the last—and about the past. The article he had been working on was one of a series for *Aussie* magazine which recalled his visit to London twenty years before.

As Bourke, or 'the bush' generally, and then the Sydney of his youth, had receded in time and memory to become moral alternatives to the present, so finally the London of the crucial period in his artistic career was fondly recalled. The 'tragedy' of his life that the Longstaff portrait had reminded him of on his return from London had become a distant memory. Today, more than three quarters of a century after his death, he is remembered not for his personal failings and decline, but for the artistic triumphs he managed to achieve against such improbable odds.

34 See the next essay, 'Sydney or the Bush', for some further remarks on Lawson's later writings.

35 Denton Prout, *Henry Lawson: The Grey Dreamer* (Rigby, Adelaide, 1963), p.287.

# Sydney or the Bush: Some Literary Images

It has frequently been observed, as something paradoxical, that although Australia from the 1890s was one of the most highly urbanised countries, its literature appeared to be preoccupied with the countryside. This 'paradox' was noted by contemporaries as well as by later commentators. In his introduction to *Australian Writers* (1896) Desmond Byrne asked whether local novelists 'who find so little material in Sydney or Melbourne' had seen what Henry James and W. D. Howells had done with their cities, and Byrne quotes the *Australasian Critic* in 1890 for the view that English readers of Australian fiction must form the impression that 'big cities are unknown in Australia'. In his *Victorian Cities* (1963) Asa Briggs makes a similar observation that 'at a time when the "muckrakers" were exposing the evils of the American cities … Australian interests were diverted from the city altogether', and gives as his chief example the work of Henry Lawson.[1]

Yet the reality for Lawson and his generation was more complex. Although in the legendary nineties there was much writing about the bush, some of it romantic and escapist, many writers were also recognising the challenge of the city. For Lawson and others of that generation there was a choice, or a tension, between the societies of 'Sydney or the Bush'. This protean phrase sums up the opposing models available to those who asked where civilisation was going in this country, what sort of people Australians were becoming. One model, the bush, was receding, the other, Sydney, was advancing disturbingly. Just as urban civilisation was to dominate rural, so the focus of urban civilisation itself was shifting to Sydney—which was assuming the role previously played by

1 Asa Briggs, *Victorian Cities* (Odhams, London, 1963), p.301.

First published in Jill Roe, ed., *Twentieth Century Sydney: Studies in Urban and Social History* (Hale and Iremonger in association with the Sydney History Group, 1980).

'Marvellous Melbourne', and becoming the largest, most progressive, and culturally dominant of the colonial capitals, the image and reality of the metropolis.

Here, as elsewhere, the modern city was a new environment and experience. As Asa Briggs also observes, the rapid urbanisation of American and Australian populations at the turn of the century raised the same questions as it had in England in the 1840s, where the phenomenon first occurred: 'What shall we do with our great cities? What will our great cities do with us? (p.75). Rural nostalgia was only one expression of this concern in the writing of the 1890s. Another was the attempt to find imaginative means of engaging with the seemingly unengageable mass existence of the city—the faces in the street by day; at night the larrikins and their doxies, made more bizarre and threatening by gaslight; the unemployed dossing out on the Domain, or down by the docks.

It is a truism of Australian literary history that writers, like the painters having to develop a new palette to depict the landscape, had to discover the forms and the diction, the conventions, to render the different environment and experience of this country. In the closing decades of last century, the modern city also demanded the adaptation of traditional conventions and the creation of new forms and images. In this period, the responses to and literary images of Sydney which predominate in the writing of this century began to emerge. How much these were based on observation of the actual city, and how much influenced by responses to the 'City' already established elsewhere—in Dickensian, modernist, or social realist conventions, for example—varies considerably from writer to writer. Yet, whether presented as a social issue, or as the local manifestation of a universal cultural tension between country and city, past and present, 'Sydney or the Bush' is a recurring if changing theme in the work of major writers in this century.

Here this theme is traced over almost a century, from the emergence of the modern city in Australia, and its reflection in literature, to the present. The sheer volume of imaginative writing set in Sydney precludes any attempt at inclusiveness, and only the most familiar works which can be associated with the city will be referred to. Considering them in terms of attitudes they reveal towards Sydney might seem quite incidental to their author's artistic concerns; yet what emerges suggests that the images of the city these writers have formed are by no means unrelated to their imaginative perceptions of life.

The varied writings of Henry Lawson contain a range of responses to the cultural dilemma of 'Sydney or the Bush': recoil from the city as the focus of modern civilisation, escape from it into an idealised pre-industrial past, or a coming to terms with it by relocating that past within the city itself. Lawson had come to Sydney from the Mudgee area as a youth in 1883. He had risen before dawn to work as a carriage hand, seen the unemployed searching the 'Wanted' columns outside the *Herald* office at four in the morning, seen the slums and the poor, and began to write about the faces in the city's streets, the slum-dwellers, larrikins, and prostitutes, as well as about the representatives of another culture 'up country'. His earliest memories went back to the last of the goldrushes, which he associated with Eureka and the movement to unlock the land; yet, as the elder son of a selector, he knew that those days when the world was wide were over, and that any radical impulses would have to come from the anonymous faces crowded into the city's streets. His coming to the metropolis after his childhood on a selection, and encountering the depression of the early 1890s was a personal experience of the major socio-economic developments and cultural divisions of the period. As the imaginative historian of Australia's transformation from a predominantly rural to a predominantly urban-industrial nation, Lawson saw the choice between an alienating, dehumanising city, in which physical and moral growth was stunted, and the countryside which bred madness, violence, and despair out of loneliness, but which could, ambiguously, also allow a dignity and warmth in human relations lacking in the city:

> Nearly every man the traveller meets in the bush is about as dirty and ragged as himself, and just about as hard up; but in the city nearly every man the poor unemployed meets is a dude, or at least, well dressed, and the unemployed *feels* dirty and mean and degraded by contrast—and despised.
>
> ('Dossing Out' and 'Camping', *Bulletin* 1893)[2]

2 Henry Lawson, *Complete Works*, I, p.303. Subsequent volume and page references, included in the text in parentheses, refer to this edition.

Among Lawson's earliest stories is the Arvie Aspinall sequence in which he seeks to bring his experiences as a carriage hand together with his sympathy for the newly discovered class of young urban manual workers. By common consent the result is sentimental, but the stories suggest the problems of adapting a literary model to observed socialreality. There seems little likelihood Lawson was aware of such contemporaries writing in English about the modern city as Gissing, Dreiser, or the Crane of *Maggie*, but one model he had from the earlier English experience of urbanisation was Dickens. A Dickensian element is apparent in Lawson's stories about city life from this early sequence, through his mature work, as in 'Mr Smellingscheck', to the late 'Elder Man's Lane' series. The urban setting in each case is not so much an observed Sydney as a literary extension of Dickens's London, a city-scape that could equally well be located in any centre of exploitative capitalism. The influence of established literary modes on his early attempts to respond to urban life can be suggested by another example, said to have been written in Surry Hills but, with its delineation of 'marks of weakness, marks of woe', essentially another version of Blake's 'London':

They lie, the men who tell us in a loud decisive tone
That want is here a stranger, and that misery's unknown;
For where the nearest suburb and the city proper meet
My window-sill is level with the faces in the street—
        Drifting past, drifting past,
        To the beat of weary feet—
While I sorrow for the owners of those faces in the street.

And cause I have to sorrow, in a land so young and fair,
To see upon those faces stamped the marks of Want and Care;
I look in vain for traces of the fresh and fair and sweet
In sallow, sunken faces that are drifting through the street—
        Drifting on, drifting on,
        To the scrape of restless feet;
I can sorrow for the owners of the faces in the street....

('Faces in the Street', *Bulletin*, 1888; I, p.48)

When, before the turn of the century, Lawson locates his image of the city—the focus of economic forces asserted against the humanity and individuality of his characters—in a specific Sydney its centre is Paddy's Market. In 'If I Could Paint', published in the *Bulletin* in 1899, he depicts the Markets as the centre of working class life:

> Paddy's Market, Saturday night—a world of types, humour, pathos, and tragedy there. The usual haggard-featured, temper-and-voice-spoilt mother, going from one entrance to another of the markets: a boarding-house keeper, with two or three grown-up, white-shirted, stand-up-and-turn-down collared (mother does all their linen herself) straw-hatted cigarette-smoking sons (boarding at home and paying twelve or fifteen shilling a week) aping men-about-town in King Street to-night. She has the ordinary load of Sunday-dinner stuff on one arm, and a great, peevish brat on the other, two or three trailing behind, or hanging on to her skirts. She turns sharply, at last, goaded to it, and says: "Be quiet, blast yer! (that I should say such a thing) where am I to get hokey-pokey money from?" I'd like to paint her and the children—and the "nan-nan" sons—hurrying past in the background. I'd call it "Nit! There's Mother". Where was she to get hokey-pokey money from? ... And in the face of Mother Grundy and to the advancement of Australia, the slums—there are miles of 'em now—and the poor of Sydney; the interiors of brothels (where little girls keep the door when "Aunty" is at the pub, or too drunk), and Chinese dens (for European and Australian types as well as Chinese—the variety of types and feminine beauty would surprise you a bit, I reckon). The Patrol of the Prostitutes at night in Elizabeth, Bathurst, College, and Hunter Streets; splendid types, some of them, and there is plenty of street light to allow of effect. Our civilisation has advanced so that these are no longer shy of light and crowds. (I, p.577)

In his unfinished autobiography, Lawson remembers Paddy's Market as about the only place he would go to on Saturday nights in his teens, and recalls again this figure of the harassed mother, an urban version of The Drover's Wife or Mrs Spicer of 'Water Them Geraniums'.

The market on Saturday night is also the focus for the critical depiction of Sydney as the centre of capitalist civilisation in William Lane's ironically entitled *The Working Man's Paradise* which, set during the shearing strike of 1889 and 1891, appeared in 1892, the same year as Lawson's first urban stories. Lane's observer is a bushman on his first visit to Sydney, who is appalled by the misery he sees in the crowd of faces in this Temple of Mammon, spending their weekly earnings to survive another working week, and by the prostitutes, larrikins, and drunkards in the streets surrounding the Markets:

> All around were like this. All! All! All! Everyone in this swarming multitude of working Sydney. On the faces of all was misery written. Buyers and sellers alike were hateful of life ...
>
> The women, the poor women, they were the most wretched of all; the poor housewives in their pathetic shabbiness, their faces drawn with child-bearing, their features shrunken with the struggling toil that never ceases nor stays ...
>
> It seemed to Ned that here was collected, as in the centre of a great vortex, all the painted and tired and ill-fed and wretched faces that he had been seeing all day. The accumulation of misery pressed on him till it sickened him at the heart.

Like Lawson, who appears in Lane's novel as 'Arty, the people's poet', Lane also seizes on a single figure to establish sympathetic contact with the crowd, a blind girl who is singing for alms:

> It was a hymn she sang, an old-fashioned hymn that has in its music the glad rhythm of the revival, the melodious echoing of the Methodist day. He recollected hearing it long years before, when he went to the occasional services held in the old bush schoolhouse by some itinerant preacher. He recalled at once the gathering of the saints at the river; mechanically he softly hummed the tune.[3]

Out of context, these echoes from 'the old bush school' might sound a nostalgic harking back to an earlier, more innocent way of life that might still be discoverable outside the city. In fact, the novel explicitly

3 William Lane, *The Workingman's Paradise* (1892; facsimile edn with an introduction by Michael Wilding (Sydney University Press, Sydney, 1980) pp.36–38. See Wilding's introduction for a detailed account of Lane's involvements and influence.

rejects such sentimentality at its literary (and for Lane, personal historical) roots in English provincial life, and sees Sydney as the centre of the exploitative capitalism that is dominating the whole continent. The alternative to this City of Dreadful Night lies in the future, in the revolution that such misery must occasion.

The City of Dreadful Night is less an image of Sydney than it is the writers' perception of a disturbance in society which stirs in them deep, ambivalent, feelings. This way of seeing the city presupposes an observer who is sympathetically concerned with humanity but who simultaneously feels cut off from the crowd. The people are seen as dehumanised by misery and vice; they are as figures glimpsed in a nightmare, the unnaturalness of their servitude accentuated by artificial lighting. The observer can only translate them back into human terms, identify himself with them empathetically, by singling out a single figure—Lawson's mother or Lane's blind girl—and by engaging imaginatively with this individual; the mass are lost, unengageable. For all the realism in the writing of these examples, they are as much an expression of attitudes against the city, and the civilisation it incorporates, as many a modernist poem, and for the good reason that Lawson and Lane are responding to the same social developments and personal anxieties as writers who were beginning to adopt quite different stylistic modes.

By 1894, only a couple of years after Lane's representation of Paddy's Market as a centre of exploitation and vice, Christopher Brennan (born and reared in that same Haymarket area) began writing the verses which would grow into the elaborate sequence of *Poems [1913]*—in which any representation of urban life seems far removed from Lane's or Lawson's.

The yellow gas is fired from street to street
past rows of heartless homes and hearths unlit,
dead churches, and the unending pavement beat
by crowds—say rather haggard shades that flit

round nightly haunts of their delusive dream,
where'er our paradisal instinct starves:—
till on the utmost post, its sinuous gleam
crawls in the oily water of the wharves;

where Homer's sea loses his keen breath, hemm'd
what place rebellious piles were driven down—
the priestlike waters to this task condemn's
to wash the roots of the inhuman town!—

The explicitly sought epic associations and the flitting Dantesque shades make apparent that this is not a particular late Victorian city but the City in history, and western literature—the fallen state of man, the obverse of the eternal Edenic state of innocence. The next poem, which speaks of 'London or Tarshish, Rome and Paris' reinforces this. Whatever the city, or whenever its period of cultural ascendancy, the emphasis is on its unnaturalness, its desolation (the familiar, paradoxical sense of isolation within a multitude), and on its nightmarish dehumanisation. This second poem, 'Ah, who will give us back our long-lost innocence', speaks of the cities as belching 'their sodden dreams of empire, lust and blood'.

As accommodation within the city, within civilisation and time, is impossible, the seeker after eternity becomes an outcast, the Wanderer:

When window-lamps had dwindled, then I rose
and left the town behind me; and on my way
passing a certain door I stopt, remembering
how once I stood on its threshold, and my life
was offer'd to me, a road how different
from that of the years since gone!

His road is Dante's *cammin di nostra vita*, a metaphor for life; and while the poem is sufficiently specific and personal in tone to suggest the poet's own experience, it is enhanced by its traditional, and general metaphoric implications. The 'town' of the poem is an image of that social conformity which the romantic spirit revolts against everywhere, in every age.

There is a deliberate specifying of setting in the Epilogue titled '1908' —'The droning tram swings westward'. As the poem after which is written 'EXPLICIT 15 December 1913', it is a summation of the themes of the *Poems*, but its 'I' is more personal and localised. The experience described is a tram ride from the city to the university in mid-winter dusk, a journey between two spires, one the university tower, the other identified by A. R. Chisholm in his introduction to the *Verse* (1960) as old St Benedict's, which used to front George Street.[4] The journey allegorises Brennan's early life in terms of remembered landmarks: his passing from the 'long-lost innocence' associated with the church to his later search for Eden associated with the tower of 'hermetic thought'. The stated intention of this epilogue is to establish some identification or sympathetic relationship with the people in the streets, to recognise that all men are in search of spiritual solace:

> their fellow-pilgrim, I must greet
> these listless captives of the street

Yet 'listless captives' hardly assists in establishing the proclaimed identification, nor does seeing them as 'pavement thralls' and observing the 'dark crowd's dreary loitering' assert sympathy. The 'lampions' orange blaze', the 'electrics' ghastly blue' and 'the gin-shop's ochrous flare' (*gin-shop's*?) are, for all their anachronistic and literary flavour, at one with the attitudes soon to be expressed by T. S. Eliot's 'Violet Hour': the saddened recognition of the artificial injection of excitement into drab lives after dusk. Brennan's lights image the 'bright banality' between these lost, deluded souls and the night in which they 'flit'.

More interesting, though, than the consistency of Brennan's attitudes with the modernist image of the city as a nightmare vision of hell is their consistency also with those of Lawson and Lane. Despite the obvious differences in levels of literary sophistication—Brennan was well aware of the French symbolists who influenced modernism in English, and his poetry is transitional between a full-blown romanticism and a disillusioned modernism—Lawson and Lane in their more realistic modes were responding similarly to the city. More fundamental than aesthetic or stylistic predilections were shared assumptions about the unnaturalness of life within it.

A different response emerges in Lawson's work after the turn of the century, and his personal and artistic decline. Although his later writings are inferior, they are interesting in terms of his response to the form of civilisation that has emerged as dominant in the new century. He idealises the country communities of the past, which he had previously presented

4 A. R. Chisolm and J. J. Quinn, eds, *The Verse of Christopher Brennan* (Angus and Robertson, Sydney, 1960), p.4.

with an unillusioned realism, and, in a similar way, comes to terms with the city by relocating the pastoral past within it. His Sydney is no longer centred on Paddy's Market and representatives of the working class; it becomes more fragmented, local and personal. He writes of his experiences in courts, prisons, and hospitals, of the areas in which he lives and their local eccentrics and non-conformists, including himself. Still referring often to Dickens, he adopts a very Dickensian recourse in the 'Elder Man's Lane' series, and writes of pockets of humanity within the otherwise unengageable city. There are urchins with hearts of gold, and Benno the bottle-o who, like Wemmick in *Great Expectations*, devotedly cares for his aged P. One especially Dickensian story, 'I'll Bide', is about a Miss Havisham type household tucked away in the suburbs. It is kept by a woman awaiting the return of her lover who went, many years before, to the goldfields. One day he returns, only to find the house has been demolished for a development. This theme of the passing of time and the loss of a more romantic past to the mechanised present sums up Lawson's preoccupation in his late writing. The young poet who had lamented the passing of Cobb and Co. coaches and crowded diggings, finally comes full circle to celebrate the picturesque Sydney of his youth, with its horse-drawn traffic and tall-masted ships at the Quay that had then seemed to him the City of Dreadful Night.

Recoil from the city, the desire to retreat from it, or into a community that is in but not of it, persist as basic responses in later writers. These are more responses to an image of civilisation than they are to Sydney in itself, yet, by definition, imaginative writers will engage us more by their larger responses than by the accuracy of their topographical, architectural, or other descriptive observations. A different response, which could be seen as latent in Lawson's acceptance of and identification with the viewpoint of his 'low' characters, is a version of pastoral in which the urban poor and working class are seen not as alienated—and certainly not as alienated from the author and his implied audience—but as true folk with their own manners, morals, customs, rituals, and folkways, as traditional peasantry relocated in inner suburban villages. The obvious danger with this mood is that the writer, in avoiding a distanced and patronising sympathy for the masses, will lapse into sentimentality and assume that his folk are more 'real' and 'natural' than the middle classes who have lost contact with the roots of life, have grown too effete to share the rude pleasures of the poor.

As twentieth century writers were attracted more frequently to urban subjects, the grey dehumanised crowds of the city were differentiated, socially and geographically, and associated with recognisable sub-urban cultures. The larrikins, who provided one set of images for disturbed and uncomprehending reactions to urban change in the late nineteenth century, became increasingly a subject for examination. Ambrose Pratt's *The Great Push Experiment* (1902) capitalised on fears that the larrikins constituted an organised threat to civilised society by sensationally depicting a 'push' as a crime syndicate. A more understanding interest in the 'pushes' is found in the foreword to Edward Dyson's *Factory 'Ands* (1906), a collection of stories mainly from the *Bulletin*, which in its first years had crusaded against larrikin behaviour and found itself involved in a libel suit. Dyson anticipated some of the success C. J. Dennis's Sentimental Bloke was to enjoy, and *Factory 'Ands* was followed by two further collections. Although in his foreword Dyson reveals a sympathetic understanding that the larrikins were more often urchins and street Arabs than psychopaths bred by industrialisation, the stories themselves imply an amused detachment from the ungrammatical prattling of his characters and the workers are seen as traditional, low comic figures.

In *Jonah* (1911), Louis Stone came to an imaginative and unpatronising understanding of the urban working class life and the larrikins. The novel opens with a description of Saturday night in Waterloo, pay night and shopping night. As in Lawson's and Lane's descriptions of Paddy's Market on Saturday night, the weekly shopping provides a means of engaging with the faces in the street. In *Jonah* the custom is described as if it is almost a pagan ceremony, with overtones of the sacrifice and the hunt; and this pattern in the people's lives also provides a pattern in the novel about them, for Stone returns periodically to such scenes in establishing the rhythms of their lives. Stone is a deft realist who works through character and situation, rather than documentation, to reveal the manners and morals of the inhabitants of Waterloo and the surrounding inner industrial suburbs. With a skilful impression of following the hazards of fortune, he shows us the contrasting lives of two larrikins, Jonah and Chook, as they graduate from the 'push' to marry and make their way in the world. The contrast in their fortunes—Jonah's rise to prosperity but personal disappointment, and Chook's contentment with his humble lot—has its share of melodramatic excess (with Jonah) and sentimentality (with Chook). But even if somewhat schematic, the contrast brings out the predatory nature of the economy in which they live—to succeed Jonah must destroy others, and himself, in the process. For this urban peasantry, life is a struggle to survive not against nature (there is nothing about the seasons or the added adversity of winter which one would expect in a European or American urban novel) but against economic circumstance. Without didacticism, Stone presents the proletariat's own view of these circumstances: they are shown as unconscious of capitalist oppression; they see themselves simply as the poor, who have always been so and always will be. Their class enemies are not 'the rich', who are remote and shadowy, but the shopkeepers, whose ranks Jonah eventually joins.

The basic rhythm of the novel is that of the generations: the larrikins and their doxies rebel against conformity and monotony; courtship, marriage, parenthood (not necessarily in that order) follow; and then a slow sinking into the pattern of their parents' lives before them. This timeless pattern reasserts itself in each generation, as in novels of rural life, and the true pastoral note is hit by Mrs Yabsley when she regrets the passing of the good old days:

> Suddenly she felt old and lonely, and wrapping a shawl round her shoulders, went out to her seat on the verandah. It was near eleven, and the street was humming with life. The sober and thrifty were trudging home with their loads of provisions; gossips were gathered at intervals; sudden jests were bandied, conversations were shouted across the width of the street, for it was Saturday night, and innumerable pints of beer had put Cardigan Street in a good humour. The doors were opened, and the eye travelled straight into the front rooms lit with a kerosene lamp or a candle. Under the verandah at the corner the Push was gathered, the successors of Chook and Jonah, young and vicious, for the larrikin never grows old.[5]

5 Louis Stone, *Jonah*, (1911; Angus and Robertson, Sydney, 1965), p.149. Subsequent page references, included in the text in parentheses, refer to this edition.

Although in her old age Mrs Yabsley sentimentalises the past in comparison with the present (which bears a strikingly cyclical similarity to it), Stone is unsentimental in his attitudes to the city. In *Jonah*, there is no idealised rural alternative to long for, at most a ferry trip to the north shore, and his characters do not constitute a pocket of humanity in retreat from urban anomie, but live at its centre, and accept it as their engageable community and environment. Paddy's Market is not an image of exploitation and degradation but a colourful festivity to mark the end of the working week; the eye of the observer is not that of an alienated author but of young Chook. The Markets contain 'the drift and refuse of a great city'; this time though it is not the shoppers who are being referred to but the treasure troves of second hand goods. The shoppers move 'like water in motion', but instead of Lane's 'vortex' of human misery they are enjoying themselves good-naturedly (p.69).

Stone uses the Sydney setting more imaginatively than simply observing the ways of life in the slums around the footwear factories, and contrasting these with the more gracious life harmonised with nature on the other side of the Harbour. When Jonah breaks out of the constraints of the inner suburbs and, on the north shore, declares his love for Clara, Stone uses the city to express Jonah's emotions:

> They had talked for half an hour, intent on figures which Jonah dotted on the back of an envelope, when they were surprised by a sudden change in the light ... The sudden heat had thrown a haze over the sky, and the city with its spires and towers was transformed. The buildings floated in a liquid veil with the unreality of things seen in a dream. The rays of the sun, filtered through bars of crystal cloud, fell not crimson nor amber nor gold, but with the mystic radiance of liquid pearls, touching the familiar scene with Eastern magic....
>
> And as they watched. surprised out of themselves by this magic play of light, the sun's rim dipped below the skyline, a level lake of blood, and the fantastic city melted like a dream. The pearly haze was withdrawn like a net of gossamer, and the magic city had vanished at a touch. The familiar towers and spires of Sydney reappeared ... (pp.180–81)

Such bejewelled prose as this, and shortly after when Jonah and Clara see the city after dusk as 'a symphony in light', gathers in many of the stock properties of *fin de siècle* and the Celtic twilight found also in the early verse of Kenneth Slessor. But in context these conventionally exotic metaphors are appropriate to allow the cityscape to express Jonah's transported emotions; they are also ironically checked by Jonah's doodling calculations on an envelope and discoursing all the while on his business plans.

The possibilities for the novel of urban life that Stone discovered have constantly been rediscovered. *Jonah* stands at the head of two related traditions: the 'larrikin' novel about the young rebel against the stultifying lack of opportunity in his own background (and the equally stultifying respectability of the dominant middle classes encircling the inner suburbs) and the urban pastoral which, like *Jonah* itself, can contain a larrikin novel within its episodic structure. Both strains have attracted many writers associated politically with the 'Left' who have been seen collectively as realists or social realists. While many of these have been content to simply name Sydney streets and suburbs and provide flat descriptions of working class life, others have aspired to capture poetically the essence of representative experience. Kylie Tennant's *Foveaux* (1939) which opens in 1912, in a period contemporaneous with *Jonah*'s, warmly embraces the folkways of the inner suburb which provides the novel's subject and title. The realism of her style is constantly heightened by a delighted celebration of the oddities and eccentricities, architectural and human, of this community; even the garbage collection is transformed into ritual and a theatrical display (Chapter IV). Other novels that continue the urban pastoral tradition are Ruth Park's *The Harp in the South* (1948) and Dorothy Hewett's *Bobbin Up* (1959) In the first, Paddy's Market on Saturday night is evoked, as in *Jonah,* to contrast its colour and excitement with the dull routine of the working week. In the second, there is a description of Tempe tip as a Vale of Tempe with its own historical and Arcadian associations (Chapter XIX). Despite a tendency to divide writers into 'mere' realists and the 'more imaginative', such a distinction is difficult to maintain. Although Chester Cobb's *Days of Disillusion,* (1926) with its Virginia Woolfish stream of consciousness technique is ostensibly a departure from realism, its details are neatly observed and untouched by metaphoric suggestiveness. The same could be said of some later writers who stylistically proclaim themselves to be experimental and imaginative beyond the range of realism, but have only a different manner, and often that at secondhand.[6]

Images of the City of Dreadful Night register the extreme of rejection in the emergence of literary attitudes towards Sydney. In Lane's novel and Lawson's early work, this imagery expresses the cultural dilemma of Sydney or the bush. At the other extreme, of acceptance, the imagery of urban pastoral resolves the dilemma by relocating the natural and the communal within the city; a version of this can be found in Lawson's later work. Although not in such pronounced polarity, these opposed patterns of imagery and response continue in the literature of this century, perhaps more because of established literary attitudes and conventions than because of a sense that the dilemma persists within society. Brennan's attitudes towards the City can be compared with Lawson's, but Brennan's are more heavily determined by literary influences (and different influences from those affecting Lawson) than by the actual city of Sydney. Similarly, later writers who ostensibly express attitudes towards Sydney can be seen as responding at least as much to images of the City established elsewhere. To illustrate this, and to trace later developments, some works by modern writers will be glanced at now. Although the author of the first book wrote only one novel set in Sydney, the opportunity of examining the impressions of a major European writer concerned with the social changes associated with urbanisation is irresistible.

D. H. Lawrence's *Kangaroo* (1923) was written after a two month stay in Australia, in 1922, the year of Lawson's death. Early in the novel occurs an often quoted passage about a first encounter with the bush, in Western Australia. But this experience of the bush as intimidatingly ancient and lonely is presented through the memory of Somers, the Lawrence figure in the novel, when he goes into the back garden of the

6 Two plays which provide examples of an imaginative use of realistic Sydney settings are Dorothy Hewett's *This Old Man Comes Rolling Home,* 1976 (first produced 1967) and Peter Kenna's *A Hard God,* 1974 (first produced 1973). *This Old Man* is set naturalistically in Redfern but employs rhythms and poetic effects, some of which are reminiscent of Patrick White's *The Season at Sarsaparilla. A Hard God,* naturalistically set in the western suburbs, uses its characters' Irish Australian lilt to convincingly infuse lyricism into the colloquial, especially in Aggie's monologue recalling her first coming to Sydney from the country.

bungalow he has rented in suburban Sydney. From the roof of the summer house, he looks out over the 'vast town' which is

> lying mysteriously within the Australian underdark, that peculiar lost, weary aloofness of Australia. ... And it didn't seem to be real, it seemed to be sprinkled on the surface of a darkness into which is never penetrated.[7]

The relationship between landscape and cityscape, Sydney and the bush, is problematical for Somers-Lawrence as it was for earlier Australian writers. His conditioned European expectation of an organic, and idealised, relationship between civilisation and nature is disappointed. Sydney may be admitted to be 'the London of the Southern hemisphere', 'a real metropolis ... One of the great cities of the world', but it is London 'made in five minutes, a substitute for the real thing', and although it is one of the great cities, it is 'without a core', like Australia itself: 'The friendliest country in the world: in some ways the gentlest. But without a core. There was no heart in it all, it seemed hollow' (p.336). The lack of 'fit' between this civilisation—part derivative, part indigenous, in a democratic way that Somers-Lawrence finds disturbing—and the landscape which contains it is imaged on the city's fringes. Somers and his wife trace this civilisation to its limits where it meets the bush at a state reserve ('a bit of Aboriginal Australia') and the sea in a litter of 'promiscuous' bungalows, tin cans, and old paper:

> The *vacancy* of this freedom is almost terrifying. In the openness and freedom of this raw chaos, this litter of bungalows and tin cans scattered for miles and miles, this Englishness all crumbled out into formlessness and chaos. Even the heart of Sydney itself—an imitation of London and New York, without any core or pith or pith of meaning. Business going on at full speed: but only because it was the other end of English and American business. (pp.32–33)

Sydney provided Lawrence with his image of civilisation in Australia,

7 D. H. Lawrence, *Kangaroo* (1923; Penguin, Harmondsworth, 1950), p.18. Subsequent page references, included in the text in parentheses, refer to this edition.

as it had William Lane or as much later it was to provide Xavier Herbert in his *Poor Fellow My Country* (1975). The vision of Herbert's Jeremy Delacey as he leaves the city by train from Central is not dissimilar to Lane's. Delacey is led by his sense of the myopic insularity and material self-satisfaction of this society to flirt with a right wing nationalist group, as Lawrence's Somers had done. Yet Somers remains sufficiently uncommitted to feel the seductiveness of lotus-eating Sydney:

> Richard bought himself a big, knobbly, green, soft-crusted apple, at a Chinese shop, and a pretty mother-of pearl spoon to eat it with. The queer Chinese, with their gabbing gobbling way of speaking —were they parasites too? A strange, strange world. He took himself off to the gardens to eat his custard apple—a pudding inside a knobbly green skin—and to relax into the magic ease of the afternoon. The warm sun, the big, blue harbour with its hidden bays, the palm trees, the ferry steamers sliding flatly, the perky birds, the inevitable shabby-looking, loafing sort of men strolling across the green slopes, past the red poinsettia bush, under the big flame-tree, under the blue, blue sky—Australian Sydney with a magic like sleep, like sweet, soft sleep—a vast, endless, sun-hot, afternoon sleep with the world a mirage. He could taste it all in the soft, sweet, creamy custard apple. A wonderful sweet place to drift in. But surely a place that will some day wake terribly from that sleep.
>
> Yet why should it? Why should it not drift marvellously for ever, with its sun and its marsupials? (p.338)

Among the novels which are most evocative of Sydney are Christina Stead's *Seven Poor Men of Sydney* (1934) and *For Love Alone* (1944). Stylistically, they range from a realistic location within the city to an expressionistic, often lyrical rendering of their youthful characters' dreams, delusions, and disillusions, which are projected onto the Sydney of the 1920s. Both open in a fishing village, identifiable as Watsons Bay, which is a community on the outskirts of the city and on the edge of oceanic and ambiguous possibilities. In *Seven Poor Men,* the centre of Sydney is seen not as dehumanised and inorganic, as the antithesis of life, but as varied and vital. It is filled with parks, birds, the scent of flowers, and a range of human activities:

> The city ran on outside. Typewriters tapped, loiterers and unemployed men lounged in the little park, a hydraulic lift wheezed up and down in the cart-dock. The City Council took up and put down tar paving which would not set on account of the heat. A man opposite developing blue prints turned on his heliotrope light, the whistle blew for the cranes . working on the Harbour Bridge, ferries whistled, a liner coming down the harbour to berth at midday bellowed, cars rattled past, the messenger boys went out for the lunches, the swallows chased each other off the red roof of the new yellow and blue building opposite . which had the blue escutcheon of the Chilean Republic's consul on its walls ...[8]

This collage of impressionistic detail presents a more diverse and objective Sydney than is perceived by the characters, who project their own dreams and frustrations upon it. Haunted by the surrounding sea's ambiguous promise of escape, they react against the economic restrictiveness and social conformity of the city. Yet, although the novel is permeated with images of poverty, both economic and spiritual, they do not coalesce into a single, and simplistic, image of Sydney as a centre of capitalist exploitation. Joseph Bagenault contrasts with his cousins Michael and Catherine by not feeling alienated nor deracinated: 'This is my city, here I was born and bred, I cannot be lost here, nothing can happen to me' he thinks during one of the novel's 'night scenes'. As he nears the area of the Markets:

> the city had become warm, hospitable, a city of hearths and yellow-silk lighted interiors; spoons clapped on soup-plates, spoons clanked in cups, sugar-basins revolved ... The street-lights were switched on and glowed warmly in a slight thick dusk, as if to prove conclusively that the day had knocked off work and gone home. Near an old garden, he noticed how the trees had taken on an inhuman air with something wild in them, as lions have, sitting unreconciled in the back of their cages licking their paws, in the

8 Christina Stead, *Seven Poor Men of Sydney* (1934; Angus and Robertson, Sydney, 1965), p.109. Subsequent page references, included in the text in parentheses, refer to this edition.

> zoo. He heard again the tapping behind him of the nocturnal prostitute just beginning her beat: fresh, odorous, with shining curls and a big bow on her neck and frilled elbows, pretty, dainty. (p.122)

In this description of a walk at dusk through the Markets area can be found all the stock elements of the modernist nocturne, including garish purples, mauves, and reds. But these are the colours of the chocolate boxes in a lolly-shop window; even the prostitute, the conventional figure of urban degradation, is 'pretty, dainty'. What is remarkable is the lack of intensity usually found in such set scenes; here there is an implicit acceptance that this is only one aspect of the human life that goes on in this setting. The City of Dreadful Night exists within a larger city; behind the windows fronting the possibly menacing streets are the clapping spoons and clanking cups of a populated city, not just a nightmare haunted by flitting shades:

> The people were all wilted at the end of a long hot day, but they hurried because they were hungry and they were anxious to get their shoes off. Sometimes they went in pairs, and the man carried the girl's shabby paper case; sometimes they did not go straight home but had something first. The ill-lighted greasy chain restaurant opposite was full of people eating ninepenn'orth of tea, pies, and toast. (p.162)

It has been objected that such passages as these are the most prosaic realism, sorting ill with the lyrical responses to the city by the romantic characters; but such realism recognises a fuller and more human variety in society than the characters are able to individually.

Formally, *Seven Poor Men of Sydney* cannot resolve its conflicting tendencies towards a Marxist concern with social injustice and a vitalist celebration of the exuberant energy of life; between a pessimistic sense of the ineffectuality of the individual, and a patient and hopeful acceptance of social life; stylistically, between lyric effusiveness, whether expressive of optimism or despair, and a descriptive and implicitly accepting realism. The result is that Sydney is captured not as an allegorised image of capitalist exploitation, nor as a realistically observed background, but as a complex and richly varied cultural ambience. The description of Mendelssohn's room in Woolloomooloo expresses this unconventional openness of response nicely; so much is admitted—the surrounding view, the other tenants, the way of life in this ghetto—that it becomes a celebration of community *and* diversity. The markedly more mature *For Love Alone* employs comparable settings to render the feelings of its heroine, Teresa Hawkins. Here, though, they are dramatically controlled to express her responses, so that, although the City of Dreadful Night reappears in the slum scenes, and Sydney is also seen contrarily as merging into the natural world that surrounds it, these are clearly recognised as projections of Teresa's feelings. Despite Teresa's Nietzschean rejection of the 'herd' life of Sydney's inhabitants, Christina Stead's detachment from this could be said to be a mood of acceptance, of recognition of the city as an image of life in all its complexity and contrariety.

Kenneth Slessor is the poet who is immediately thought of as 'a man of Sydney', the title of Douglas Stewart's book on him. Slessor accepted the city as a major source of his images for his meditations on Time, Memory, History, the vitalist surge of life and the ever present premonition of death. Yet it is in his prose, such as his *Portrait of Sydney* (1950) or *Life at the Cross* (1965), that he is more directly concerned with the city and expresses his affection through detailed evocation of its scenes. In his collected *Poems* (1957) there are surprisingly few pieces specifically related to Sydney, though more frequently it provides the implied setting. The early 'City Nightfall' in its strained figures and conceited irony is redolent of Arthur Adams and the *fin de siècle:*

> Smoke upon smoke: over the stone lips
> Of chimneys bleeding, a darker fume descends.
> Night, the old nun, in voiceless pity bends
> To kiss corruption, so fabulous her pity.

'Late Trams' affects a different form of detachment, one reminiscent of Eliot's 'Preludes':

> That street washed with violet
> Writes like a tablet
> Of living here; that pavement
> Is the metal embodiment

Of living here; these terraces
Filled with dumb presences
Lobbed over mattresses,
Lusts and repentances
Ardours and solaces,
Passions and hatreds
And love in brass bedsteads ...

More characteristic though is 'William Street' which in four stanzas reverses such modernist attitudes by celebrating the sensuous and whimsical appeal of the city at night:

The red globes of light, the liquor-green,
The pulsing arrows and the running fire
Spilt on the stones, go deeper than the stream;
You find this ugly, I find it lovely.

The emphasis here, as with 'Ghosts' trousers, like the dangle of hung men/ In pawnshop windows, bumping knee by knee' is on the imagination's transformation of mundane reality rather than on the reality so transformed. A favoured situation in Slessor's poems is to have the imaginative observer behind a window pane, detached from the reality which stirs his memories and meditations. So Captain Dobbin

Now sails the street in a brick villa, "Laburnam Villa",
In whose blank windows the harbour hangs
Like a fog against the glass,
Golden and smoky, or stoned with a white glitter,
And boats go by, suspended in the pane,
Blue Funnel, Red Funnel, Messageries Maritimes,
Lugged down the port like sea-beasts taken alive
That scrape their bellies on sharp sands
Of which particulars Captain Dobbin keeps
A ledger sticky with ink,
Entries of time and weather, state of the moon,
Nature of cargo and captain's name,
For some mysterious and awful purpose,
Never divulged.

He is the chronicler of the sea beyond his room, that 'cemetery of sweet essences' from which he imposes Memory and History on 'the blind tide/That crawls it knows not where, nor for what gain'. A similar assertion of the imagination against the boundlessness and flux of the sea is found in Slessor's finest poem, 'Five Bells', an elegiac reminiscence of his friend Joe Lynch who was drowned from a ferry. The atmosphere of the Harbour—its lights, sounds, the reflections of the city in its waters at night—pervades the whole poem. Sydney provides a rich image of life, even though the poet is detached from its immediacies and brought to question its ultimate significance.

The major writer who has engaged most often with Sydney and its suburbs is Patrick White. The map his novels, short stories, and plays leave in the reader's mind follows the broad contours of class differences and life styles in the suburbs and leaves the central city as a Babylon populated chiefly by patent leather ladies of the night, pissing sailors, and orphic drunks. Images of Sydney as the modernists' neon-lit nightmare abound in his work, yet so also do versions of pastoral, both on the suburban fringes and close to the city's centre; and over the course of his work can be discerned a shift from a mannered recoil from the City towards a form of acceptance. The opening of his second novel, *The Living and the Dead* (1941) is a modernist set piece presenting London's Victoria Station at night, and a character who wishes to make some contact with 'the faces in the street'. Sydney first appears in his next novel, *The Aunt's Story* (1948), and the description of the city at night (Chapter V) is painted in the full modernist spectrum of violet, crimson, and purple. A similarly conventional attitude affects *The Tree of Man* (1955). When Stan Parker goes to Sydney in search of his son Ray he finds himself in an 'ant-world', *fourmillante cité*:

> So Stan Parker went on his way over the asphalt. Once he thought he saw Ray looking at him from a window, but was mistaken apparently. A young woman who was pinning some material to her bust pulled down the blind. In one street two cars rammed each other, crushing the occupants. He went on, sad to think that the impulse to run to their assistance had been taken from him; it would have been different on a dirt road. Now he no longer looked at people, but for the names of streets nailed to corners. He went on, over a rime of rotting vegetables, and

old newspapers, and contraceptive aids.[9]

Only in the most incidental way could this be identified with Sydney. It is a generalised image of the modernist City: dehumanised ('it would have been different on a dirt road'), depersonalised ('he no longer looked at people, but for the names of streets'), sterile and unnatural (the contraceptive aids), it is the obverse of the sense of community and an organic relation with nature that the Parkers have in the countryside, which by the end of the novel has become a suburb. Such cliched depictions reach an hysterical pitch in the frequently quoted description of Himmelfarb's journey into the modern Babylon of Sydney in *Riders in the Chariot*, a catalogue of perjorations both inherited and characteristically the author's own: the neon's greens and purples colour 'the pools of vomit and the sailors' piss', the breasts of blue-haired grannies roundly assert themselves 'like chamberpots in concrete', and the city meets the sea in 'a scum of French-letters'.[10]

The play, *The Season at Sarsaparilla* (first produced 1961) has a quite different tone. A satiric comedy of Sarsaparillan life subtitled 'A Suburban Charade', it is almost affectionate in its presentation of the ritualised routines of the middle class. 'Life', vitalistic and instinctual, is within or behind these routines, not outside them. The recurrent off-stage sounds of a pack of dogs pursuing a bitch in season images the underlying reality of the cycle of nature that the events force most of the characters to recognise. The births, copulations, and deaths that occur are not presented as aberrations revealing how man in modern mass urban-industrial society has lost contact with the roots of his nature, or the well springs of life, or whatever. They are life, as the callowly 'artistic' Roy with his escapist dreams recognises at the end, and, as young Pippy learns, they will recur 'Over and over and over. For ever and ever and ever'. What might seem disconcerting about this apparent acceptance of the norm is that it implies through Judy and Roy a rejection of ambition and critical detachment. Other characters are also shown as coming to an undeluded appraisal of their self-images. Is therefore no course other than acceptance of the majority life-style to be entertained? Yet this is

9 Patrick White, *The Tree of Man* (1955; Penguin, Harmondsworth, 1961), p.273.

10 Patrick White, *Riders in the Chariot* (1961; Penguin, Harmondsworth, 1964), pp.391–92.

failing to recognise what is at the centre of this version of urban pastoral—the Boyles, the characters who have all the life. Ern the sanitary man and Nola his ripe, childless wife are in middle-class suburbia but not of it; they are presented as freed from middle-class affluence and inhibitions, closer to the natural and instinctual, to 'real' life, or Life. This relocation of the folk and traditional pastoral values within the city setting is found elsewhere in White's work around this time: in, for example Whalleys in the short story 'Down at the Dump', or Mrs Godbold, the only survivor of the *illuminati* in *Riders in the Chariot.* A qualified suburban-pastoral note also pervades the next novel, *The Solid Mandala* (1966). Like *Riders* it is set on the frontier of suburbia as it encroaches on an older, rural way of life: but, as in *The Season at Sarsaparilla* the mockery of suburbia is more mellow. There is the impression that life on Sydney's fringes is no worse than elsewhere, indeed that it is preferable to the world of war and revolution on the other side of Mrs Poulter's television screen.

In *The Vivisector* (1970), the artist Hurtle Duffield wanders around a city which is presented with a descriptive realism remarkable after *Riders in the Chariot.* His whereabouts are located by simple references to the Quay, the Domain, or Central Railway. Spewing drunks and leather-mouthed prostitutes are still encountered, but they do not coalesce into an image of rejection; in fact, Duffield, during an early bohemian phase, takes up with a lusty young whore. In later years he retreats from his wealthy patrons and admirers behind the pretentious facade of his house in Flint Street, and into the urban-pastoral world of Chubb's Lane:

> The back staircase to his house opened on Chubb's Lane. Here the clothes-lines and corrugated iron took over; ladies called to one another over collapsing paling fences; carts were parked and serviced, and dragged out on shrieking wheels. In the evening young girls hung around in clusters, sucking oranges, sharing fashion mags, and criticising one another's hair as though they had been the artists. There was a mingled smell of poor washing, sump oil, rotting vegetables, goatish male bodies, soggy female armpits, in Chubb's Lane.[11]

In *The Eye of the Storm* (1973), the Sydney setting is even more

11 Patrick White, *The Vivisector* (1970; Penguin, Harmondsworth, 1973), p.264.

detailed: the family house that was originally at 'the unfashionable address' of Centennial Park, flats in Kensington, Watsons Bay, and the Parramatta Road. There are still pissing sailors, to express Dorothy's disdain; still condoms on the beach at Watsons Bay to image Basil's disgust; and there is Mrs Hunter's perception of life of the city that mingles pastoral and satire:

> The life of Sydney was streaming past and around, you could sense as well as hear, pouring out of factories and offices: by this hour men in bars ... had begun inflating their self-importance with beer; ambulances were hurtling towards disasters in crumpled steel and glass confetti; in semi-private houses, mothers would have started sponging little boys, their still empty purses, while nubile girls looked in glasses to pop their spots cream their skins dreaming of long-hoped-for but unlikely lads.[12]

But these familiar images are now used with detachment by the author to express what in context are recognisably the characters' responses to situations. The City is distinctively Sydney, not simply a hazy, conventional emblem of modern man's fallen state.

One aspect of Sydney life that remained peripheral in most imaginative writing until recently is the bohemianism that has long been a feature of Australia's oldest, largest, and least easily characterised city. In works of autobiography, biography, and reminiscence, the tracks of generations of bohemians can be mapped around the *Bulletin* office, the Quay and of bohemians can be mapped around the *Bulletin* office, the Quay and the University. In the 1890s, Victor Daley, Julian Ashton, Arthur Streeton, Norman Lindsay, and others were drawn to Sydney as the metropolis of Australasia.[13] Lindsay's *Bohemians of the Bulletin* (1965) opens with an account of the Quay area in these years. In his autobiography, *Naught to*

12 Patrick White, *The Eye of the Storm* (1973; Penguin, Harmondsworth, 1975), pp.100–01.

13 Since this essay was written, Graeme Davison has published a very detailed description of Sydney's 'urban frontier' and its literary bohemia in the 1890s: 'Sydney and the Bush: An Urban Context for the Australian Legend', *Historical Studies* (1978), 191–209.

members of the Dawn and Dusk Club, the Lindsays, Daley, the Quinns, Ashton, and Favenc. Norman Lindsay's son Jack, in *The Roaring Twenties* (1960), remembers a later generation —and Christopher Brennan's daughter. In *Seven Poor Men of Sydney* there are 'Lindsays galore' in the Roman Cafe (and possibly Brennan also), but the scene is glimpsed from outside, as such scenes most usually are in fiction until recently, despite the strong and continuing tradition of an intelligentsia (and lumpen-intelligentsia) identifying themselves as a 'push' at variance with society at large. This 'push' sees itself as a libertarian enclave within a conformist, even repressive society; a community of individuals sharing the same unillusioned values, folkways (especially in relation to drink, sex, and drugs), and mythic past replete with heroes. It is a community that accepts the city and has its own watering-holes and corroboree grounds within its familiar territory—while at the same time having the satisfaction of breaking others' taboos.

An 'inner urban tribe' Frank Moorhouse calls them in his early story 'Apples and Pears' and describes their nomadic life-style:

> Drinking from beer bottles in grimy kitchens. Dancing to worn rock and roll records. Talking about authoritarianism and Zen and about Burroughs and Ginsberg Sending up your friends, sending up yourself. Talking just beyond what you know. Always being tempted out that little way further beyond your knowledge. Wading out in the beer. Always more books to read. Someone else to know about. Always another party. Always someone's affair finishing. Another affair starting. Another person gone to North Ryde Psychiatric Centre. Another lesbian. Another pill. Another idea about going interstate. Another way of making an easy quid. Another idea about going to the country and living like a primitive.[14]

14 Frank Moorhouse, *Futility and Other Animals* (Gareth Powell Associates, Sydney, 1969), pp.19–20. For discussion of a distinctive Sydney tradition in intellectual life see C. M. H. Clark, 'Faith', in Peter Coleman, ed., *Australian Civilisation* (Cheshire, Melbourne, 1962), pp.85–87; Geoffrey Serle, *From Deserts the Prophets Come* (Heinemann, Melbourne, 1973), pp.233–36; John Docker, *Australian Cultural Elites* (Angus and Robertson, Sydney, 1974), pp.131–65. [See also Peter Kirkpatrick, *The Sea Coast of Bohemia: Literary Life in Sydney's Roaring Twenties* (University of Queensland Press, St Lucia, 1992).]

Moorhouse's linking of discrete stories through recurrent characters in this first collection, and *The Americans, Baby* (1972), captures the transient 'feel' of relationships in this community of young people at variance with what they perceive as society's norms. As well, and this comes out more markedly in his subsequent collections, especially *The Electrical Experience* (1974), the 'bush', the countryside seen as the repository of uncomplicated traditional values, is still an alternative to Sydney for many of his characters.

The early short stories of Michael Wilding and his novels *Living Together* (1974) and *Scenic Drive* (1976) also accept Sydney as a fully adequate ambience for contemporary social comedy. In *Aspects of the Dying Process* (1972), his story 'The Sybarites' is a lush evocation, through the consciousness of a new arrival, of Sydney's pagan and erotic promises. Other stories in this collection bring out well the drifting quality of relationships within the city's bohemia, as its life is experienced by the narrators. 'Somewhere New', which dryly observes a cultural climber's hectic efforts to locate himself at the centre of avant garde cosmopolitanism (which is always relocating itself somewhere else), heightens a difference in attitude between writers of this and earlier generations. Christina Stead captures the earlier ethos, in the way her characters are persuaded that the cultural capital, the true metropolis, lies elsewhere, most probably London; and they are haunted by an awareness that Sydney is merely provincial. For Moorhouse's and Wilding's characters, the world has come to Sydney. Through the media they are affected by the same political causes, ideological issues, fashions and fads as prevail internationally. Through contact with visitors from abroad they realise that provincialism is a universal affliction within the international culture; even Americans, such as Moorhouse's Becker, suffer from it. But provincialism is also seen as having its positive connotation—as being the way of life of those who belong to the distinct location of Sydney, the ground for an authentic variety of that contemporary culture.

Beyond this, though, are the true provinces. There is still the choice between 'Sydney and the Bush', as the poet Les Murray reminds us by seeing the city from the countryman's point of view:

> Uncle Clarrie reckoned when he knew Sydney first, it
> was a lazy dangerous town five stories high

with razors up lanes, trams crushing stained corn,
                hawkers spitting,
straw hats on the ferry, shopgirls indignant about
                everything—
It was never a village. But now it'd hold even more
people who never in their lives have to know the score.
                (From 'Explaining to the Fencers')[15]

Although over what is now almost a century, literary attitudes towards Sydney have broadened and diversified, the historical opposition of city and country continues to re-emerge, as in this poem. More often though it has manifested itself, not as a preoccupation with a locally rooted cultural division, but as a more general concern with the course that modern civilisation has taken, a concern shared by literature written elsewhere over the same period. Even so, the continuance of traditional responses to and images of Sydney have confirmed its metropolitan status within Australian writing. In our literature, Sydney represents the City, in a variety of images which have both reflected and affected attitudes towards urban life.

15 First published in the *Sydney Morning Herald*, 10 June 1978.

# A. A. Phillips as Critic

As for untold thousands of other secondary school students, my first encounter with the name A. A. Phillips came through textbooks with such titles as *Presenting Ideas, In Fealty to Apollo, An Australian Muster,* and *Thinkers At Work*—the title of the last in red letters on a green cloth cover, or at least this is the image memory brings to mind, and with it other associations.

Writers of textbooks must be among the least lionised of authors, and here I should like to take the opportunity of acknowledging one student's gratitude to A.A. As one who had difficulty with such elementary exercises in logic as Pythagoras's Theorem, rote memory of which was necessary in the public examinations, I was excluded from the science stream. Even the low level of mathematics we 'humanities' students had to achieve seemed impossibly demanding. Algebra and geometry were taught, as were the classics to Tom Tulliver, with never a hint as to their place in the scheme of things. Language, or at least English, conveyed the pleasures of literature and the fascination of history; but these were regarded as peripheral pursuits, even feminine distractions, compared with the hard, central, masculine disciplines of a mathematical kind.

*Thinkers At Work,* our textbook for the 'clear thinking' section of the obligatory English paper, which was written by A.A. and A. Boyce Gibson, opened up other possibilities. It suggested that language, rather than simply being the vehicle of 'soft options' could, indeed should, be used with precision and rigour, and that it could also lead to discoveries. Gratifyingly, many who could fill their physics or chemistry exercise-books with symbols had difficulty in English classes with isolating 'essential factors' or perceiving 'slides' in a writer's use of term. When

---

First published as the introduction to *Responses: Selected Writings by A. A. Phillips* (Australia International Press, Kew, Vic., 1978). A. A. Phillips died in 1985.

confronted with the problems of the 'real' world, with the causes of epidemics or the interpretations of aerial photographs in war-time, many a budding physicist or chemist revealed limitations as a 'clear thinker'. Perhaps because of the compensation it allowed, 'clear thinking' became a passion. I dreamed of teaching it myself one day, of the satisfaction of revealing to others the structures of thought, or deceitful snares, that lay just below the surface of language, and which only needed, to expose them, the keys which *Thinkers at Work* provided.

Other early encounters with A.A.'s name (though I doubt if I saw the connection then) were in the Saturday Literary Supplement of the Melbourne *Age*. The 'Lit. Supp.' was an institution greatly revered by teachers of English, who urged their students to study the model essays provided by the paper's second leader (usually whimsical, always studiously unprovocative) before turning to the reviews and articles in the supplement. In the suburban steppes of Melbourne in the 1950s, the Saturday *Age* held out the glittering promise of metropolitan cultural sophistication—theatre, film, music, painting and books—to the starved souls of school-teachers and some of their students. Colin Bennett, Geoffrey Hutton, Ian Mair and A. A. Phillips were some of the fixed stars in this cultural firmament glimpsed from afar. After twenty years, my memories of A.A's reviews merge into a general impression of an astonishing familiarity with writers ancient and modern, a manner both magisterial and idiosyncratic, and—to a reader whose notion of literary 'appreciation' were formed by presumed knowledge of what the examiners would expect at the end of the year—a recklessly oblique approach to the subject in hand. Those openings that avoided the obvious, straightforward, and dull approach, the telling of appropriate anecdotes, the maintenance of an individual and intimate speaking voice despite the severe limitations on length: these characteristics worried me, profitably I hope now, as they were so contrary to what we were told would be 'expected' from us.

Later, when I escaped from the suburban provinces into the inner keep of metropolitan culture, the University of Melbourne, A.A. was still a presence, at least behind the scenes. There was then no course in Australian literature, though Australian History was well-established. It stirred many of us into adopting a proletarian tie-lessness, singing bush ballads, and sensing for the first time in our lives that there was an Australian culture—even one worthy of our serious undergraduate attention. Dimly, connections became apparent between what was presented in the History course and what was appearing in local periodicals, which I began to read at this time. Manning Clark, Geoffrey Serle, Ian Turner, Brian Fitzpatrick, Stephen Murray-Smith, Vance Palmer, and A. A. Phillips were amongst those who were not only debating and defining what our culture was but who could also be seen and heard around campus, as staff or visitors. Not only were they living, unlike most whose work we studies, they were living in our society. One evening, Vance Palmer gave a reading which included Lance Skuthorpe's 'The Champion Bullock Driver', 'The Backing of the Colt' passage from *Such is Life*, and his own 'Josie'. Ballads were sung by Miles Maxwell, son of Ian Maxwell the Professor of English who introduced the guests (and who on such occasions used to claim not to have read much Australian writing). Excitingly, the evening suggested that Australian culture could find as appropriate a place in the English Department as it had already in History.

When, after this, I took the newly established honours course in Australian Literature, A. A. Phillips's still fairly recent *The Australian Tradition* was a constant reference. I seem to remember that Mr. Phillips and others who had been propounding a democratic social and literary tradition were found to be sadly ignorant of the rigorously disciplined 'new' criticism that seemed so fresh and revealing when it reached Australia, thirty years after its emergence in Cambridge and Nashville, Tennessee. Mr. Phillips and others had recklessly misappropriated such technical terms as 'tradition' without appreciating the mysterious, quasi-theological associations they held for the initiated. They confused social with literary concerns (disturbing during the Cold War period) and paid scant heed to such central literary shibboleths as 'texture', 'ambiguity' or 'organic form'. In short, they were trampling across what was intended to become a well-weeded and fenced-off campus lawn.

Some students on the campus who had a different interest in Australian writing were those who were already determined to become writers themselves. Another memory of A.A. as an incorporeal presence around the university is of one of these writers-to-be asking if I had seen A.A. 'in action' at any literary meetings—'He's quite terrifying'. For him (and he did go on to become a prominent writer), A.A. was the epitome of impassioned and aggressive Australianness. His impression is worth recalling because, I imagine, it was fairly general at that time.

Those were the days when it was much easier to be regarded as extreme, or eccentric, or nonconformist, when *Meanjin* was considered 'left wing'—with a hint of subversiveness. Among students I knew, A.A. had acquired something of a reputation as a literary nationalist and a formidable guest of the Literature Club—though he can only remember addressing them once on an Australian topic. When finally I did see him for the first time, standing up in the audience and speaking in his characteristically deliberate and forceful manner, I thought him more impressive than 'terrifying'.

Eventually I met this presence who had haunted my school and undergraduate years when I spent some weeks at Wesley College as a student teacher. A.A. the Senior English Master, with cushion, stick and, invariably, a cigarette was obviously the respected 'character' of the common room. But how would he, with his slight build, close-clipped moustache, spectacles, and gentleman-of-the old-school manner, handle a class of strapping adolescents such as I had been observing? I received his permission to sit in on a Matriculation literature class and found that the answer was, very well indeed. It was no impressive 'demonstration' lesson for my benefit. A.A. walked in, arranged cushion and walking stick to his satisfaction, reminded the dilatory that the essay list for the year was behind the door, that they should select a topic and get on with it, and then talked to the students individually or in small groups while the rest went on with the projects he had devised for them. A.A. refused to dictate notes, the prevailing form of instruction at this level, and guided the students to acquire familiarity with the authors and texts themselves.

It was only after his retirement from Wesley that I came to know Arthur personally, and to discern the links between what had seemed to be the very different worlds he moved in. School mastering was his chosen profession, and he remained dedicated to it for fully fifty years, but his interests spilled over naturally into broadcasting, editing anthologies for the schools and the general public, writing for newspapers and the new periodicals as they emerged, acting and producing, participating generally in the life of the *community* (a key word in his criticism). As well, friendship with writers, editors, academics and theatrical people, and contacts through the position he has built in numerous associations over the years (including six, politically lively years as president of the Victorian Fellowship of Australian Writers) had kept him in touch with a wild range of individuals and groups. Personal acquaintance also provided the opportunity to confirm what I suppose every reader of his criticism would suspect from his favouring metaphors related to judicious seasoning and superior vintages—he had a discriminating palate for food and wine and was also a good cook.

Angell Arthur Phillips was as old as the century. His own twenties and thirties coincided with those decades he has often referred to in his writing—decades of comparative aridity and striving to stimulate local art and literature, or to recapture some of the cultural efflorescence at the end of the nineteenth century. In a number of essays he recorded this sense of deprivation, and also the sense of excitement towards the end of the 1930ss when the poetry of Slessor and Fitzgerald seemed to confirm the promise of a new beginning. Yet the barrenness these recall was that of the native culture. It was not that he saw Australia as uncultured.

The Melbourne of his youth was not the constellation of suburbs I remember, and cheerfully disparage, in a way I'm sure he would not have approved. His family background related him to the quite vigorous colonial culture of late nineteenth-century Melbourne. His great-grandfather, the Reverend Solomon Phillips, had arrived in Australia, newly-married, in 1830. He was assistant minister of the Bridge Street Synagogue in Sydney until 1852, when he moved to Melbourne and went into business. He returned to Sydney to become first Minister of the Macquarie Street Synagogue, and on retirement in 1874 moved again to Melbourne. His son, Arthur's grandfather, became a solicitor in Melbourne in 1860, thus founding a family association with the law, and was a member of colonial Melbourne's literary circles: he contributed to the *Melbourne* and *Victorian* reviews, belonged to literary societies, was president of the Shakespeare Society—his lecture 'The Jew in English Literature' was published in pamphlet form—and played a part in establishing the university's Law School. His home in East St Kilda was eventually acquired by Dame Mabel Brookes. His eldest son, and Arthur's father, M.M., studied law at Melbourne, taking both the Supreme Court Prize and the Exhibition in the History of Philosophy. After a time in the family's legal firm, he entered the public service to become eventually Master in Equity and the first Public Trustee. He also served as president of the Shakespeare Society, was active in university government, and chief president of the Australian Natives' Association. M.M.'s youngest sister, and Arthur's aunt (whom he used to visit when at Oxford) was Marion Phillips, who became a member of the House of Commons and whose *A Colonial Autocracy* (1909), researched while she was at the London School of Economics, remains a classic study of Macquarie's period based on documentary sources. A cousin of M.M. was E. Phillips Fox the painter, who studied in France and later returned there to live. One of Arthur's cherished heirlooms was a fine example of the work of this most mellow of the Australian Impressionists.[1]

Arthur's mother shared her husband's interest in literature and education. Under the name 'Phillip Ray' she wrote stories and articles for the *Argus,* the *Australasian,* the *Bulletin,* and the *Weekly Times.* During the First World War she published a novel, *White Feather.* Prominent in philanthropic, educational and cultural organisations, she was active in the foundation of the Free Kindergarten movement and organised the appeal to establish Women's College at the university. She was a keen theatre-goer, like her husband, and a good amateur actress. She played Mrs George in Shaw's *Getting Married* with the McMahon Players; and a one-acter she wrote was put into rehearsal by them. While growing up, the young Arthur was not conscious of cultural deprivation. One memory is of Ellen Terry, then on a lecture tour, visiting their home: 'It was my first close-up of a Great, though she was a weary and half-blind old woman.' As well as visits to theatres and concerts, there was also a good library at home; and Arthur's youthful impression was that Melbourne was a remote cultural dependency of London which maintained contact through visiting theatrical companies, musicians, and books and magazines. He was, he says, a good deal protected from feelings of national inferiority: at home and school, Melbourne Grammar, he had the sense that patriotism was a matter, first of all, of loyalty to the empire, though this was not in conflict with some degree of national pride.

After a brief taste of law when he went up to the university,

1 Victor Cohen, 'Reverend Solomon Phillips and his Descendants', *Australian Jewish Historical Society Journal and Proceedings* 3 (1940): 73–84; Len Fox, *E. Phillips Fox: Notes and Recollections* (the author, Potts Point, 1969). Unacknowledged quotations in this essay are from conversations or letters.

Arthur switched to Arts and pure English, and left it to his elder brother to continue the family legal tradition with distinction. The vocation Arthur had in mind was not then a usual one for a member of the professional classes, but his parents supported him after he had decided to become a schoolmaster. In his English course there was no Australian literature, indeed little literature beyond 1860. The Literature Society did bring writers in—Bernard O'Dowd, Frederick Maccartney, and Vance and Nettie Palmer, who came to promote the Pioneer Players. These though were invited as local Melbourne writers, rather than as 'Australian' writers—the term then would have suggested the coarse bohemian Sydney variety. Arthur can remember being unimpressed by the *Bulletin,* or *Vision,* and finding *Triad* more to his taste in those years. As a student he had a poem published in *Melbourne University Verse,* and began organising a national selection of undergraduate poetry. *Australian University Verse* appeared in 1922 with an introduction by John Le Gay Brereton. E. H. C. Oliphant made the final selection to avoid any suggestion of partisanship for a particular university. Included were R. D. Fitzgerald, Jack Lindsay, Ian Maxwell and A. A. Phillips. Among contemporaries at Melbourne were W. K. Hancock, later the distinguished historian, and R. C. Bald, who took the exhibition in Arthur's final year and was to become a professor at Columbia.

After completing his degree with distinction, Arthur spent some time teaching before going to Oxford to undertake the Bachelor of Literature. No training in research was offered and the topics suggested—for example, early ballad production of the eighteenth century—failed to inspire him. As he had intended to do the Oxford Diploma of Education after the B.Litt., and now wanted to drop the latter, the master of his college, Sir Michael Sadleir, offered to tutor him in a private study of educational issues until he could begin the diploma the following academic year.

> It proved a wonderful chance for contact with one of the most knowledgeable and vigorous minds in the field of my main interest. It was also valuable because the tutorship system is the most valuable aspect of Oxford education and B.Litt. students didn't have tutors. I remember one ploy of Sadler typical of the demanding and stimulating Oxonian mode. Having listened to me read my essay for the week, he commented, 'You advance such-

and-such a theory. What do you think Plato would have said about that?' After I had done my best to ventriloquise for Plato, he went on, 'Yes, that seems a reasonable interpretation. Now, what would Lenin have had to say about it?'

On completing the Diploma, Arthur returned to Australia and in 1925 commenced his career at Wesley College which was to continue until 1971. A. A. Phillips the literary critic did not emerge until later. In the early 1930s, he made a start in broadcasting over what was soon to become the Australian Broadcasting Commission, and after this was instituted he continued to broadcast in programmes like 'Books Worth Reading' for many years. Otherwise, he was active around societies, giving talks and judging competitions. When, in 1932, the English Association in London asked the local branch to submit some Australian poems for inclusion in an empire anthology, Arthur came into closer contact with Australian writing. Percival Serle, who was also on the committee, lent him books from his library, and after the selection was made, Arthur realised that there was more good local writing than he had been aware of and he decided to explore it. He then went to the bookshop Frank Wilmot was running, and made his acquaintance—the beginning of his admiring friendship with the poet—and asked him for all the worthwhile Australian books he could buy: 'I relied on him to do the choosing—with due regard to the slenderness of my purse'. Arthur joined a private discussion group with Wilmot and Serle, another with Bernard O'Dowd and Marie Pitt, as well as larger public bodies such as the Home Reading Union. But he felt that his most important association was with Dolia Ribush and his dramatic productions from 1936 to 1948. 'Ribush's devoted artistry, and the contacts I made through him—his home was the nearest thing to a *salon* that Melbourne had, though it was more bohemian than patrician—were the strongest influences on me at a critical period of my life.'

It was not until 1945 that he first contributed to the still fledgling *Meanjin*, the publication with which his name has been most closely associated ever since. 'Their Sweet Jargoning' was an attack on the pretentiousness and sloppiness of some of the magazine's previous contributors. His first major article on Australian literature, 'Henry Lawson as Craftsman', appeared in 1948. Some years earlier he had given Commonwealth Literary Fund lectures that had included some discussion of Lawson. Then, when asked by the P.E.N. Club to again judge their annual prize, he disqualified himself by saying that he was to be an entrant and drew upon lecture to write the essays on Lawson which won the prize. Hearing him read it at a P.E.N. meeting, editor Clem Christesen requested it for publication in *Meanjin*. It was not until the mid-1950s that he began reviewing regularly for the newspapers.

The core of A.A. Phillips's criticism is to be found in *The Australian Tradition*. The original edition appeared in 1958, the same year as Russel Ward's *The Australian Legend,* four years after Vance Palmer's *The Legend of the Nineties,* and three years before the long-awaited appearance of H. M. Green's *A History of Australian Literature*. As a later generation of historians has realised, the period in which these studies appeared was an important stage in the development of cultural awareness. The fact that such *books* appeared was significant in itself. Discussions postulating a democratic social and literary tradition, which these studies have in common, can be found, particularly in *Meanjin*, during the Second World War and the post-war decade of reconstruction. By the mid-1950s there was a large enough readership with interest in our culture for book-length studies to appear. This was a new departure, or a long-interrupted continuance of a development that had languished after the turn of the century.

Elsewhere, I have outlined the broad context of the debate between 'localists' and 'universalists' on the issues relating to Australian writing.[2] Here I want to consider A.A.'s stand in relation to the extreme positions of 'aggressive' literary nationalism, on the one hand, and a disdainful formalism on the other. In compiling *The Australian Tradition* sub-titled 'Studies in a Colonial Culture', A.A. drew together the most related of the essays he had published from the late 1940s onwards, chiefly in *Meanjin*. In his preface to the second edition (1980), he recalled that he had chosen this title for 'the air of combative paradox' it presented at a time when 'it was pretty generally assumed that the Australian community was too young to have any traditions'. He was successful

2 See my *Criticism* in the Australian Writers and Their Work series (Oxford University Press, Melbourne, 1974).

in provoking reaction, and his coinage 'the cultural cringe', seen as the keynote to the collection, passed into currency as a term to condemn anything short of unreserved confidence in all things Australian. This might suggest that its creator was espousing such an attitude. To look again at the conclusion of 'The Cultural Cringe' is to realise that he was saying nothing of the sort. He sees the most important development that Australian writing had made in the previous two decades as being in the direction of being unselfconsciously Australian—a phrase that places him in some very conservative company in terms of the same cultural debate during the 1890s. The public are seen as not having progressed correspondingly because they still share an attitude of colonial inferiority about their own culture. Instead of the Cringe, or the Strut, A.A. preferred 'a relaxed erectness of carriage'.

Perhaps the most succinct statement of the basic ideas underlying the essays in *The Australian Tradition* can be found at the end of 'The Democratic Theme'.

> The wind which blows from the far country through the mind of the Australian democrat is the spirit of the nineties. As a literary influence it is obvious not so much in political conceptions ... as in the inheritance of certain humane values ... In many of our writers there is the same belief in the importance of the Common Man, the same ability to present him without condescension or awkwardness, the same square jawed 'dinkum' determination to do without the fripperies, the modes—and sometimes the graces—of aesthetic practice, the same unembarrassed preference for revealing the simple verities rather than the sophistication's of human nature.[3]

With the Palmers and H. M. Green, and the historians Manning Clark, Russel Ward, Ian Turner, and others, A.A. saw this tradition coming down from the 1890s. What he saw as uniquely Australian about it was that it was written of and about 'the Common Man'. A radio talk for 1944, 'Dickens and Democracy', reprinted in this book, is an early example of this interest in implicit class assumptions in literature, and

3 A. A. Phillips, *The Australian Tradition: Studies in a Colonial Culture* (Cheshire, Melbourne, 1958), p.56. Subsequent page references, included in parentheses, refer to this edition.

A.A.'s refusal to distinguish ultimately between literary and social values. The essay on Lawson, originally published in 1948, which opens *The Australian Tradition,* provocatively develops this interest in class attitudes by beginning:

> When the Australian writers of the nineties achieved a revolution in nineteenth century Anglo-Saxon letters, setting fiction free from the cage of a middle-class attitude and a middle-class audience, they set themselves problems of technique as well as of subject matter. (p.1)

Another contention in 'The Democratic Theme', which recurs elsewhere in his criticism, is that in writing for and about the Common Man these writers dispensed with the conventions and 'aesthetic practice' of their time. Again in 'The Craftsmanship of Lawson'—with the essay on Furphy, one of the first close examinations of an Australian writer's style—openings of stories by Hardy, Kipling, O. Henry and Conan Doyle are contrasted with some of Lawson's to show how his craftsmanship was the search for the style and the form which would allow him 'not to tell stories for their own sake, but to reveal the Australian way of living and the ethic informing it' (p.3).

In 'The Family Relationship', later writers like Katharine Susannah Prichard and Frank Dalby Davison are seen as continuing this tradition in that they write 'a rough-hewn prose in the dinkum tradition with a touch of slap-dashery' (p.84); and this slapdash quality is viewed as an expression of the national character. When we see this tradition associated with preference for 'the simple verities rather than the sophistication's of human nature' (p.56), we find a view similar to those perceiving two streams in American culture—the genteel, Brahmin, Highbrow and Paleface versus the native, democratic, Lowbrow or Redskin. And A.A.'s terms—the Australian writer's preference for a 'pragmatism' which excludes the 'exaltations of the mysteries' (p.88)—suggest some correspondence to that disjunction between the real and the ideal discerned by a long line of American critics. Yet, according to A.A., he was not aware of American criticism and its similar concerns with the issue of an independent native tradition when he was writing these essays. (Later, in his review of a collection of American criticism he suggested that the local equivalent of 'Redskins' and 'Palefaces' could be 'Abos' and 'Pommies'.)[4] The end of 'The Family Relationship' looks forward to the resolution of 'the colonial dilemma', when the native stream and the European, with its acceptance of 'mystery' and 'incertitude', will converge. The comment, added in a footnote, that in the then recently published *The Tree of Man* Patrick White had succeeded 'in reconciling a sympathetic interpretation of Australian life with a keen feeling for the spiritual mysteries' (p.88) is prophetic—though for years after this was written White's novels were made the centre of dispute between the democratic traditionalists and the universalists. A.A's characteristically independent approach avoided commitment to either extreme.

The postulation of an Australian democratic tradition furnished an historical 'reality', which could be seen as having helped form the present, and as offering it relevant ideals. Between the period when this tradition was being propounded and the past which was being re-examined, there had already intervened what A.A. calls the 'Neo-Ninetyism' of the Jindyworobaks and P. R. Stephensen. Like the historians, A.A. should be seen as trying to revaluate a past which, as Vance Palmer pointed out in *The Legend of the Nineties,* had already become mythic. As the whirligig of time brings the 1950s and 1960s under scrutiny, we need to remember the context in which *The Australian Tradition* appeared, and the qualifications added in A.A.'s later writings. The view of cultural history that underlies the book is that of the pendulum-like swing of attitudes between colonial subservience and national assertiveness, and the implication of the sub-title is that the period in which the essays were written and collected together was one still subject to this swing. It is not, then, a static image of two opposed sets of attitudes, one of which is preferred by the author. The attitudes are seen as complementary, mutually reactive, and combining in different proportions in different decades. The tension between them is seen as historically inevitable, and as needing to be worked through rather than avoided. Perhaps the book's focus on individual writers has obscured for some readers this discerning perception of cultural history, which provides the themes relating the separate essays. And it is not a book preoccupied with the past; instead it looks forward to a resolution of

4 Review of Harold Beaver, ed., *American Critical Essays, Age* [Melbourne], Saturday, 27 February, 1960.

'the colonial dilemma', though it is mercifully free of pontification on how this might be hastened. A.A. avoids the danger of a nostalgic infatuation with the past, with what he calls, 'Neo-Ninetyism', as a 1962 *Meanjin* essay emphasises:

> The trouble with the traditionalists is that they are traditionalists, and have lost the sense of forward movement. They follow the tracks of pioneers ... who followed no man's tracks.[5]

When A.A. came to select from the varied writing he had published over the preceding thirty years for *Responses*, he deliberately avoided the kind of thematic unity found in *The Australian Tradition.* Readers who know only that, and his book on Lawson,[6] might see him as exclusively preoccupied with Australian literature, chiefly of the 1890s period. *Responses* complements the earlier books by revealing his wider interests. The range of subjects is much broader, as also is the range of publications these essays were originally written for, and together these allow the reader to form a more varied impression of his work as a critic. The earliest pieces in the collection were written for radio. They are among the earliest broadcast scripts preserved in the Australian Archives, and include A.A's contribution to the programme 'Standard Works I'd like to Burn' for 1950—his talk on Pope, which in his preface to *The Dunciad Minor* A. D. Hope refers to as a source of inspiration (and much of the mock epic's scholarly apparatus is attributed to 'A.A.P.').[7] As well as writing for *Meanjin* (and providing editorial assistance), and *Overland,* A.A. began reviewing for newspapers in the later 1950s: for the *Age* (most frequently), the *Sydney Morning Herald, Nation,* and later, *Nation Review.* In selecting from the considerable volume of his literary journalism for *Responses,* he chose a high proportion of reviews of Australian authors. These, he felt, would be more likely to be of interest to readers of the collection than his opinions on English, American and European books of all kinds—which, rather

5 'The Literary Heritage Re-assessed', reprinted in *Responses*, pp.72–81.

6 A. A. Phillips, *Henry Lawson*, Twayne's World Author Series (Twayne, New York, 1970).

7 A. D. Hope, *Dunciad Minor: An Heroick Poem by A. D. Hope: Profusely Annotated by A. A. P. and A. P.* (Melbourne University Press, Melbourne, 1970), pp.v–viii.

than Australian books, occasioned the bulk of his newspaper reviewing. Almost half of his reviews were concerned not with imaginative writing but with wider cultural, and political, concerns, such as education or government support for the arts. These facts should remind us that, like A. G. Stephens and Vance Palmer before him, his interests were much wider and more cosmopolitan than his more familiar writings might suggest.

Stephens, Palmer, Phillips ... there does seem to be a relationship between them that goes beyond their having been seen as 'literary nationalists'. Their names in sequence suggest elusively some pattern in cultural history, though not a line of simple descent from the 'Red Page Rhadamanthus'. They can be seen as the most prominent, and forcefully individualistic, critics who countered indifference towards Australian culture in successive periods. They were not alone; and their criticism, examined more fully, forces qualification of the received stereotypes we have of it. But that they were, however unintentionally, responsible for such stereotypes of the Australian Critic is a large, if inaccurate, measure of their achievement. Unfairly simplified as their views have been, at least they were recognised as provocative gad-flies with unfashionable interests; discomfortingly, they wrote against the grain of complacent dismissal of our own culture. Vance Palmer can confidently be seen as an influence on A.A. because of his pervasive influence on cultural life, especially in Melbourne, from the 1920s onwards. His views of the interdependence of national culture, democratic values, and the literature which expressed both had their fullest influence on *Meanjin.* An affinity between A.G.S and A.A. that one can sense—beyond their obvious common commitment to Australian writing—is more a matter of style and, with this, of stance. Both employ a direct, confident, vigorously colloquial manner that is provocatively pointed, a style that suggests the writer has matters of personal urgency to express in a pithy, down-to-earth way and has no time for, or patience with, academic jargon or affectations.

Although he can rise to the impassioned eloquence we find at the end of 'The Democratic Theme', A.A.'s preferred critical style tends towards terseness. In this he is very reminiscent of Stephens; both prefer brevity, not only in their sentences but also in their paragraphs. Their concern is with their judgements, or the direction of their arguments, rather than with proliferating analytic detail; their natural unit is the essay rather than the book. They prefer a personal, informal engagement with an implicitly immediate audience, rather than to write formally and impersonally for 'ideal' readers, or posterity. Theirs is style—in the best sense of these words—of the teacher and the journalist, who know they have only so much time to make the points they want urgently to make—so they need to make them sharply, vividly, memorably.

In a review of a collection of American criticism A.A. wrote:

> Professionalism gives a critic's work a valuable solidity. It gives the brooding time needed to hatch the eggs of thought. But unless the critic can also retain the essential impulse of the amateur, his work will be as dead as mutton.[8]

'The essential impulse of the amateur' was his attempt to give an account, to himself and to others, of the delight that he found in a work of literature. Speaking as 'a rank amateur' at the UNESCO seminar on the arts in Australia in 1968, A.A. contended that professionalism in literary criticism tended to distort responses by shifting the emphasis from 'delight' to 'significance'. Not that he disregarded significance—'Every work of art ... is also in some measure a statement, intellectually apprehensible, about the process of living'—yet if the critic is preoccupied with significance at the expense of delight (his example is F. R Leavis with *Hard Times*) he misleads his readers. In this address on 'The Responsibilities of the Critic' A.A., like A.G.S. and Vance Palmer, saw himself as a mediator between the 'life' of literature and the lives of its readers. And if, he maintained, a fascination with forms leads a writer away from life and his readers, it is the critic's responsibility to speak up on the reader's behalf. Without being in any way daunted, he may have felt on this occasion at the University of Sydney that he was taking a stand against the more obscurantist tendencies in academia, an attitude not unprecedented in his writing.[9] Be that as it may, it did not prevent the University of Melbourne from recognising that its former student had become 'widely regarded as the doyen of Australian literary critics' when in 1975 it conferred on him the Doctorate of Letters.

8 Review of Beaver, ed., *American Critical Essays*.

9 An extract from this address appears as 'Reader and Writer' in *Responses*, pp.152–54.

# Patrick White: Twyborn Moments of Grace

By the end of the 1970s it was clear that critics were deeply divided over the nature of Patrick White's work and his achievement. At that time, I attempted to identify their fundamental differences by asking whether White was to be seen as a traditional novelist with a religious or theosophical view of life, or as a sophisticated, ironical modern—mistrustful of language and sceptical of ever being able to express what might lie beyond words?[1]

Since then, literary criticism has registered some changes, and shocks. Indeed that term, 'literary criticism', has come to suggest the kind, or kinds, of exegesis and evaluation that prevailed in the ages that preceded our own brave new theoretical world. (I speak in general terms but have contemporary Australian academia specifically in mind.) How, I wonder, would a new reader, one coming to White for the first time through his most recent novel, *The Twyborn Affair* (1979), perceive him?

In imagining this 'new' reader I have in mind a younger generation, particularly of students, who need not have encountered White's earlier novels and criticisms of them, and for whom the terms and concerns of Anglo-American New Criticism which affected the academic reception of White's work from at least the 1960s on are likely to be less immediate than those of Continental and North American theorists who have been influential during the last decade or more; for instance, Mikhail Bakhtin, who looms large on the program for this conference and in the October 1984 issue of *PMLA*.

Knowing such readers, especially among graduate students, I begin

1 In my *Patrick White* (Macmillan, London, 1980; St Martin, New York, 1980).

---

A paper presented at the Modern Language Association Conference, Washington, D.C., 1984; 'the Twyborn moment of grace' is the concluding phrase of White's autobiography, *Flaws in the Glass* (1981).

to speculate on how White's most recent novel might answer to their interests.

My imagined new readers would be suspicious of such enshrined concepts as 'the novel', or even 'literature'. They would see these as 'privileging' and 'valorising' assumptions which should be subjected to sceptical reappraisal. Their interests would be in 'writing': in 'texts', their 'discourses', their 'strategies', and their 'intertextual' relationships with other writings. Their reading of 'Theory' would encourage them not to attempt to construct a single, stable interpretation of a text but to 'deconstruct' it: to search for the paradoxes embedded in its discourses and concealed gaps or 'absences', and to celebrate the 'play' of diverse meanings these reveal.

Such readers coming to *The Twyborn Affair* innocently—that is, approaching it as a contemporary fiction and not as the latest (and a very late) step in White's long and much discussed development—would, I conjecture, discover a text that demands 'decoding', in that it explicitly plays with contradictory possibilities of significance, and deconstructs itself in its unfolding.

The opening of the novel invites us to recognise its mode as that of comedy of manners *à la* Edith Wharton, whom Mrs E. Boyd ('Joanie') Golson is reading. It invites us to read it as a study of repressed sexual attraction between wealthy married women holidaying on the French Riviera before the first World War, as a period comedy in which New World naivety and insecurity encounter Old World sophistication, and decadence. This mode is sustained through Joanie's voyeuristic point of view while at the same time being ironised by the reader's 'modern' awareness that the object of Joanie's infatuation, Madame Eudoxia Vatatzes, is 'male'. This drag-show comedy culminates in the Vatatzes 'entertaining' the Golsons with a Chabrier piano duet (or duel) and M. Vatatzes's appalling display of bad manners—a scene exquisitely embarrassing for the Golsons, and farcical for the reader because a disruption of the social and literary conventions lovingly evoked in the establishment scenes.

Clearly, linguistic as well as literary play is being indulged in. The comedian as the letter 'E' confuses signifiers and signifieds, names and genders, and relationships within the Twyborn family. Admittedly, these confusions may pose only initial difficulties for readers, who either struggle to sort them out for themselves or wait for the narrative to clarify them (unless they have already lost their innocence through reading reviews). However, that readers cannot be sure, initially at least, which 'E.' is being referred to (and desired) nor of his or her gender signals a deliberate playing against the conventions that the opening has lead them to expect. And even though the innocent reader discovers in Part Two that Eudoxia is 'really' Eddie Twyborn, who becomes Edith Trist in Part Three, the radical indeterminacy of signifiers, linguistic and sexual, and the indeterminacy of gender itself, continue throughout as the novel passes into, and mixes, other modes.

Other discordant elements, other kinds of writing, also enter early to upset the readers' expectations. Angelo Vatatzes's obsession with Byzantine history seems calculated to perplex in that it introduces, through his confused consciousness, highly specific but, for most of us, unfamiliar reference. Helpfully, in a traditional humanist reading of the novel, A. P. Riemer has elaborated the arcane textuality and etymological play ('bugger' is derived from 'Bulgar', *OED*) behind these lengthy passages.[2]

I'd like to suggest further that the 'subversive strategy' behind them is that they 'defamiliarise' our, admittedly stereotyped, literary expectations of how European culture will be presented, *à la* Edith Wharton or the early Henry James, in a novel opening in the Edwardian period and presenting the comedy of New World manners encountering those of the Old. White's Australian variation on this by now time-honoured 'international theme' intercuts Vatatzes's Levantine memories and Byzantine fantasies with Joanie's equally 'untypical' reveries over her personal, and homoerotic, past in the New World.

Another early example of discordance is that odd, seemingly excrescent interlude with M. Pelletier, the sour keeper of the beach kiosk who masturbates over the distant, androgynous, Hellenic figure of Eudoxia in the sea. Is this a disgusted Flaubertian parody of Romantic afflatus, with the *petit bourgeois* voyeur presuming to imagine that he has glimpsed the transcendent. Or is it, having in mind another voyeur masturbating on the strand, a blurring of Joycean epiphanies, high and low? (In *Ulysses*, Cissy, object of Mr Bloom's desire, herself ejaculates, 'Oh, will you ever forget the evening she dressed up in her father's suit

2 A. P. Riemer, 'Some Observations on *The Twyborn Affair*', *Southerly* 40 (1980), 12–29.

and hat and the burned cork moustache and walked down Tritonsville Road, smoking a cigarette?'—which is not unlike Joanie's obsessive memory of Eadith ('E.') Twyborn's cross-dressing prank.)[3]

M. Pelletier's moment of 'tremulous abstraction' may seem no more than the result of a 'sordid ejaculation', as inconsequential as those other 'expostulatory ejaculations' of the coffee pot as it boils over on the rickety little spirit lamp. But for him, as he returns to this world and the damp newspapers presaging the coming war, it remains 'a triumphant leap into the world of light and colour' which he craves, into the poetry he has never written and the love he has never expressed for (and note the gender mix) 'Simone or Violette—or Mireille, Fernandel Zizi Jacques Louise Jeanne Jacques Jaccques ...'.[4]

This incident, we might say, oozes semiosis. Yet its counterpoising of Romantic and anti-Romantic attitudes and styles is so diffused with ironies that it seems pointless to ask whether M. Pelletier has truly glimpsed transcendence or only, laughably, presumed he has. Assuming readers 'know' by this stage that Eudoxia is 'male', they might feel they are joining with the author in relishing the dramatic irony at Pelletier's expense. But any sense of shared superiority is then undercut by the play on 'ejaculation' (Pelletier's and the coffee pot's), which insists that any 'significance' is merely coincidental, an etymological accident, an empty effect of writing.

This brings us directly, if uncertainly, to what seemed the issue in White criticism throughout the 1970s. What was it precisely that his characters' perceptions of 'pure being' signified? Discussions then focused on such epiphanic moments as M. Pelletier feels he has experienced. Whether or not the majority of commentators saw White as successful—and those that didn't found something like 'tremulous abstraction'—they agreed on seeing him as attempting to 'realise' in language what new readers would now recognise, and knowingly dismiss, as the 'transcendental signified'. If, however, M. Pelletier seems too peripheral a character and this episode excrescent, we might consider a moment of transcendence for Eddie himself in the central section of *The Twyborn Affair.*

3 James Joyce, *Ulysses*, (Bodley Head, London, 1937), p.337.

4 Patrick White, *The Twyborn Affair* (Cape, London, 1979), p.76. Subsequent page references, included in the text in parentheses, refer to this edition.

This section rings satiric changes on the conventions of the Australian novel rural life—conventions which White has returned to intermittently since his first published novel, *Happy Valley* (as *The Twyborn Affair* also returns to the London of *The Living and the Dead* and the southern France of *The Aunt's Story*). The moment occurs when his feeble-minded workmate Denny invites Eddie home for a beer and to meet his wife Dot and their baby. Once there, within a setting that is one of White's familiar moral landscape, where rocks suggest an irreducible core of reality and life is stripped to its essentials, Denny dandles the infant that, unsuspected by him, is the issue of Dot and her father, Dick the rabbiter.

As she contemplates her husband blissfully salivating over the baby, the frazzled, feral Dot is momentarily touched, we are told, by a 'revelation'. But then there occurs a 'violation of grace' when Dick, father both of Dot and her daughter (and, as a rabbit-skinner, another kind of *pelletier*?), approaches on horseback. Denny drives 'Dadda' away with oaths and gunshots. As Eddie rides away he wonders 'whether he wasn't leaving the best of all possible worlds' (pp.276–78).

This scene is so encoded lexically and conventionally that it can be read as both low satiric, but not unsentimental, rustic farce and as an ostensibly blasphemous allegory of the Holy Family and the Incarnation. Again, it is parodic and portentous at the same time; and for White's 'old' readers, what it is parodying would have to include all those much discussed 'epiphanies' in his own the earlier novels. A frequent criticism of those earlier 'revelations' was that they were granted only to an elite and denied to the caricatured 'normal' members of a society from which these visionaries were alienated. Here, Eddie's Panglossian but provisional epiphany is bodied forth by the caricatures, as though White were revisiting ironically not only his own earlier texts but that wider text that by this time constituted 'Patrick White'.

Yet another example occurs towards the end of Part Three, in which other modes and conventions are operating. Eadith recalls an Australian captain having told her/him during the first World War of his furtive coupling with a 'Frog' woman in her farm-house, and how he felt they had been enfolded by giant wings. While the captain, a caricature of crude Australian maleness, insists he believes in 'nothun', what he recounts could be interpreted as an experience of the Holy Spirit, despite the lowness of his diction and the iconographically incongruous imagery (cockatoos rather than doves). Remembering this towards the end of her life, Madame Eadith Trist reflects that 'In certain circumstances, lust can become an epiphany' (pp.417–19). While yet again an 'old' reader might ask whether this is a portentous gesturing towards a deeper, religious significance, or a parody (and self-parody?) of literary pretensions to incarnate the transcendent through language, 'new' readers, rather than agonising over White's precise 'tone' or 'stance', might less problematically see him as his maximising the play, and clash, of disparate signifying codes.

The Christian lexicon—so often the stabilising element for 'old' readers of White's previous novels—continues to pervade *The Twyborn Affair.* It enters in Part One with Eudoxia seeing Joanie Golson's appearance as a 'Visitation' and dreading her 'Second Coming' (p.33), and becomes most pronounced in Part Three. Like the play with the letter 'E' in the first section, the play on the brothel-as-nunnery/nunnery-as-brothel in the final section foregrounds a radical ambiguity. Is it elevating prostitution by equating it with the religious vocation, or degrading that vocation to an institutionalisation, and therefore a profanation, of divine love (as prostitution is of human love)? Or is it freely, 'irresponsibly' indulging in the elaboration of a given trope which turns the conventional world upside down?

The latter would be my answer: the brothel/nunnery is a classic catachresis in the pornographic tradition (Diderot and Sade readily come to mind) invoked here to play with, and against, readers' expectations of decorum, of clear and proper distinctions, fictional, social, and sexual. Another level of literary style (but problematically 'literary' for 'old' readers?), that of pornography, is being added to the predominant mode of international comedy of manners in Part One and, in Part Two, White's return to Australian topoi and his own local moral landscapes. Behind White's texts there have always been (inescapably the Barthesian would mutter) other texts; here they include his own, and fictional parallels with his now widely known life-history, the extended text that is 'Patrick White', in an act of flamboyant auto-intertextuality.

Now, of course, one does not have to be a 'new' reader at all to discern such diverse discourses running through this text. With *The Twyborn Affair,* the process of 'deconstruction' is inverted. Instead of disparate literary conventions, dissonant lexical codes, and radical ambiguities lying beneath its surface, they obtrusively are the surface. Structurally foregrounded (shades of *The Aunt's Story*) are the narrative jumps from Eudoxia to Eddie to Eadith and to Eddie again (and back and forth within these), and jumps in the fictional modes and literary styles that mirror his/her search for a life-style.

Pervasively there are the linguistic play with, and clash of, religious and psychoanalytic codes (all those oneiric passages in which the characters indulge their polymorphous perverse propensities); farcical disruptions, as when Reg and Nora Quick 'cooeee' around the country house garden in Part Three; the shifting, partial perspectives—through windows, reflections in mirrors, peepholes on the brothel of life—which turn the reader into a voyeur. All of these would frustrate any 'old' reader's attempt to reconstruct the narrative in accordance with traditional expectations of a consistent central character and situation, a single authorial point of view, and a single, stable 'meaning'.

Such an attempt would fail not because there is insufficient characterisation, situation, motif, etc. to be interpreted along conventional psychological-realist, and liberal or Christian humanist lines but because there is an excess of, and conflict among, such interpretative possibilities. This novel could be read one-dimensionally, as White's earlier novels have (variously) been read, only at the cost of repressing its often outrageous play with its readers and its transgressions of linguistic, literary and social codes.

Responding to these transgressions, my 'new' reader would almost certainly be reminded of Bakhtin's carnivalesque-grotesque tradition in fiction. The carnivalesque masquerade, in which the normal world is turned upside down or inside out, and the 'other' (the rogue, the fool, the clown—or the hetaera) becomes, in the case of *The Twyborn Affair*, queen for a day, has an obvious appropriateness, not only for the brothel-scenes but also the cross-dressing masquerades that run throughout the novel and subvert notions of a 'natural order'.

In this light, *The Twyborn Affair* could be seen as in a venerable, if subversive, tradition and its author's playfulness on so many levels simultaneously in accord with Bakhtin's summary of this mode's functions:

> to concentrate inventive freedom, to permit the combination of a variety of different elements and their rapprochement, to

> liberate from the prevailing view of the world, from conventions and established truths, from cliches, from all that is humdrum and universally accepted.
>
> And so, to offer instead, 'a new outlook on the world, to realise the relative nature of all that exists, and to enter a completely new order of things'.[5]

We seem also to have entered a completely new order of things also for the interpretative and evaluative exercises we used to call 'literary criticism'. If *The Twyborn Affair* seems calculatedly to answer to those interests that characterise my 'new' readers, how will they read (or re-read) the earlier novels? Will they find that White changed course with this latest novel, or that, at least since *The Aunt's Story,* he has been both the 'readerly' novelist explicated and evaluated by earlier commentators and a self-consciously literary, ironically playful, 'writerly' novelist—a postmodernist in the most literal sense that he has absorbed earlier twentieth-century experiments with fiction, and also a postmodernist in our current sense of scepticism towards any of the absolutes postulated in even the recent past?

If you want (as many have wanted) to seize on White's statement that he sees himself as essentially an old-fashioned writer,[6] and to present him as adopting such modes as the historical novel, the comedy of manners, or the *Bildungsroman* for traditional ends, then the protean nature of his work will allow this. You will focus on *The Tree of Man, Voss, The Vivisector, A Fringe of Leaves,* possibly *The Eye of the Storm.* If, however, you wish to present him as a proto-postmodernist, then you will stress *The Aunt's Story,* possibly *Riders in the Chariot, The Solid Mandala,* and—the winning card in your pack—*The Twyborn Affair.* But really, of course, he is and always has been both; and my unsurprising conclusion is that, as critical interests and emphases continue to shift, White's work will continue to answer to them, as it has answered to different, and opposed, interests in the past.

5 Mikhail Bakhtin, *Rabelais and His World,* trans. Helene Iswalsky, (MIT Press, Cambridge, Mass., 1969), p.34

6 Thelma Herring and G. A. Wilkes, 'A Conversation with Patrick White', *Southerly* 33 (1973), p.139.

# Frank Moorhouse: A Retrospective

Today, publication in the United States represents for probably most Australian writers, and readers, the same kind of recognition that publication in England did for so long in the past. Until toward the end of the nineteenth century, when the establishment of local presses coincided with conscious effort to develop a native literature, London or Edinburgh offered the Australian writer virtually the only chance of publication. A consequence of this cultural colonialism for this century has been a tendency to distinguish between 'characteristically' Australian writing published locally and the more 'international' writing by Australians published elsewhere—even though this has often been confused by consideration of the writers' country of birth or residence, their concerns, and the continuance from last century of the debate over the appropriateness of absolute 'universal' or relative 'local' critical criteria. There is nothing unusual about this in the history of a comparatively new literary culture, nor that 'metropolitan' recognition was sought and welcomed (with London, historically, providing the metropolis of letters). Writers who published abroad, however, often suffered delayed recognition in their own country: the most familiar examples among novelists would be Christina Stead and Patrick White, who from the beginnings of their careers published in London and New York. Although today the more artificial aspects of this distinction between local and international writing have faded, there still remains a 'metropolis', a perceived source of influence, of critical and financial success, but it is now much more likely to be located by Australian writers in New York than London.

For Australian readers, conspicuous recent examples of novelists who are winning 'international' recognition through publication in the United States would include: Thomas Keneally with *Confederates* (Collins, Sydney and London, 1979; Harper and Row, New York, 1980), David

First published in *Modern Fiction Studies* [Purdue University, U.S.A.] 27 (1981).

Malouf with *An Imaginary Life* (Chatto and Windus, London, 1978; Braziller, New York, 1978), and Roger McDonald with his first novel, *1915* (University of Queensland Press, St Lucia, 1979; Braziller, New York, 1980). As well, the new generation of short fiction writers has appeared in American magazines, including Murray Bail, Morris Lurie, and Michael Wilding in the *New Yorker*; and Peter Carey's collection *The Fat Man in History* has been published simultaneously by prestigious houses in London and New York (Faber, London, 1980; Random House, New York, 1980). Such examples could be multiplied, yet (and to come to the point), well-deserved as this recognition is, an element of adventitiousness enters into its achievement, in that the writers who attain it are not the only ones whose reputations are high among Australian readers. Conspicuously absent from the examples just given is Frank Moorhouse, who is generally seen as among the most original and substantial of the writers who emerged in the late 1960s and the early 1970s. There seems some perversity in his not having received international recognition through publication in America, because the impact of American culture on Australia is a recurring subject in his fiction—and the book with which he first established his reputation is entitled *The Americans, Baby.*

Moorhouse's most recent collection of stories, *The Everlasting Secret Family* (1980), appears after a decade in which he published five others, including his first. It was also a period of distinct social, political, and cultural change, a period he has captured in a collection of 'new journalism', chiefly his own, titled *Days of Wine and Rage* (1980). Like this, *The Everlasting Secret Family* also has aspects of a retrospective collection. The early books—*Futility and Other Animals* (1969), *The Americans, Baby* (1972), and *The Electrical Experience* (1974)—were each subtitled 'a discontinuous narrative'; this is the form that Moorhouse has made his distinctive, though varied, means of structuring his fictions, and employed in *Conference-ville* (1976) and *Tales of Mystery and Romance* (1977). While individual stories can be read (and some have been published) separately, the interlinking of characters and themes relates them in each volume. As well, some characters reappear from volume to volume; and a story from the first recurs in the second, one from that in the third, underscoring the sense of a 'family' relationship, or, one might say (not inappropriately, given its psychological associations), a 'polymorphous' relationship within each collection and among them all. The effect is that while the stories move through discrete social levels, generations, and locales, they also imply an elusive pattern of interaction, one in which connections are *not* made as they would be in a traditional novel.

Although Moorhouse is committedly a writer of stories rather than novels, his composed collections are among the most original, extended fictions of the past decade, and his discontinuous forms are essential to his view of the ways things happen and of the discreteness and fragmentation of individual experience. What happens does not 'develop' as in a continuous narrative, yet there is the sense that all is not random, disconnected, arbitrary. *The Everlasting Secret Family* develops, in the senses of further revealing and imaginatively extending, these relationships underlying his work to date. Although not subtitled 'a discontinuous narrative' as the first collections were, *The Everlasting Secret Family* contains such sequences in the first and third of its four sections. Readers expecting again a 'family' relationship among all the stories (and they would be right to do so) will find that in mode, mood, and subject these form more radically distinct groups than in any of the previous collections. The book appears a 'retrospective' in that each section develops different aspects of Moorhouse's characteristic manners and concerns, whereas the book as a whole (as its predecessors did successively) moves into different areas and new stylistic modulations.

The first group of stories, 'Pacific City', offers scenes from provincial life in an earlier generation—a classic subject of realist, and ironic, fiction. Although in comparison with other writers of 'contemporary' fiction (and his near contemporaries) like Murray Bail, Peter Carey, and Michael Wilding, Moorhouse is not so manifestly experimental in style and has tended to locate his fictions in immediate experience, to be ostensibly more the realist than the artificer, the realism of this opening sequence is in a very literary, artistically self-conscious mode. The town which is to be the site of the projected Pacific City is already familiar from earlier collections, especially *The Electrical Experience,* and is perhaps not unlike the town a hundred miles south of Sydney that the author himself (born 1938) came from. But it is also, with traditional literary and cultural associations, the Town as against the City, and a microcosm of the Society (as well as of a society in a particular time and place) that in all times frustrates the Artist and the Seer. In this consciousness of—even parodic awareness of—archetypes, the 'Pacific City' sequence is closer to Patrick White's first novel, *Happy Valley,* than it is to traditional fiction about Australian country town life. And Moorhouse's style, in the particulars of his relocating classic themes in an alien environment, is not essentially different from White's: the predominant sense of 'slice of life' realism is, at the same time, working figuratively, to transcend (and render arbitrary) that notional categorical separation into metonymic and metaphoric modes of writing posited by some theorists.

Irving Bow, 'the proprietor of darkness' in the story so titled, and proprietor of the Odeon Cinema, is the focus for the ironic comedy in these stories which contrast mundane existence in the small town with the Life of the imagination, of dreams and visions, but also of deceptions and delusions. Left money by his mother, Bow has built his Odeon facing away from the town toward the projected Pacific City (the year is 1927). With its plaster statues of the Muses in the foyer, it is his temple of art and promise of the Golden Age to come, advanced by electricity, when Pacific City will be a pleasure resort like Baden or Nice and the Odeon the centre of its public life. But unsuspected by the townspeople who accept as real the illusions the cinema offers them, it is also a most transpontine theatre (my archaic flourish; but justified by 'The Crying Organ' story, in which a troupe of strolling players protests at competition from the cinema and topples the statue of Thalia). In the stories' own images, it is Bow's castle, Romanesque balcony and all, his retreat from the desert of the town; and, as keeper of his temple's mysteries, Bow is the proprietor of darkness in another sense—he is the dark stranger in the lives of the town's more attractive pubescents whom, with their compliance, he temporarily enslaves while he poses as a jaded Emperor. Or he shows 'Passion's Slave' again to Dr. Trenbow in a private screening. His associates in the town are others who feel apart from it: Trenbow, whose ambition is to pursue the study of human psychology in Vienna; Backhouse, the newspaper editor, who aspires to Fleet Street; Scribner, the town's bohemian of mysterious means, who is reputed to be an old Balliol man. 'The Town Philosophers' Banquet' gathers together these and other luminaries, including Branton, who is regarded as a classics scholar, although he teaches something else at the local school, and Selfridge, the athlete returned from the Amsterdam Olympics, who brings a body balm back from Greece (or Bow wants to think it's from Greece). Bow entertains them in the cinema's banquet room; as the guests discuss physical pleasure over the wine, the children of a Sicilian immigrant, dressed in Grecian costume, dance before them, their performance culminating in a mime of seduction. Afterward, Bow is left with the athletic but sleeping Selfridge, trying to delude himself from his balcony that 'Pacific City and its glittering noise, automobiles, and neon gas lights, had already arrived'.[1]

The ironically Platonic associations of this story's title and the Hellenic allusions (including pederasty) within it convey the timeless nature of Irving Bow's dissatisfactions and his idealisation of the City. His 'lonely unrespectability' is both specific to this town and time and simultaneously the romantic idealist's perennial sense of estrangement. The other 'philosophers' also feel exiled from an ideal metropolis. 'The Science Club Meets' brings them together again, around the body of a two-headed calf, to hear Bow lecture on the cinematograph. Afterward, the secretary reads a letter from the Institute of Patentees, London:

> 'Our correspondent says that little groups of patentees were still discussing points from the lecture among themselves on the stairs well after the close of the meeting.'
>
> The secretary looked up. 'That's all.'
>
> They sat there in silence, wanting so badly to have been among the small groups of patentees who gathered on the musty but well-polished stairs of the Institute in Westminster, the portraits of Faraday, Edison, Stephenson and Isambard Kingdom Brunel on the walls, the gas lights being turned out by the caretakers who told them to hurry along as they talked excitedly about Rynder's talk and spilled out into the spring air, pulling on their caps, going then maybe to a comfortable English public house for a pint, each giving guarded information about his latest theory, invention or calculation.
>
> McDowell broke the wistful silence by moving in a quiet voice that the report of the Institute of Patentees be received. (p.51)

1 'Frank Moorhouse, *The Everlasting Secret Family and Other Stories* (Angus and Robertson, Sydney, 1980), p.36. Subsequent page references, included in the text in parentheses, refer to this edition.

This sense of not fully belonging, of being spiritually estranged, remote from the true cultural centre (whether it be a fanciful classical Athens or Rome, imagined contemporary London or Vienna, or the idealised but never to be built Pacific City) pervades these stories. At the realistic level it captures the colonialist and provincial consciousness of this generation. At the metaphoric, and consciously literary, level, it insinuates the irony that such delusions of a finer, fuller life in some other place and time are perennial. The 'Pacific City' sequence closes with 'To Be Continued', quietly underscoring this recognition of the timeless conflict between the real and the ideal.

The complex play against the conventions of local literature is especially apparent in 'The Illegality of the Imagination', a reworking of the traditional subject of the child lost in the bush. Conventionally, this subject should oppose a sense of community to the inhospitality of the bush, but Bow's alienation from both the landscape and the people of the countryside expresses the author's rejection of conventions that would sentimentalise life in this place, at this time. After a premonition of death, Bow finds the child, which is then thrashed by its father, and later loses itself in the bush again, never to be found. The 'illegality' of Bow's imagination in conjuring up an image of the boy's skull on his naked body, and then remembering how the boy clung to him, corresponds with Moorhouse's own in venturing outside the conventions which traditionally prescribe how such subjects should be presented.

If Irving Bow, the corrupt master of illusions, is perceived as a type of the artist, forced into silence and exile, finding no one amongst his kindred to take his confession, but speaking the truth cunningly to the townspeople 'in a way that it would not be understood' (p.8), then the next section, 'The Dutch Letters', can also be seen as having problematical implications for art. The author-narrator tells us that he has found some letters in the student's room he is occupying during a conference, and he divulges their contents in full. The discovery is not accidental: the writer, curious to the point of invading the privacy of others, has actually broken into the student's locker and searched for the secret trap that conceals the letters in a writing cabinet. For the reader, the 'status' of this story is uncertain: is it a *conte trouvé* (to use the title of one of Moorhouse's uncollected stories), and are the letters genuine? Or are the letters, and the writer-narrator, the invention of another writer who likes to play on the boundary between fact and fiction? The writer in this fiction is unable imaginatively to penetrate the lives, empathetically enter the relationships, that the letters present. All he can do is to document these documents, producing a jumble of discordant footnotes. The writers of the letters refuse to be 'written'; their experiences remain intractable to this writer. From him the reader has a confession, such as Bow, another furtive voyeur, wanted to make. From Moorhouse, the writer 'behind' this narrator, we have—what? Either the dramatic presentation of the gap between the recorded experience of others and the missing imaginative version that a 'real' writer would create from it, or a confession of a violation of others' secrets and of imaginative failure on the part of the real writer.

The third section, 'Imogene Continued', is the most extended example of 'discontinuous narrative' within *The Everlasting Secret Family* (though the possibility of the whole collection being a variation on this form needs to be kept open). It is in the mode most frequently associated with earlier collections, in which the author plays the roles of acute, ironic observer of contemporary manners and comic realist who blurs the edges between fact and fiction. Although such a characterisation ignores the variations that exist between the previous collections, it has its point in summarising readers' expectations that Moorhouse will speak the truth about social and sexual relationships (even though, like Irving Bow, he may speak it in such a way that it is not understood). Set at the same conference as the preceding 'Dutch Letters,' this section introduces a range of contemporary intellectual and political types, some at least being sketched from life; and the ritualistic procedures and group behaviour at the conference are so drolly observed that the sequence reads rather more like 'new journalism' than fiction. Yet the sequence raises problematical questions about the relationships between these ostensibly distinct categories of 'reportage' and 'fiction' and contains its own authorial confessions.

Cindy, one of the academics attending the conference, and a former lover of the narrator (the same writer-narrator who had searched the student's room in the previous section), is raped by some delegates from the Aboriginal ghetto in Sydney. Her reaction to this, complicated by her vicarious guilt over the injustices accorded the Aboriginals historically (and the fact that the conference is being held in Queensland, where the police have a reputation for brutality and racism); the narrator's own reaction, affected by his past conditioning and earlier affair with

Cindy; and the further complication introduced by their discovering that one of the Aboriginals involved is a convicted child molester confuses their attempts to make rational, detached, mature responses. They find, in a variation of the wording in a lecture they attend, 'only the interaction of confusing things.' The subject of this lecture, John Anderson, Professor of Philosophy at the University of Sydney from 1927–1958, had provided, through his empiricist rejection of totalising systems of thought, a rationale for generations of 'Libertarian' Sydney bohemians. Cindy and the narrator (like Moorhouse himself) had been Libertarians in their youth; the irony is that they find themselves experiencing, emotionally and confusedly, that 'interaction of complex things' which intellectually they hold as their understanding of life. It is an irony at the expense of the narrator, who establishes himself first of all as jauntily detached and self-possessed. While in public he retains this confidence, continuing to clown and to participate in the regressive antics of the conference, inwardly he is under the pressure of these personal confusions.

In the context of Moorhouse's work as a whole, these admissions of uncertainty by the writer-narrator must seem confessional for the author also. The Libertarian subculture, influenced by Anderson's thinking, is presented in Moorhouse's earliest collections, and their discontinuous narrative structures can be seen as fictional demonstrations of Anderson's 'interaction of complex things'. Cindy is a character in these collections, and a story from the first reappears in this latest among the documenting notes to 'Imogene Continued'—in which she admits to lying about the experience on which that earlier story was based. Such a play with fact and fiction seems designed to counter conventional distinctions between the author 'in the story' (who reveals Cindy's secret to others) and the 'real' author (who reveals it to us) and to be an admission that Moorhouse shares his narrator's or persona's uncertainties which he draws so confidently into his fiction.

The final, and title, sequence begins by asserting the conventional distinction between author and narrator. The author notes that this 'erotic memoir in six parts' has been prepared from various sources; the narrator remarks: 'This was originally to be published privately and circulated privately. I do not in any way wish to harm the conservative forces in this country. In so far as this memoir touches on political things (and caution delimited this severely) it does so simply as a fact of our lives.'

But having come to this after the preceding sections of the book, the reader is likely to be wary of such a disclaimer from one of Moorhouse's narrators and to suspect the opposite is being hinted at. Yet 'The Everlasting Secret Family' departs from realistic modes to embrace the conventions of high pornography: the vaguely specified setting in time and place, Gothic suggestions of sacrilege and defilement associated with rites and vestments, and a classic concentration less on luridly described physical encounters than on the psychology of dominance and submission. But the classic, conventional theme of the abasement of self and the subjugation of others through the senses is played upon by this being a homosexual confession. A decadent set of conventions is revitalised by regaining its power to shock the contemporary imagination.

The narrator had been seduced by his lover, a politician, when he was a schoolboy; now he is a willingly submissive slave, chained by the telephone to his master's fickle whims, abused and manipulated, but also furtively rebellious in his promiscuity. In time, he obeys the instruction to initiate his master's son into the "secret family':

> I was joined to a line through history which went back to the first primitive tribal person who went my way, who took a virgin boy lover, and every boy who became a man and took, in due turn, a boy lover, through to Socrates. I had played a part now in the continuation of that chain. I had played my first part as a child in becoming a man's lover. I had now played my second part. I now belonged fully in that historical line. It was a way of passing on and preserving the special reality, a way of giving new life, the birth for the boy of a new reality, a joining of him to a secret family, the other family. To belong to that chain is to belong to another life. (p.204)

In the high artificiality of its mode, this sequence departs from the varieties of realism preceding it in the collection. It can be seen as purely imaginative, fictional play, a calculatingly provocative virtuoso flourish by an author who, like Irving Bow, is a 'proprietor of darkness,' indulging the 'illegality' of his imagination and, uncertainly, as a fable to be read, decoded, in political and psychological terms. In its engagement with taboo subjects and its revelation of secrets, it teasingly suggests possible 'secret' and 'family' relationships with the earlier sections in different modes: the politics of personal, and especially sexual, relationships—the dissembling, manipulativeness, and treachery that enter into these—and the deceptiveness, even deviousness, of the art that presents them. Where, though, there is only 'the interaction of complex things' in the earlier sections, in 'The Everlasting Secret Family' there is the narrator's discovering in his transported imagination a significance, a continuity, and an order in life—but a travesty of these traditional moral and literary positives. Here, clearly, the collection is implicitly rejecting any simple disjunction between the realistic, true-to-life, and the consciously fictional, true-to-art. Playing with the complicating possibilities between these opposed extremes, it constitutes a retrospective of Moorhouse's development to date.

Moorhouse's first collection, in which the story Cindy alludes to in *The Everlasting Secret Family* appears, was first issued by a publisher of 'girlie' magazines at the end of the 1960s.[2] Following the success of *The Americans, Baby,* it was later reissued by Angus and Robertson, traditionally the major publisher of Australian writing since the late colonial period. Angus and Robertson have continued to reissue *Futility and Other Animals* to meet rising demand and have published subsequent collections of Moorhouse's fiction. The early stories were, in the main and on the surface, about being young in Sydney during the Vietnam war and experiencing the tensions induced by the prevailing subcultural ideology of 'liberation'—political and sexual. A number of these stories had been rejected by editors of literary magazines (hence publication in popular but hardly cultural 'girlies'), not only because they were considered as riskily indecent but also because they were counter to what it was felt an 'Australian' short story should be about: more 'representative' characters and a more normative set of attitudes. Moorhouse was consciously opposing such stereotypes and in an interview has commented upon his own earlier attempts to write such stories:

> They were humanistic. They were kind to the working class. They were sympathetic to kangaroos. They were everything that

2 *Futility and Other Animals* (Gareth Powell Associates, Sydney,1969).

> Australian short stories should have been at that time. Social realism writing. It has to pretend to be realistic, and also at the same time to be the vehicle for sentiments, liberal sentiments.[3]

The narrative manner of *Futility and Other Animals* is realistic, but it is not the vehicle for liberal humanist sentiment. Rather, the stories present detachedly, without conventional judgment, the pressures of immediately contemporary experience and the conflicts between how the characters feel and the way they think they ought to feel.

In a prefatory note the author describes these characters as a 'tribe—a modern, urban tribe' sharing an environment that is 'both internal—anxieties, pleasures, and confusions—and external—houses streets, hotels...'. These experiences, the inner Sydney ambience, and the reappearance of various characters in different stories provide the common elements in this 'discontinuous narrative'. Although unconventional when it first appeared, because of its departure from the more 'representative' characters and settings and the more 'normal' situations of short stories then, it now seems more obviously a 'first' collection, preoccupied with youthful rites of passage (and it is a book that has continued to appeal to new generations of readers). In the main, its stories are about growing up, leaving home, coming to the city from the country, or returning there; first love affairs, hetero- or homosexual; and finding a peer group, a life style, an ideology, especially the anti-ideology of Libertarianism. 'Liberation' imposes its own stresses, conflicting with the desire for simple, secure relationships on the part of those who have rejected the 'bourgeois' romantic concept of love, and, additionally, for the women, with their desire to have children. While the characters' emotional experiences are often 'immature,' Moorhouse's ironic distance from them is characteristic of his own mature manner, which is marked by direct, dramatic presentation of a voice or voices and by a preference for freshly colloquial, metaphoric language. Even the authorial 'stage directions' for the dialogue (as later quotation will show) are conveyed by 'low' or homely concrete diction and comic metaphor rather than by abstract and polysyllabic description. The first story in *Futility and Other Animals* would seem implicitly to

3 'There's No Such Thing as a Gay Novel', interview with Frank Moorhouse by Martin Smith, Sydney *Campaign* [Sydney] 21 (1977), p.19.

acknowledge an early debt to Hemingway for this astringency of style and dramatic shaping.

*The Americans, Baby* opens with a fine example of this mature and characteristically ironic manner, 'Dell Goes into Politics', which carries over some of the concerns of the first collection.[4] It looks (or it did when it first appeared) very much a stereotypical 'Australian' short story about the return of a girl to her family in a small country town after living in the city. Her 'going into' politics is no more than her shouting out in the local pub, traditionally a male preserve, the anti-Vietnam slogans she has acquired from her Trotskyist lover in Sydney. Her family and friends, the rural working class, are embarrassed, even frightened. Dell's father tells her, "There's only one way to get along in this world—shut up". '"What do you know about politics?" her mother said, suspicious, as though she's suspected she might also know about sex' (p.7), and then comforts herself with the ignorant thought that 'They don't let women into Parliament anyhow' (p.8). Harry, the boy Dell had thought of marrying on her return, looks 'as if he'd got a bee flying around him' when she asks if the politician in the pub is State or Federal—'Christ, Harry, that's about the least you can know' (p.4). The ironic registering of the impact of the war on public consciousness depends on the story being read against the conventions of a rural realism that sentimentalise the workers as a progressive class. As well, there is the impact of the war on individual consciousness with the revelation of Dell's bad faith. Her shouting 'Why don't you bring the boys back from Vietnam?' (p.5) is a displacement of her real concern, an evasion of the fact that she has come back home because she is pregnant. The nexus between politics and sex assumed by the revolutionaries in Sydney is here played with ironically.

The second story, 'The American Paul Johnson', introduces Carl, a radical student in Sydney, who thinks he should exploit an American he meets because he represents ideologically the 'enemy,' but instead discovers his own homosexuality through the encounter. Like the first story, this is a study in bad faith that reveals the private, emotional anxiety beneath a public involvement in politics. 'Becker and the Boys from the Band,' which like many of Moorhouse's titles contains an ironic

4 *The Americans, Baby* (Angus and Robertson, Sydney, 1972). Subsequent page references, included in the text in parentheses, refer to this edition.

allusion (here to the play, then current, about New York homosexuals) introduces Becker, a Coca-Cola executive from Atlanta, Georgia. He seems another inauthentic figure, the creature of the corporation who would rather be back home, preferably playing piano in a jazz club; but his consciousness of his 'inauthenticity', his shrugging acceptance of his own limitations, makes him the most positive character in the book. In a time-honoured American tradition, Becker is the innocent abroad, in a country as remote to him as the moon ('Becker on the Moon', written after the U.S. moon landing, is another story in the collection), but, with a twist to the conventions, he is, ambiguously, liberated or corrupted in this New World of speed freaks, drag queens, and aggressively emancipated women.

Two other Americans appear in the first group of stories. Angela, in 'The Girl from *The Family of Man*' (she claims her photograph as a child appears in that collection), is the epitome of a new variety of primness—countercultural selfrighteousness—whereas the narrator, who beds her, is uninhibitedly vulgar, lecherous, and aggressive. Hugo, in 'The Story of Nature' (who is carried over from *Futility and Other Animals*), is a 'nuclear refugee' from the States, a scientist turned primitive who piously throws away Cindy's contraceptive pills in attempting to impose his values on their relationship. These stories present variations on a conflict between instinct and ideology over a range of characters who seem unrelated and socially peripheral—an impression important to the collection as a whole for the way changing sexual attitudes and radical political attitudes recur in the different worlds of city and country, business and the counter-culture, but in no simple, coherent pattern.

The sixth story, 'The American Poet's Visit', is one of two described as an 'interlude', and these, strategically placed in the collection, move to the centre of contemporary consciousness in the 'metropolitan' Libertarian subculture influenced by Anderson's critical, or negative, ideology. The interludes also move closer to the author, who is elsewhere 'invisible'; in the interludes he is the author as schlemiel, employing a self-deprecating irony as his defence against both life and the reader. 'The American Poet's Visit' fictionally recounts Kenneth Rexroth's actual reception by Sydney Libertarians in the late 1960s, capturing their ingroup smugness but also their doubts and defensiveness when confronted by a figure from the truly metropolitan, indeed cosmopolitan, counter-culture. The second interlude, 'The Girl Who Met Simone de Beauvoir in Paris', captures comically the threatening aspects of the women's movement for insecure males, and there is another painful reminder of their provincialism in the fact that de Beauvoir was met *in Paris.*

Between these comic interludes are stories about Dell's boyfriend Kim and his revolutionary friends, about Becker, another about Hugo; and there is 'Five Incidents Concerning the Flesh and the Blood', which, in tone and form, is quite distinct from these other stories about characters already introduced. Yet the thematic contrast it establishes between the rational, organised, and lifeless, *and* the spontaneous, instinctual, and vital, between 'the fleeting pleasures' and 'the groaning hours', opens up implications of a wider vision of life than the characters in the other stories, immersed in their subcultural preoccupations, can discern. In a self-consciously literary, perhaps too explicit way it points to a preference dramatically implied elsewhere in the collection for the vital and honest, if also messy and vulgar, as against the controlled and rationalised. The structuring of the collection also seems to assert this preference. Although after the second interlude there are stories about Becker's 'liberation' from life in the corporation (he ends up playing piano at the Silver Spade, Surfer's Paradise) and the story of Dell's rebelling against sexual indoctrination before returning home, to emphasise these narrative lines would be to give too 'novelettish' an account. *The Americans, Baby* has the length and the substance—in terms of psychological density, significant themes, contrasting characters, and social settings—for a novel, yet it deliberately avoids developing situations and relationships as a novel would. It even wilfully resists conclusion, the drawing together of latent relationships between characters and events, by ending with 'The Letters to Twiggy', which shows an exceedingly 'rational' but obsessive and sexually repressed mind quite out of control.

Through its structure, the collection presents a different view of the way things happen, the ways in which they do not form a simple, coherent, significant literary pattern, nor, in social terms, constitute a 'community' of experiences. It implies a view of contemporary Australian society that departs from received literary and sociological stereotypes such as the city and the country, 'Sydney or the Bush', an imposed Anglo-European tradition and a native, populist culture, 'authentic' working class values and 'inauthentic' middle class attitudes. Moorhouse's characters include Coca-Cola executives (as Americans, the transmitters of the dominant contemporary culture), a self-made, small town businessman, T. George McDowell, rural working class Dell, and varied representatives of the new class of predominantly young, predominantly middle class intellectuals, or lumpen-intellectuals; but all feel displaced, feel peripheral to their sense of a cultural centre. The discontinuous form, which sets up subtle and elusive refractions between the stories, cannot be considered in purely formal terms: it raises questions beyond these, and some of the most analytical commentary has come from social historians and cultural critics. But the drawing out of the ideological implications of what is dramatised, although an essential part of a full reading, cannot alone account for the book's qualities: its usually wry but at times exuberantly comic observation of the ways of the contemporary world, and its underlying perception of life as conflict, which cannot be resolved or avoided by observing abstract precepts. More abruptly than any other book of its decade, *The Americans, Baby* moved Australian fiction into the contemporary.

With this second collection, Moorhouse won national recognition and the reputation of being an accurate and acute observer of contemporary manners and morals, a reputation reinforced by his journalism and writings on the media. In the period which saw the emergence of a self-consciously 'new' fiction, Moorhouse clearly appeared more the realist than the fabulator. He continued to play a traditional role of the imaginative writer—a critical observer of social life—that many of his contemporaries were prepared to relinquish for formal and stylistic experimentation. Yet such broad distinctions, as were then forced, between 'realistic' and more 'imaginative' writing can have a dubious validity in particular cases. Not accorded equal recognition with his realism was Moorhouse's own, if less flamboyant, concern to 'make it new' formally and stylistically, as well as mimetically. This commitment has become more apparent as each book since *The Americans, Baby* has departed in its own way from its predecessors, and from readers' expectations formed by the first collections.

*The Electrical Experience* begins with the elderly businessman T. George McDowell in his small town talking to Becker about his daughter Terri and the problems of young people today.[5] Terri is the disturbed young woman in *The Americans, Baby* who 'liberates' Becker from the corporation and launches him on his uncertain career as a jazz pianist. The finest of the Becker stories in that preceding collection reappears here, but in the very different context of McDowell's life. George is a self-made and successful manufacturer of soft drinks, who had first visited the United States as a youth in 1923 and been influenced by the efficiency and technological progress he found there. The stories present, out of strict chronological order, revealing moments in George's life: Terri's birth during the bush fires of 1939; her conception, or at least George's conception of family planning; his changing his name to follow progressive business practice; George as a young man struggling to overcome shyness and meeting Zane Grey during the depression and the approach of the second World War; and finally as an old man suffering a stroke. Externally, he lives in the same South Coast town as in the later 'Pacific City' stories—in which he also appears (as do Backhouse, Trenbow, and Scribner in these). Yet the town, or his perception of it, is different from Irving Bow's, that historical and spiritual outsider. George's town is located much more specifically, and more one dimensionally in time—especially through the photographs, recipes, technical tips, and folk sayings which are included among the collection's 'fragments'—though it is still as much a mental as a physical environment. He identifies with the town in a way that Bow cannot, believing that 'You had to find the right-size place for the size of man you were' (p.4), and the town is George externalised and extended.

With his Elbert Hubbard individualism and rural communalism, his Rotarian's respect for service and efficiency, and his sexual repression, he epitomises a past ethos that conflicts with that of his daughter's generation, the contemporary urban intelligentsia whom he sees as 'gipsies.' The contradictions in his life—psychologically, between his instincts and his sense of propriety; philosophically, between his individualism and his communalism, and between his rationalism and the larger questions that Rotary cannot answer—are 'discontinuities' articulated through the stories. But the major discontinuity of the book is that between his generation and his daughter's, which is brilliantly

5 *The Electrical Experience* (Angus and Robertson, Sydney, 1974). Subsequent page references, included in the text in parentheses, refer to this edition.

emphasised in the final story, 'Filming the Hatted Australian'. In it, a group of young film makers in Sydney, which includes Terri, is making a documentary about 'the prejudices, the beliefs, the life-style' (p.184) of the self-contained Australian of George's generation. They corner their specimen as though he were a primitive anthropological survivor and then proceed verbally to flay and dissect him. The sudden shift in temporal perspective and the disturbing shift in values capture the discontinuities within apparent social-historical continuity.

At this mimetic level, *The Electrical Experience* is immediately impressive as imaginative social history—both for its capturing of the individual's experience of social change through McDowell and through the motif of the transforming and dislocating effects of electricity. Like Moorhouse's other collections, this is not discontinuous with the world outside the book; yet neither are the language and the form transparent means of presenting a simple fictional version of historical processes, as the account above might suggest. In form and language, the book (a discontinuous unity in a way the thematically more complex *The Americans, Baby* is not) departs from conventions of literary and cultural realism, from received notions of 'the typical,' and from deterministic assumptions about personal and social development. The chronologically disordered structure works against naturalistic assumptions of causation; and George McDowell is not a representative 'product' of his time and region—when the film crew in the last story selects a 'subject' to fit its stereotype of George's generation, it chooses someone quite different from the same town. George expresses an ethos that in his own mind is more American than Australian; and it is through his expressing it, his language, that the reader is made conscious of Moorhouse's artistic concerns, which go together with his critical engagement with Australian society.

McDowell is a simple man with a simple language: 'I do not care for words in top hats. I believe in shirt sleeve words' (p.9). The 'invisible' Flaubertian narrator, using George's lexicon, creates gently, even affectionately, with superior irony, the gap between how George thinks and speaks and how we perceive him. This stylistic method is capable of the most delicate and subtle comedy when the author detaches himself by isolating George's favourite words and phrases within quotes. Like Irving Bow at the very beginning of the 'Pacific City' sequence, and the narrators of the other collections which follow *The Electrical Experience,*

George has a preoccupation with language. Language expresses and creates the contradiction between his outward confidence, his gregariousness and garrulity, and his inner shyness and uncertainty. This contradiction is apparent in the opening story, when he reflects that:

> Life's experience had taught him that never once had speaking to a stranger been anything but to his advantage. Although inherently shy as a young man, he had learned early to talk to someone as if they owed you money. In all his life, including his world travel, the only person with whom he had been unable to converse in good fellowship was his daughter Terri, and this was a source of some distress to both [him] and Thelma. (p.10)

Yet even with his wife, Thelma, intimacy is inhibited; and George's inhibitions reveal themselves through the embarrassed and evasive syntax of his thought:

> He observed that the limitations and restrictions on the matter of sexual indulgence, placed by Thelma in their marriage, sometimes aroused him, her unwillingness, he had perhaps the sort of personality which was, which savoured, well, the restraint she imposed, the limitations on when, and her refusals. And now and then, though rarely, he imposed himself on her, and the silent, wordless impositions he enjoyed too. It had to do; he speculated, with the basic economic principle of scarcity. Though really, this aspect of their lives he did not truly understand and did not ponder over much and which was not to say, either, that they did not conduct their married life *correctly.* (p.16)

George is fond of such economic notions—'Man's know-how was his personal capital. The bank inside his head' (p.52)—and mechanical metaphors—he sees children as society's 'replacement parts.' They encapsulate the rationalised view of life which his language systematises. His language defines his character and ethos. It cannot comfortably accommodate intimacy, nor what he alludes to as the 'Great Mysteries', his dim and resisted apprehensions of the more transcendent values of religion and art, which would demand different vocabularies.

Through his language, T. George McDowell creates his public and speechifying self; and his adoption of this form of his name (which Backhouse tells him looks 'Americanized') suggests his consciousness of verbal role-playing. Moorhouse's own consciousness of language, as an essential part of his 'content' and not merely the vehicle for presenting it, is displayed with mastery in the final story. The abrupt shift, in diction and pace, into the speech of the young urban intellectuals contrasts them with their 'subject' and his generation. They make aggressive, even sadistic verbal assaults on Frederick Victor Turner to provoke and then to destroy his defences. They are self-righteous both in their presumed artistic justification for their deceptions and provocations, and in their assumed moral superiority to the racism and sexism of a stereotype they despise (but have relentlessly 'created' for the film). The easy ironies they achieve are not approved by the author-narrator in the story, nor are they consistent with the more comprehending, affectionate ironies of the book as a whole. Implicitly, the intention is the opposite of the film makers': toward an empathetic understanding of what it was like to be George McDowell, to see the world his way, and to feel that it is collapsing in the present. With *The Electrical Experience,* Moorhouse's ironic range, and the flexibility and precision of his control over dramatised language, made it obvious that as well as being a powerful 'realist' he was also among the very finest of 'stylists.'

The first of the dozen 'episodes' comprising *Conference-ville* is entitled 'In Flight Sadism'; in it, the author-narrator flying to a conference meets 'a conversational sadist,' the academic who is going to introduce his paper, that is, he adds, if the conference eventuates.[6] In this book, language is more markedly an essential dimension of what is being realistically, and critically, presented. Moorhouse, playing the same uncertainly fictional role of author-narrator as in the middle sections of *The Everlasting Secret Family,* registers confusions that are not only expressed through language but arise from it, as he attempts to define his 'position' in response to conflicting information and demands from others. At the conference there is incessant squabbling over and playing with words, the counter for counter interpretations of reality, while the author inwardly broods over his inability to find a coherent grammar of response for the comically varied situations he discovers himself in.

6 *Conference-ville* (Angus and Robertson, Sydney, 1976. Subsequent page references, included in the text in parentheses, refer to this edition.

Others have their confident positions, readily identifiable and entailing ready linguistic responses for interpersonal political skirmishes; the author has only his critically detached awareness of how their language reveals their positions, and the inadequacy of his own.

As a serially arranged collection of 'episodes' (part of its original conception was that it could be issued as a magazine serial), *Conference-ville* differs from the earlier books in having a linear narrative development (though what 'develops' remains problematical). It is closer to the novel, or at least novella form, but its more simple coherence can be seen as issuing from the author's preoccupation with what would prevent him from writing a novel. It is a non-novel about the difficulties, the impossibility of writing, in a form so traditional and confident of its conventions as the novel, about how we live now, in Australia in January 1976. The novel that is 'unwritable,' because about experiences which cannot be engaged truthfully and fictionally at the same time, would be about the effects of the *coup d'état* of November 1975 when the reformist Labor government, the first for a quarter of a century, was dismissed by the Governor-General, with suspicions that this unprecedented 'destabilisation' had been engineered by the C.I.A. The resulting 'cold civil war' and the impossibility for the author of reaching a confident 'position' in interpreting these events provide the subject of Moorhouse's non-novel. Lacking such a position, and being in actual circumstances which created confusion and induced 'paranoia' (but then there was Chile), he cannot present a clear, coherent fictional interpretation, even a confidently paranoid, 'new' fictional response to a plausibly paranoid political reality. The implicit discontinuity becomes that between confident fiction and uncertain experience.

Ostensibly personalised 'new journalism,' with many public figures referred to as appearing at the actual conference on which it is based, *Conference-ville* also engages with some concerns of the 'new' fiction. It is literature as process, writing about being a writer, confessing inadequacies and betrayals ('You could've changed the names at least,' one character reproaches the author (p.116) in the last episode). The author-narrator engages with the 'unwritability' of contemporary life, registering his defeat in assuming honestly an authorial position that would allow him to organise, control, develop, and shape meaningfully the 'interaction of complex things' he has encountered. This uncommitted, sceptical position of the author-narrator, so precisely caught by the other author, or other self, behind him is this book's artistic strength: it turns the apparent negations of commitment into a positive open stance and shapes the uncertainties of writing about the contemporary into a taut set of images.

In the opening episode of *Conference-ville*, the academic 'conversational sadist' mentions another (and actual) Australian writer who had been 'the darling of the literary scene in the late fifties,' who had broken 'new ground' but whom no one reads today. The author-narrator winces:

> He meant me. It could happen to me. Not yet the darling, not yet unread.
>
> I chattered on, but damned Markham had set my mind on anxious literary introspection ... will my other books be just obsessional pacing over the same initial life experiences ... or attempts to reproduce what had succeeded earlier ... worse, selfconscious attempts to 'break' with the preoccupations of earlier work ... rationally conceived fiction ... no heat ... no madness. (pp.4–5)

Moorhouse's next book shares with its predecessors the characteristic of breaking 'new ground,' and although it is exceedingly self-conscious, in a problematical way, the 'heat' and the 'madness' are there from the very beginning:

> The Malaya restaurant, city of Sydney, my mouth burning with sambal, splashed with chilled beer, tasting only hot and cold. My psyche also running hot and cold. They are back. Milton and Hestia are back from the States.
>
> Milton's hand on my shoulder. Our first physical touching since his return. It rings through me. I can't hear the message. It's a confused line.
>
> 'Well, I'm glad you're both back,' I say suddenly, pleased with my spontaneity and correctness.[7]

7 *Tales of Mystery and Romance* (Angus and Robertson, Sydney,1977), p.2. Subsequent page references, included in the text in parentheses, refer to this edition.

Contrary to the fears of the author in *Conference-ville, Tales of Mystery and Romance* impresses less as a 'rationally-conceived fiction' than as a series of virtuoso stylistic performances by the author, who as a zany version of the same 'narrator, or set of clowning variations on the authorial self, dances with desperate playfulness on the indeterminate boundary between truth-telling and story-telling—or lying.

The title suggests a self-conscious literariness, with its nineteenth-century Gothic evocations of the fantastic and the erotic; and the preoccupations with perversion, incest, metamorphoses, drug-induced fantasies, and death of an earlier decadence are comically translated into a contemporary version here. The 'tales' (the tale being to the story as the romance is to the novel, in claiming a greater imaginative 'latitude'?)[8] are set in a variety of typefaces to correspond with the discontinuities in mood between them; but despite this visual reinforcement of their tonal differences, the personality of their common narrator and the pattern of his emotional life emerge progressively. He is a thirty-seven year old poet-philosopher from Concord—the Sydney suburb, not the rural seat of Transcendentalism—who finds himself between two worlds. One, which is lost to him, is that of his family, childhood security, first love, marriage and fatherhood, the world of conventional domesticity: 'A cold quandary blows permanently on the moors of abnormality. The cheery lighted house of normality is a distant stage set' (p.94). The other is the world of Milton, his distant and beloved, his erstwhile intimate friend (but never, fully, his lover), his academic alter ego. Milton is now into a whole new 'scene'—Transcendental Meditation, Yoga, the occult, living in a commune with Lance and Karrine, Hildergarde, Margit, Tina, Sheena ... all, the narrator ruefully observes, under-thirties names. Although scornful, the lad from Concord with his Low Anglican, Boy Scout, small capitalist, individualist background is hurt by Milton's serenely frenetic pursuit of the now scene. He remembers that last year they were supposed to be nonhappy people, always freaking out; now it's satori, meditation, and deep relaxation. In a classic display of displaced, frustrated rage, he attacks a member of the Hare Krishna who accosts him on the street, embarrassing Milton and Milton's new friend: a most droll

8 A reference to Nathanial Hawthorne's oft-quoted distinction between novel and romance in his preface to *The House of the Seven Gables.*

presentation of his insecurities which have been intensified by Milton's countercultural cant.

For Milton, the narrator is pathetically passé, vulgar in his pursuit of 'volupté,' inauthentic:

> 'Look around you,' he said, and I did, and he exasperatedly said, 'no, I mean around your scene—not the oval—hasn't it come home to you. Haven't you noticed we are all into a different trip now. It isn't champagne breakfasts. It's not watching the rosy fingers of dawn at the Taxi Club. It isn't throwing people into swimming pools, it isn't expensive dinners and mock speeches, and it isn't going to ethnic night clubs and joining in the handkerchief dance, having your photograph taken with the belly dancer, putting dollar notes down the crevice of her breast, it isn't getting your photograph in the newspapers wearing a cowboy hat, it isn't appearing in public places in drag, it isn't being seen arm-in-arm with two negresses in New Orleans. Oh you know that I mean, the scene has changed. And look at your age.'
>
> Listening carefully to what he said, I replied, 'You make it sound *first class*. The long years of penury have led me into wild excesses. Like Raphael de Valentin, I have dreamed of a life on a princely scale and now I can make the dream come true. My bills for champagne alone are enormous. Under the influence of Eugene Sue I see myself as a dandy, for I have a horror of the solemn imbecilities indulged in by the English with their much vaunted sang froid. I suppose you are troubled by my white house gowns with gold tasselled girdles?'
>
> 'Your dabbling in effeminacy doesn't interest me. But I'll tell you another thing it isn't—it isn't dodging being a real person by hiding in irony, self-concealing humour, hiding behind ambiguity, double-edged humour, switching of persona, self-deprecation—that's all so much shit.' (pp.97–98)

The dynamics of their conflict are verbal; the systems that clash, linguistic. Milton tells him that, 'You must let go of words like "decide," "intellectualize," "explain"' (p.122). (The 'must' is good.) The narrator suspects that Milton's copy of the 'Desiderata', purportedly found in Old St Paul's, Baltimore, and dated 1692, is a fraud on internal linguistic evidence. Yet beneath his verbal braggadocio and glib sententiousness is the underlying sadness of the clown. The central, revealing story here, 'The Loss of a Friend by Cablegram', is also the central story of the collection structurally.

In this, the narrator, visiting his ex-wife, receives Milton's telegram rejecting him for his new lifestyle. As he is attempting defensively to explain, she is reading from his notebook cryptic entries, some in the first person, others in the third, that reveal the confusion of his thoughts and values, and his theory of 'the distortion of information by fictional suction': 'The attention of the audience, the reporter's expectations, the audience's expectations even in conversation, drag you away from the complicated, ragged reality, from say, pointlessness, away from stray and unrelated material towards a distorting order, a distorting sensationalism' (p.83). The discontinuities of mode and mood throughout the collection find their centre here in the discontinuities of a personality that is overwhelmed by consciousness of the 'complicated, ragged reality' and refuses to accept 'a distorting reality' from among those offered in the language and value systems embraced by others. The narrator is vulnerable, exposed, accused by his wife of being on the very edge of reality; and in tone this is much more a 'confessional' story than most of the others (excepting the one in the form of letters to the same ex-wife), bringing out the lonely and uncomfortable integrity underlying the comic surface elsewhere.

*Tales of Mystery and Romance* is both satisfying and enigmatic. A book of brilliant comic surfaces and rhetorical flourishes, yet one that conceals or complicates as much as it reveals. The presentation of the narrator's various selves is as much the real action as his encounters with Milton and his ex-wife; but the confusions and uncertainties of this narrator are dramatised with such confidence that we cannot completely identify him with the author. The implications for art are enigmatic. 'Lying and fiction are brothers? But not twins,' we are told (p.79), but which is which here—which lies, which secrets? Is the author, again like Irving Bow in the next collection, speaking the truth in a way that it will not be understood? Or, in accordance with the jottings in the narrator's notebook, is the truth being presented without the distortion and sensationalisation of fiction? With *Tales of Mystery and Romance,* Moorhouse may seem to have moved across the spectrum from his early critical, realistic engagement with social experience to that mode in which the only sure subject is the style, and the only true value the act of writing itself. Yet the pattern of his work is not so simple, as such a simplistic distinction would assume, and as, in its retrospective aspect, *The Everlasting Secret Family* makes clear.

In form, in theme, in social 'subject matter,' and personal preoccupations, this latest collection looks back but, appropriately from a writer who has emphasised discontinuities between all levels of experience, including the artistic, in no simple way. 'Pacific City' returns to the lost world of T. George McDowell, but from a different perspective, and shows Moorhouse the subtle, delicately ironic stylist. 'The Dutch Letters' and 'Imogene Continued' return to the narrative stance of *Conference-ville*, to the immediacies of personal and public life, and to the tensions between them; they show Moorhouse in his most commonly recognised and easily identified role as the witty, acute, but sceptical intelligence critically engaged in defining and interpreting contemporary social reality. While the title sequence apparently disrupts this emerging retrospective pattern, it also exhibits another characteristic of his writing: his continuing to break 'new ground' and old taboos, and to break also from his readers', his patrons' expectations, which could otherwise imprison him like the narrator in this sequence. In drawing together and further developing these different aspects of his work to date, *The Everlasting Secret Family* makes apparent the continuance throughout his varied books of his simultaneous concerns with experience and art: with finding the appropriate forms, styles, and authorial stances for engaging experience—past and present, personal and social, real and imaginative. Each may be discontinuous with the other, but discontinuity would seem to presuppose some continuity to depart from, and this latest collection suggests the 'familial' though 'secret' relationships between them all which provide his work with its unique, imaginative pattern.

# 'The Ways We Live Now'
# David Williamson

> *Australia has always seemed a very crude society, and this play explains better than most why so many Australians of talent chose to live in Britain and America ... If this is Australia, the Aborigines should have won.*

So opined English-born Clive Barnes in January 1974, reviewing an Off-Broadway production of David Williamson's *The Removalists* for the *New York Times.* Barnes had already seen London's Royal Court production (in July-August 1973) of this play which, first performed in Melbourne and Sydney 'alternative' theatres two years before, had quickly won its young writer a national reputation. By the time Barnes reviewed the play, that reputation was becoming international, for at the end of 1973 Williamson had won the London *Evening Standard*'s George Devine Award for Most Promising Playwright.

Barnes's assumption that a play, realist (though also absurdist) in mode, mirrored a whole society, or reflected the perceiver's stereotyped impressions of that society, had not been shared by this London counterparts. Although Harold Hobson of the *Sunday Times* felt that the play was evil, pandering to the audience's worst instincts by offering scenes of violence that (curiously) he thought belonged more in the brothel than on the stage, other London reviewers had been more receptive to this black comedy of machismo run riot, in which two policeman meddle in a domestic dispute and end up bashing the husband to death. Most of them saw the play as a psychological-cum-moral fable with implications extending far beyond the particulars of its Australian setting and the issue of police violence.

---

First published in *Critical Survey* [Oxford, U.K.] 6 (1994) with the title '"The Ways We Live Now": David Williamson's Recent Plays'. For a more up-to-date and detailed account see my *David Williamson: A Writer's Career* (rev. edn, Currency Press, Sydney, 1996).

But when Williamson's third big success, originally commissioned for the opening of the Sydney Opera House's Drama Theatre, *What If You Died Tomorrow*, opened at London's Comedy in September 1974, B. A. Young in the *Financial Times* struck a note similar to Barnes's. His view was that if the play's characters—a doctor turned novelist (as Williamson was an engineer turned playwright), his new woman, his parents, his publisher, and his attractive female editor—represented the Australian intelligentsia, then 'Australia need take no further steps to reduce immigration, for no decent person could possibly want to live there'. Again, though, others found that the setting was incidental to its qualities, this time as comedy. Herbert Kretzmer in the *Daily Express* thought it showed that 'life in Australia is just as awful as it is elsewhere', and Charles Lewsen in *The Times* thought that, while the battle for a writer's soul could be set anywhere, the first act at least had 'guts and implies a passion that I do not see crowding the stages of England'. The *Evening Standard*'s Milton Shulman found that it continued to display 'the witty, candid and virile writing style' that had won Williamson the paper's Most Promising Playwright award the previous year.

What really provoked an indignant outburst of cultural superiority among London reviewers was Michael Blakemore's production of *Don's Party*, which opened at the Royal Court in March 1975. Written immediately before *The Removalists* (their first productions had overlapped in Melbourne's alternative theatres), *Don's Party* is a virtuoso display of eleven characters interacting while the election results, which most are hoping will change their lives, are coming through on the television. The lives they hope will be changed by a Labor victory reveal themselves as, in the first half, the males pursue the females, and then, in the second, their wives gang up on them with bitter revelations and recriminations. After the revels of election night turn sour, life reverts to drab normality—as do national politics because the conservative government is returned. The style is larrikin Chekhov, with the outrageous sexual language and antics of the priapic Cooley masking a traditional theme of youthful, romantic ideals and illusions succumbing to the disappointments of middle age and tired marriages.

Herbert Kretzmer in the *Daily Express*, under the heading 'One Party Worth Avoiding', advised those thinking of migrating to Australia to see the play first, after which they would happily 'settle for a bedsitter in Neasden'; he concluded, 'I hated every minute'. Arthur Thirkell in the *Daily Mirror* decided, on the evidence the playwright offered, that 'his country is strictly for morons'. B. A. Young's variation on this (in the *Financial Times*) was 'a nation of Yahoos', and he approvingly quoted his own warning against migrating to Australia. Irving Wardle of *The Times* confessed he found it hard to respond warmly to plays by Commonwealth writers that 'hold up their compatriots to ridicule for audiences in the old country'.

Productions of later Williamson works in London attracted quite different reactions. When *The Club*, which the *Guardian*'s Michael Billington said used sport as a metaphor for corruption 'in a way that no recent English production gets anywhere near', opened at Hampstead in January 1980, the same Irving Wardle found it 'blissfully funny'. The *Sunday Times*'s reviewer was also commendatory but puzzled by the mildness of the language in a play from Williamson, and from a former penal colony. In June the same year *Travelling North*, which in striking contrast to *The Club* is about an ageing couple, opened at the Lyric, Hammersmith. A number of reviewers found their way into discussing it by observing that it upset preconceptions that it would be boozy and brutal, and then invoked the names Chekhov and Miller. Although *The Perfectionist*, a stylish comedy of manners about the battle of the sexes under feminism, had a run at Hampstead in mid 1983. its real success overseas came the next year at the Spoleto Festival in Charleston, South Carolina. Clive Barnes described the play and the Sydney Theatre Company's production as 'stunning'.

However, the assumption by Barnes and some of the London reviewers that the earlier plays directly mirrored Australian society was a not-too-distorted antipodean reflection of the reception they had already had in Australia. There too, reviews have not only been mixed, but also often concerned with he same sort of question that *The Removalists* raised in Clive Barnes's mind: what sort of a society have we here, if this play is an accurate reflection of it? One would like to complicate this by pointing out that Williamson's dramatic images of his own socicty arc by now prolific (he has averaged nearly a play a year over the last two decades, as well as film and television scripts); considerably varied in their subjects and tonality; and as much comic and satiric as realist or 'naturalistic'. But such qualifications should not deny that much of the unprecedented popular, but also critical, success Williamson has enjoyed has been attributed first of all to his casting himself in the role of 'storyteller to the tribe', regaling Australian audiences (in the first instance) with stories of the ways we live now. Audiences flock to each new Williamson play expecting to see the mirror held up to aspects of human nature, here and now, and to be amused by these—and these audiences help the large state-subsidised companies profitably meet their statutory obligations to include Australian plays in their seasons ( a very different situation from when Williamson's earliest plays were produced in fringe theatres, and a situation to which his success has been central).

It has become a commonplace of the local higher journalism that Williamson the dramatist has served as the 'chronicler' of the professional middle classes over the past two decades, the intimate 'diarist' of the generation that grew up to enjoy the educational opportunities and general affluence of post-World War II Australia. This is the generation of the playwright himself (b. 1942), the generation of probably the majority of his immediate audience, and certainly the generation of the majority of his characters who, from play to play, have matured along with both the playwright and his audience. Obviously there are limitations to this uncritical interest in the plays' *mimesis*, their representation or reflection of a changing society, rather than in their *making*, their modes, their moods. Yet, equally obviously, a purely formal reading of the plays as literary texts, rather than as 'scripts for performance' (as Williamson perceives them—though they are widely prescribed by universities and schools), would overlook the social, and political, contexts in which their initial audiences see them and respond.

For example *The Club*, that 'blissfully funny' play about the politics of sport, had its première in Australia after the 1975 constitutional coup that deposed the Labor government Don and his friends had been hoping for earlier, and during a period of bitter disillusion with the treachery and duplicity of politics. To Australian audiences of that time, the play could hardly fail to imply that metaphoric dimension that Michael Billington was also alert to when it was produced in London a couple of years later (whereas reviewers of the American production were more taken by the parallels with the current politics of gridiron). Clearly, plays take on resonances from the circumstances of their first productions, which in the case of Williamson's means the contemporary Australian social and political context. But equally clearly, as successful revivals of his plays at home and productions overseas have shown, they are not restricted to these; and productions elsewhere have not been limited to the English language—witness the Warsaw production of *The Removalists* during Solidarity's resistance to military dictatorship. How to recognise this further dimension conferred by production, how to relate dramatic texts to the contexts in which they are realised, without reducing those texts to sociological documents or, through their productions, to cultural-historical moments, is a critical problem that playscripts pose with particular sharpness.

In the decade since *The Perfectionist,* Williamson had five more of his 'stories' of the 'ways we live now' produced, plays that reflect power struggles between classes and genders, plays that register the impact on Australian life, private as well as political, of Thatcherite or Reaganomic ideologies—and of the boom, all too soon followed by the bust, in the global economy. Yet, while his 'chronicling' of the times continues, these plays are markedly varied in their mode. A summary of what they are 'about' is not going to provide much sense of their formal and stylistic differences; however, perhaps both subject and form can be accommodated by seeing them as versions of moral comedy, or comic moralities. They are varied also, if the reviewers' opinions are to be respected, in their levels of achievement—and, in the local theatrical context, they can be seen as implying ripostes to his critics.

*Sons of Cain* (1985), which drew not unfavourable comparisons with David Hare's *Pravda* when it played on the West End, can be seen as responding to those of his unkinder critics who had been accusing him of no longer writing about 'real' working-class people and challenging issues (as in *The Removalists*), but pandering to his middle-class following and their fascination with seeing what Williamson himself dubbed their own 'pseudo problems' on stage. *Sons of Cain* engages with then topical controversies implicating cabinet ministers, magistrates and police chiefs in conspiracies to pervert the course of justice, with drug trafficking, and with the role of the press in exposing such networks of corruption. At the same time, it also confronts the challenges of how to raise these disturbing issues without the play itself becoming an exercise in the investigative, and ephemeral, journalism it portrays; how to balance topical satiric realism with moral comedy. Especially through the central figure of the crusading journalist Kevin Cassidy, 'last of the macho illiterates'. *Sons of Cain* recaptured that 'larrikin' flavour of the earlier satiric comedies which critics claimed they were pining for.

*Emerald City* (1987) could also be seen as responding to accusations that Williamson had 'sold out', though tonally it is quite different from its predecessor. Set in the Australian film world (and Williamson, who had been involved simultaneously in the emergence of modern Australian theatre and cinema, continues to be a major figure here), *Emerald City* has marked personal elements that would not be lost on local audiences. Yet to call it 'autobiographical' would be misleading as to its pitch: it combines, at the institutional level, wild satire (but also sharp analysis) of the conflicts over values in the industry—the values of a distinctive national art form versus those of internationally commercial entertainment—with, at the personal level of screenwriter Colin's marriage and his agonies over integrity, comedy of more sophisticated manners reminiscent of *The Perfectionist.* As its title, with its allusion to *The Wizard of Oz,* might suggest. *Emerald City* is also a consciously 'literary' play presenting a comically detached slice of the contemporary Australian writer's life.

*Top Silk* (1989) bears superficial comparison with *Sons of Cain* in the contemporary issues it embraces: political and police corruption, drug addiction, teenage suicides, the increasing homelessness caused by development. Its focus, though, is more on the personal, on the family, than on an institution like the newspaper in the earlier play. While Trevor Fredericks, a barrister, is grooming himself for leadership of the opposition state Labor Party ('the party of compassion'), his genuinely compassionate public solicitor wife Jane bribes the police in an attempt to assist a lover from her schooldays who is on drug charges. Whereas this former lover, although a drop-out academically and a drug-user, is adored by his family, the professionally preoccupied and politically ambitious Trevor is at odds with his wife over the unrealistic expectations he has of his none-too-bright son. The stage is set for a morality in which he must learn that 'the politics of compassion' begin at home.

With its structure of a well-made melodrama, *Top Silk* is redolent of turn-of-the-century social problem plays. Its neat coincidences and reversals involve both husband and wife with a right-to-life Attorney General who wants to keep Trevor out of politics; Trevor is also involved with a right-wing international media mogul who offers to support him in return for Trevor's assistance in extending his empire (the mogul—shades of Rupert Murdoch—has adopted American citizenship). All culminates in an implausible court scene in which the brilliant barrister, in an attempt to win back his wife's affections, saves her former lover from prison. But Williamson refuses the final consolations of melodrama, a sentimental reconciliation of Trevor with his wife and son—the only consolation the play offers comes at the end of its first half, and from the media mogul who expects a swing away from the right and towards more compassionate politics in the 1990s. This departure from Williamson's more usual open resolutions makes the mood of this morality about the need for 'compassion, integrity, honesty' in personal and public life uncharacteristically pessimistic, and its mode only equivocally comic.

Although *Top Silk* played around Australia to the usual capacity audiences, the reviewers were not impressed. Williamson declared that his next play, *Siren* (1990), would be totally devoid of any redeeming social message. But, in its opening scene, the members of the Task Force Against Corruption, holed up in a town on the coast in an attempt to entrap a corrupt alderman, introduce themselves to the audience like Vices in a traditional morality—the cardinal vice in his 'contemporary love story of sorts' is lust for sexual conquest. Liz, the only female member of the Force, who comes from three generations of ear, nose and throat specialists—'and in this bloody country you can't do much better than that'—cannot help exploiting her sexual powers, and sleeps in turn with the three male members, who are decidedly not from her genteel social background. With its strong elements fo bedroom farce (though bedroom farce in the age of AIDS, and crossed with film noir), *Siren* seemed a deliberate, though updated, throwback to *The Coming of Stork* (1970), one of Williamson's earliest confronting comedies—and an answer to critics who were asking when was he going to write 'gutsy' comedy again. The reviewers (who, in any case, had not been all that impressed the first time around) were appalled by the politically incorrect gender stereotypes with which *Siren* provocatively confronted them; however, they did not deter audiences from attending the play's simultaneous première productions in Melbourne and Sydney. While audiences furnish no record of their reactions, it is clear that Williamson —an unprecendentedly popular playwright at home—is closer to them than he is to his critics, and that they respond to his entertaining engagement with topical but also perennial moral issues.

Liz, the siren of the title, who lures male power figures on to the rocks of divorce or separation before abandoning them, is the central character. The battle of the sexes has been a staple element in Williamson's writings from his earliest plays, and those who read *The Removalists* or *Don's Party* 'straight', as realistic records of social behaviour, seemed unaware that they had emerged from an 'alternative' theatrical milieu committed to satirically attacking 'mateship' or machismo. Since at least *The Perfectionist*, in which the 'story' is told by the wife in a sequence of flashbacks (indicating the increasing use of cinematic techniques in his writing), Williamson has created a succession of dominant female roles; and this itself might be seen as a reflection of shifting fortunes in the real-life battle since the early days of modern feminism and *The Removalists*. Certainly Margaret, the 'narrator' of the most recent play to be produced, *Money and Friends* (1992), seems with her penchant for younger men a contemporary independent matron, though she discovers to her embarrassment that her latest toy boy is the estranged son of one of her holiday neighbours.

*Money and Friends* shows the bourgeoisie—an ecologist turned media personality, a corporate lawyer into development, a surgeon anxious about his investments, and their wives—at their leisure in their neighbouring beach houses. Socially, Crystel Inlet is an artificial environment because it is unlikely that in their working lives they would encounter each other, or the academics Margaret, a historian, and the widowed Peter, a mathematician (who cannot make sense of that summer's prescribed reading, A. S. Byatt's *Possession*). Peter is the confidant of all, especially the wives, but he is unlikely to be there next summer because, in the days of economic optimism, he went surety for his brother; now he stands to lose his holiday house. Will his better-heeled friends come to the rescue?

The Currency edition of the text has a prefatory note by Robert Gottliebsen of *Business Review Weekly* on the bursting of the 1980s property boom, no doubt a more than merely topical concern to many members of the audience around the country (and at the time of writing this, the play has settled into a long run in Los Angeles). But, with all its topicality, *Money and Friends* has strong elements of the most traditional, and moral, comedy. This in the Australian production was emphasised by an entr'acte, interpolated by the director, in which the characters, bedecked with carnivalesque beach wear and equipment, blundered around the stage like *commedia dell'arte* figures. While topical social types, the characters are also humours: the pessimistic surgeon, with a wife he finds dismayingly cheerful, is the Melancholy Man; the ecologist preoccupied by the continuance of his genes, and expecting a child by his new wife, is the Obsessive; the corporate lawyer of Sicilian descent, married to a social climber, is the Braggart. Peter, the confidant of all, is persuaded by Margaret to tell his 'friends'–who have not rallied to her call to assist him financially–the truth about themselves, rather than consoling them as before. 'Ibsen in the Antipodes' the *New Yorker* had dubbed Williamson when *The Club* played on Broadway, and, playfully, *The Wild Duck* is the text 'behind' *Money and Friends*.

> PETER: Did you ever see a production of Ibsen's *The Wild Duck*?
> MARGARET: No. I can't bear Lutheran guilt.
> PETER: This idiot called Gregers starts telling everyone the truth because he thinks it'll be good for them. It ends up ruinning everyone's lives. Conrad and Alex won't ever speak to me again and I'm not counting on any more quiche. [*He indicates the sugar bowl*] Despite massive amounts of sugar even the Lorikeets steer clear of me these days.[1]

All ends well, though, and instead of Ibsenite gloom there is a contemporary, parodic verion of the hurriedly reached curtain to traditional comedies.

Nearly a decade ago, surveying Williamson's plays up to the early 1980s, John McCullum traced the contours of the 'new map of Australia' they offered; he also charted the shifts in Williamson's subjects and style without, wisely, postulating too neat a congruence among these various contours.[2] Since then, as Williamson has updated his map, his play within and across a wide range of predominantly comic stage traditions has become more noticeable—though admittedly this has not been met with unalloyed critical acclaim. Play with conventions is simultaneously part of what the individual plays are 'about': the 'stories' about 'the ways we live now' cannot be extricated from the

1 David Williamson, *Money and Friends* (Currency Press, Sydney, 1992), p.60. All the Williamson plays referred to are published by Currency.

2 John McCallum, 'A New Map of Australia: The Plays of David Williamson', *Australian Literary Studies* 11 (1984), 342-54.

self-consciously theatrical structures that mediate, and complicate them. Such theatrical self-consciousness implicitly invites the question of what, uniquely, theatre can offer audiences in an age in which film and television provide most of their experience of drama and dramatic presentations of a current agenda of issues (power, politics, class, gender, ethnicity ...). Williamson, himself a scriptwriter highly sought after by international film and television interests, yet foremost a playwright committed to the continuing viability of serious yet 'accessible' theatre, is still coming up with answers to that question.

# The Advancing Wave: Australian Literary Biography Since 1980

'Who left the gate open?' asks Chris Wallace-Crabbe early in his lively chapter on 'Autobiography' in *The Penguin New Literary History of Australia* (1988), 'How did autobiography disguise itself? Or were the rules of the game changed for some clutch of reasons?' He is observing that autobiographies have begun to receive a great deal more critical consideration, at a time when 'the construction of all literary canons has become subject to radical questioning'. Such questioning (not least of the assumed categorical distinction between 'imaginative' and 'non-fictional' prose) has led to the admission of autobiography into the class of 'serious literature', even though the genre he is surveying seems to be a 'parody, or at least a black-and-white caricature' of other literary genres. For while autobiography also claims to refer to life, 'it does so a good deal more crassly', thus raising what he calls 'all those coarse, nagging questions about whether it is art ... or merely documentation.'[1]

*The Penguin New Literary History* itself is clearly intended to contribute to such questioning of canons and neatly demarcated genres, yet it contains no chapter on—nor even discussion of—another form which also claims, however crassly, to refer to life: biography, especially biography of literary subjects. This is a noticeable blind spot in a volume that proclaims itself to be concerned with 'new' perspectives, for an observable development in Australian literary culture over the last decade and more has been interest in the theory and practice of biography, and

1 Laurie Hergenhan, ed., *The Penguin New Literary History of Australia* (Penguin, Ringwood, 1988), p.560.

First published in Margaret Harris and Elizabeth Webby, eds. *Reconnoitres: Essays in Australian Literature in Honour of G. A. Wilkes* (Oxford University Press, Melbourne, 1992).

the admission of literary biography into modes of 'serious' literary and cultural historical discourse.

At the beginning of the 1980s, and then unfashionably, Wallace-Crabbe regretted the lack of biographies of such major writers as Furphy and Lawson, and of such influential figures as Archibald and Stephens.[2] The situation here was then in marked contrast to that in the United States and the United Kingdom, where successive generations, or even decades, were continuing to bring forth new biographies of the perceived major writers, as well as adding new subjects to their literary biographical pantheons. But since the appearance of Axel Clark's *Christopher Brennan* in 1980, a steady succession of full-length, well-researched, and critically considered biographies of major literary figures has provided much of what had been so conspicuously lacking earlier: Sylvia Lawson's *The Archibald Paradox* (1983), Craig Munro's biography of P. R. Stephensen, *Wild Man of Letters* (1984), Gary Kinnane's *George Johnston* (1986), Brian Matthews's *Louisa* (1987), Brenda Niall's *Martin Boyd* (1988), W. Wilde's life of Mary Gilmore, *Courage a Grace* (1988), Chris Williams's *Christina Stead* (1989), Penne Hackforth-Jones's *Barbara Baynton* (1989).

Already the 1990s have seen the publication of the first volume of Axel Clark's *Henry Handel Richardson* and John Barnes's life of Furphy, *The Order of Things* (both 1990); and, among others, Geoffrey Dutton's *Kenneth Slessor,* Colin Roderick's *Henry Lawson* and David Marr's *Patrick White* (all 1991). While deceased figures predominate overwhelmingly as the subjects of 'full-dress' biographies, recent collections of interviews with contemporary writers indicate the reading public's interest in the manifold personal and cultural matters that 'biography' comprehends. Also broadly biographical are David Walker's *Dream and Disillusion* (1976) and Drusilla Modjeska's *Exiles at Home* (1981), both literary and cultural-historical studies that share characteristics of what Leon Edel has termed 'group biography'.

The list I have given does not attempt to be exhaustive, nor can it be up-to-date. Nevertheless, it will serve to make the points that not only have there been many more Australian literary biographies of late, but also that many, if not most, of today's practitioners of this traditional

2 Chris Wallace-Crabbe, 'Australian Literary History', *The Literary Criterion* [Bangalore, India] 15, Nos 3 and 4 (1980), p.141.

form of literary history and criticism are academics. This might invite speculation that the New Critical orthodoxies prevailing within Australian academies in the past may have inhibited the production of literary biographies, though there are earlier examples scattered over time, among them Colin Roderick's life of Rosa Praed, *In Mortal Bondage* (1948) , Brian Elliott's *Marcus Clark* (1958), and Ann-Mari Jordens's *The Stenhouse Circle* (1979). However, it is more likely that the 'lead time' between the establishment of courses and postgraduate studies in Australian Literature, combining with the protracted nature of the individual biographical projects, had the effect of masking much of the interest that actually existed before it became so apparent in the 1980s.

Instead of further discouraging academic interest in this once supposedly 'discredited' form, the more theoretical, and sceptical, critical climate prevailing over the past decade has clearly encouraged it, and not only among practitioners. Indications of this are special issues of journals devoted to autobiography and biography, the focus on these genres at the 1989 conference of the Association for the Study of Australian Literature, and the adoption of them by the Humanities Research Centre of the Australian National University as the theme for its programme in 1990. Such interest might seem paradoxical, when the key orthodoxy in the prevailing 'post-structuralist' climate is often assumed to be 'the death of the author'; but, to be consistent, a thorough-going scepticism which assumes no category, even 'Literature', to be 'privileged' is obliged to accept the biographical as another manifestation of 'writing'—and to engage with some theoretical issues. Can precise generic boundaries be drawn between history, biography, fiction? (a question made less abstract, and more provoking, by some recent practitioners in all three genres). If biography is more than 'mere documentation', should it then also be considered aesthetically, as an imaginative construction of characters and events that seeks to confer an aesthetic, ultimately imaginative (but not imaginary) unity and significance on any life's ragged pattern—or lack of pattern?

Axel Clark's *Christopher Brennan* (1981) was first in the wave of Lives of major literary figures that swelled throughout the 1980s and is maintaining or even gaining momentum. Having its origins in a doctoral thesis, and subtitled *A Critical Biography*, it provides one contemporary model for the literary Life: as a vehicle not only for textual and contextual scholarship but also for closely argued evaluative criticism. However, it still observes the traditions of the genre by presenting a chronologically ordered, narratively interrelated account of Brennan's 'life, times, and work'—as so many nineteenth century biographies announced themselves in their titles or subtitles. But how else would a biographer present his subject?

A life story is what readers traditionally understand by, and expect from, a biography. Yet, although we have read much about *la pacte autobiographique* in recent years—the understanding autobiographers enter into with their readers that, however artful, inventive and imaginative they may be, the Lives they offer are not fictions—the conventions operating between biographers and their readers have not been much considered by critics, though they have been exposed and played with openly by some biographers (and writers of fiction). Perhaps these conventions have not received much theoretical consideration because they are too obvious; but, if so, why do we still read so often those reviews in which the subject of the biography becomes the sole focus of attention, the biography itself remaining unconsidered, invisible as a writing performance, while the reviewer, as one who knew the subject, or whose knowledge might only extend to having read the undiscussed biography, becomes the surrogate authority?

These conventions assume that biographers understand their subjects 'intimately' from their exhaustive researches and that as omniscient narrators (but preferably not obtrusive know-alls) they will present coherently shaped Lives of their central characters, however chaotic the actual lives may have seemed to contemporaries, and even to the subjects themselves. In constructing their chief characters, literary biographers will display the extent and inwardness of their acquaintance with their subjects' writing; for the most significant part of a writer's life—that part which has lead biographers and readers to be interested in the first place—has been lived imaginatively and through the act of writing. Not the facts alone but the biographers' perception of the imaginative import of these facts for their subjects and their subjects' writing becomes the nexus between scholarly or 'mere' documentation and 'criticism'—and, however the latter term might be understood at this moment, it would seem to involve empathy. John Barnes's teasing out of the elaborate relationship between Joseph Furphy and his fictional alter ego 'Tom Collins', a relationship which culminated in *Such Is Life*, provides a instance of that insightful combination of empathy with an author and an intimate acquaintance with his work that readers expect. Empathy, though, as Colin Rodrick's *Henry Lawson* shows, need not necessarily entail sympathy.

At this crux of life history and criticism there can be links or cross-overs between the two modes of 'the biographical'. If autobiographers often play at being critics by inviting readers to join in mockery of their own quoted juvenilia, biographers often (and perhaps should?) reciprocate by attempting to become vicarious autobiographers: to imagine what it must have been like to grow up in such a family and social setting, have such an education, come to more or less simultaneous consciousness of sexuality and a literary vocation, and (as is so often the case in Australian literary autobiographies) to consciousness, or rejection, of national and class identity. Inevitably, both the *auto-* and the *bio-* versions of this mode of *graphos*, of life-writing, have a succession of overlapping topics which, if they have not been scripted already by the subject as direct or indirect autobiography, can be provided imaginatively by the biographer. These rites of artistic passage offer biographers potential writerly moments, opportunities for infusing documentation and interpretation with a 'literary' element akin to the autobiographer's own—and, in most cases, the biographer has the advantage of rounding off the story by attending (at least vicariously) the autobiographer's final passage and last rite, and by observing posterity's regard, or not, for his or her literary remains.

Axel Clark's pact with his readers—and because, in the Australian context, the appearance of *Christopher Brennan* provided an unprecedented instance of 'critical biography' I want to consider it in what might seem disproportionate detail—is one he shares with the majority of his fellow biographers. That is, the story he tells will posit a significant pattern to the life and work of his subject—a life now dispersed into the heterogeneous collection of texts cited at the end of this Life. This pact he fulfils generously, presenting his previously legendary (which also meant cloudy) figure in the overlapping contexts, social-historical, intellectual and literary-cultural (both national and international) that the manifold sources document. While drawn from, and constrained by, these sources his Life is not 'mere documentation' but an interpretative construction that perceives a pattern of consistency in Brennan's life and works where previously a marked, and culturally significant, contradiction had been presumed.

This pattern is announced in the opening paragraph of *Christopher Brennan* (and, as Brian Matthews's *Louisa* demonstrates, openings are significant). By declaring that unlike Henry Lawson, Henry Handel Richardson or John Shaw Neilson, Brennan was not affected by any disturbing experiences or change in his early years, Clark situates his subject within a field of Australian literary biography—though, at the time he was writing, such a field could have been envisaged only fitfully by his readers. Rather than positing any trauma or disruption as central to his subject's development—another implicit situating move, countering the mid-century assumption of Leon Edel and others that 'modern' biography was characterised by its awareness of psychoanalytic insights—Clark's opening proclaims a consistency in Brennan's character in terms of his religious orientation, his desire for the absolute, and his conviction that he was set above the mass of humanity. In the subsequent narrative, and critical exposition, these character traits are made to marry 'naturally' with Brennan's writing, so that his personality and his poetry can be shown as developing together, each illuminating the other.

As readers of literary biography, we recognise that such an assumption of mutuality between the subject's life and work is fundamental to the genre's existence. But clearly this enabling premise, or necessary fiction, runs counter to the orthodoxies of most varieties of criticism this century, from the early T. S. Eliot and New Critical reactions against Romantic expressionist theories to post-structuralist inversions of our seemingly 'common sense' understandings of authors and texts, writing and reading. As always, there are exceptions, and Leavisism with its touchstone of 'sincerity' was an academically influential example; but while Leavisism admitted the biographical by assuming the indivisibility of a writer's 'sensibility' and expression, its practice was committedly 'literary critical' and primarily directed to evaluative readings of the works. Within the context of academic criticism prevailing in Australia when *Christopher Brennan* was published, its subtitle, *A Critical Biography*, may very well have appeared to some as anachronistic, if not oxymoronic.

As critical biographer, Clark seeks the sincere expression of personal emotional experience in Brennan's verse—and is most often disappointed. Brennan's models for his versification and diction (and Clark is sharply observant in placing him in the mid-to-late Victorian context) prove unfortunate when 'sincerity', the direct communication of 'felt' or 'authentic' feeling, is the criterion invoked. Few, if any, of Brennan's poems suggest that personal experience is their subject, and even those that might suggest this to the biographically-informed lack immediacy of reference or the sense of a direct expression of emotion. For Clark, the already vexed critical issue of Brennan's diction registers and compounds a deeper problem, that of the unsuitability of Brennan's 'raw material'—his '[T]angled, uncertain (and sometimes transparently immature) feelings'—for such an ambitious Symbolist project as *Poems [1913]*.[3] That is, a more fundamental limitation than Brennan's concealing his 'raw material' behind a screen of Swinburnian or Patmorean verbiage is seen to be his inability to 'contact' his true feelings (p.137).

While it is understandable, indeed expected that a biographer should want to uncover the personal element in the work of his subject, this approach overlooks or dismisses what could be interpreted as Brennan's calculated impersonality, his assumption of archetypal poetic roles, most memorably that of the Wanderer. Clark discerns the personal within the impersonal but then finds this personal element inadequately expressed. He sees the Wanderer, Brennan's major persona in *Poems*, failing in his quest to discover the absolute, as Brennan himself is seen as failing in his personal quest to discover it through poetry. But Clark is not arguing simply that Brennan's work is the failure of Brennan the man (to paraphrase Barthes's dismissive summary of Baudelaire's biographers as crude reductionists[4]). The Wanderer might fail in his quest, but Clark considers 'The Wanderer' and the 'Lilith' sequences to be among Brennan's finest achievements. In them Brennan does not fail as a poet; even though biographically they mark his turning away

3 *Christopher Brennan* (Melbourne University Press, Melbourne, 1980), p.90. Subsequent page references, included in the text in parentheses, refer to this edition.

4 Roland Barthes, 'The Death of the Author', *Image-Music-Text, Essays Selected and Translated by Stephen Heath* (Hill and Wang, New York, 1977), p.143.

from poetry as his vocation, and their completion coincides with the beginning of his 'slow, terrible descent' (p.175).

Thus, while (with some exceptions) Brennan's verse fails to provide this biographer with sincere expressions of his subject's inner and emotional life, Clark elegantly traces congruities between the life and the work. One might want to quarrel—as one should with any challenging critical argument—with aspects of this congruity. Some, following G. A. Wilkes would see the Wanderer's 'failure' to discover the absolute, and Brennan's similar failure over the course of the cycle, as the realisation of the Romantic ironies implicit in the undertakings of both the poet and his persona, ironies Brennan wrote about in 'German Romanticism: A Progressive Definition'.[5] However, even if one prefers to emphasise those elements that allow a more positive interpretation of the cycle's resolution, the facts obdurately remain: the poet did not sustain an interest in pursuing new versions of his quest and Brennan's personal life began to deteriorate noticeably after 1902. For any reader wanting to qualify Clark's reading of *Poems*, these facts constitute a larger, interpretatively constraining context which cannot easily be dismissed as 'mere', and irrelevant, documentation.

At a time when, in the academies, literary biography seemed to have fallen into an abyss somewhere between the old New Criticism and the new post-structuralism with its scepticism towards author/ity, *Christopher Brennan* demonstrated how this traditional form could still provide an engaging and imaginative focus for scholarship and criticism. The impersonal mode of most of Brennan's verse and the issues relating to his diction justify Clark's extended passages of interpretative and evaluative argument. While these are more concentrated critical discussions than the majority of subsequent literary biographers have felt the need to incorporate, others who have taken a poet as subject also engage closely with the work. With Kenneth Slessor, Geoffrey Dutton similarly confronts the challenge of writing about an elusively impersonal poet and, in this case, of relating his work to an enigmatic and recessive personality. In *Spirit in Exile: Peter Porter and His Poetry*

5 A. R. Chisolm and J. J. Quinn, eds, *The Prose of Christopher Brennan* (Angus and Robertson, Sydney, 1962), pp.379–95.

(1991), Bruce Bennett employs a traditional biographical framework, to focus on his subject's work—its characteristics, context and reception —and so provide the fullest consideration Porter's poetry has received so far.

Most biographies, though, have been of prose writers. With George Johnston and Martin Boyd, Gary Kinnane and Brenda Niall were working with subjects whose central works were commonly regarded as 'autobiographical', as unproblematical projections of their creators' experience and personalities. Johnston's David Meredith trilogy parallels the lives of its author and his wife Charmian Clift (who, as a writer herself, doubled Kinnane's subject). Boyd's Langton series follows the outlines of his own family history—and Boyd had also published two autobiographies. What was there for biographers to do with these self-constructed subjects, except create their own versions of what had been provided by the subjects themselves in another genre? Here the spectre of biography's own vicious hermeneutic circle raises itself (as it has in reviewers' minds with studies of Henry Handel Richardson): the biography that is presumably intended to illuminate the life and the works takes for its most substantial evidence the work itself. While their biographies are as different as their subjects, Kinnane and Niall both direct their scholarship and their critical perception to dissociating their subjects from the 'authorised' versions of their lives that readers have formed from their novels. The process could be seen as the opposite of Axel Clark's or Geoffrey Dutton's. Rather than detecting the traces left by the writers' personalities on their impersonal writings, Kinnane and Niall explore the differences between the subjects' actual experiences and their fictional versions of these. They show how these differences have been achieved through such imaginatively reconstructive processes as conflation and substitution.

Brenda Niall makes genealogy—so often a stumbling block for other biographers, or their readers—an appropriate, indeed essential, element for a fuller understanding of Boyd and his works. Her unearthing of a monied convict ancestor, a seemingly unlikely skeleton in the Boyds' vaults, is a scholarly coup to match Kinnane's subtle interpretative surmisals on the processes, not necessarily conscious, by which Johnston transformed his memories into fiction. But in both *George Johnston: A Biography* and *Martin Boyd: A Life*—the indefinite article in each subtitle reminding us of the biographer's own subjectivity—scholarship and interpretative acumen become, as in Clark's *Brennan*, means to a higher end: not merely the reconstruction of the subject's life, but the construction of 'A Life', a work with characters, settings, scenes, conflicts, in which while every word may be true the overall truth aimed at begins to overlap with some of the expectations that readers bring to fiction. Clearly, as in 'literary autobiography', the qualifier in 'literary biography' can allude not only to the subject but also to the biographer's own narrative skill and other artful qualities. By now we have enough, and sufficiently varied, examples to recognise that biography can not only add to our understanding of writers and writing, and so to 'serious' literary and cultural discourse, but also to the sum total of writing itself.

Equally clearly, the epithet 'literary' also entails some echo of that now seemingly obsolescent phrase 'literary criticism'. In a possibly futile pursuit of a taxonomy, one might be tempted to position Axel Clark's explicitly 'critical biography', or Bruce Bennett's *Spirit in Exile*, at one end of a conjectured spectrum, and at the other a Life of a literary figure that restricts interest in the works to their being—in terms of their composition, publication and reception—simply events in the history of the subject. Happening upon this declaration in the preface to Colin Roderick's *Henry Lawson: A Life*, 'This book does not aim at dealing with his works except insofar as they bear on his personality or his creative method',[6] one might feel that such a test case has been discovered. But restricting interpretation of Lawson's writings in these ways proves not to preclude evaluation of either the subject or his works. As examples, we find Roderick observing of Lawson's 'Brighten's Sister-in-law', which he sees as a prose reworking of the earlier ballad 'Harry the Carrier's Boy', that 'the rewriting of early verse as prose tales had not yet become decadent practice ' (p.224); and of *Children of the Bush* that 'The verses ... showed an advance on his earlier verse. In the opening lines of "Unknown" he struck the true note of poetry' (pp.233–34). However external or objective the intended interpretation, an essentially subjective element enters with the biographer's unavoidable assessments of both the work and its producer —and the moral hero of Roderick's Life of Lawson turns out to be the publisher George Robertson.

6 Colin Roderick, *Henry Lawson: A Life* (Angus and Robertson, Sydney, 1991), p.xi. Subsequent page references, included in the text in parentheses, refer to this edition.

David Marr's *Patrick White: A Life* illustrates well the ambivalence with which 'literary' can adhere appraisingly to the execution of a biography as well as descriptively to the subject. Marr begins his story just before Easter 1910, with a plain woman in a big hat standing at the altar for her marriage to Dick White; and like Leon Edel, who found his 'scenic' method for his *The Life of Henry James* (1953–63) in the fictional practices of his subject, Marr continues his narration through vividly presented moments and a style that bear a happy affinity with White's. For his final scene, set almost eighty years after Ruth Withycombe's marriage, he chooses that early morning when Manoly Lascaris and White's literary agent, Barbara Mobbs, scatter the ashes on a lake in Sydney's Centennial Park. The significance of the lake White chose for this rite being 'ringed with a scurf of plastic and broken glass' will not be lost on readers of White's fiction and his autobiography *Flaws in the Glass,* and in its biographical way this scene, which ends with Lascaris and Mobbs turning towards the house to begin another day, Milly the terrier bounding ahead through the grass, is congruent with the conclusions without closure of White's novels.

Marr's narrational procedures in *Patrick White* are 'literary' not only because he, like numerous other biographers, adopts or adapts many of the techniques of fiction, but also because his own biographical imagination is so steeped in the details of his subject's works that (more extensively than White himself in *Flaws in the Glass*, 1981) he can signal to readers of White's work the likely impact on the young Paddy of experiences which will surface as personal preoccupations in the mature Patrick's writings half a century or so later, though without insisting on any deterministic or other interpretive inference. Given the already massive and discordant chorus of commentators on the White canon, Marr wisely does not allow himself to become diverted from his story by the interpretations and evaluations of others, nor does he deliver disquisitions on the works himself; but he provides full and often fascinating details on the inspirations for each work, and details also of their production, reception, and commercial fortune (or lack of it). As with Roderick's *Henry Lawson*, one expects *Patrick White* will stimulate future biocritical studies which will take Marr's researches and emphases as their points of departure.

The consolidation of biography as a respectable mode of literary discourse during a decade when such discourse became a 'site of contestation' within Australian academies had, as noted previously, its seemingly paradoxical side. The unprecedented appearance of so many literary biographies coincided with the circulation of post-structuralist concepts which, by denying 'bourgeois' individualistic notions of the autonomous (and creative) self, challenged the form's basic assumption that a revealing relationship could be established between a subject's life and work, between life history and imaginative production. While, manifestly, the currency of these concepts did not inhibit writers of literary biographies, it placed them (at least in the minds of many of their readers) in the position of having to validate this enabling assumption through their individual practice—and also to provide their own answers to questions that, in the abstract, seemed vexed: what was 'criticism' and what was its relation to 'biography' in the age of the 'decentred subject'? Their answers, like their practice, proved various, no doubt allowing some readers to see the conventions of the form, or particular biographies, as accommodating their social-constructionist interests in authorship, others as satisfying their traditional critical and literary historical expectations. But at least two literary biographers engaged openly with some of these theoretical questions and issues.

While Sylvia Lawson's *The Archibald Paradox* (1983) follows the familiar contours of a life-history, her subject is 'decentred'. When the young John Feltham, then Jules François, becomes J. F. Archibald, editor of the *Bulletin*, 'What he was turned into what he did'[7] and the subject's life-story 'disappears' into 'The Great Print Circus' he provided for writers and readers in a colonial culture. At this point, her subject becomes not so much a text as the sub-text to the writings of those he edited, a sub-text to be interpreted within the context of that colonial culture, with its paradoxical sense of both its distance from the metropolis and its need to create its own centre. When, in the account of his later life, Archibald reappears from under the text he orchestrated he becomes 'part of the recent history of madness' (pp.xi–xii), a footnote to the Foucaultian perception of insanity as a social construct.

Reminiscent of Sylvia Lawson's 'Great Print Circus' is Brian Matthews's use of music hall routine in *Louisa* (1987) to present the variegated voices and concerns expressed in the *Dawn*, Louisa Lawson's paper for women. Unlike Sylvia Lawson, Matthews's dramatised

7 Sylvia Lawson, *The Archibald Paradox* (Allen Lane, Ringwood, 1983), p.117.

biographer is apprehensive of his subject disappearing into the text Louisa edited and into the history of the same colonial society. Wistfully, this biographer dreams of being able to write a conventional biography, of being able to leave 'the networks of problematics' behind and to write 'rounded periods of biographical prose, flowing from and dictated by meticulous research'.[8] Does he, though, have enough material, not only to give the sense of 'a full life being lived' but to stop him from inventively filling the gaps and thus 'sliding from biography to phantom biography and from both into a disguised form of fiction'? (pp.5–6).

Matthews's biographer and 'Owen Webster'—the alter ego the biographer creates to allow an alternative voice—rehearse these 'problematics' in a series of exchanges over their work in progress. Central to their arguments is the relation of documentable record to story, of facts to fiction. The biographer in his desire to tell a story and develop a character, a character by whom he has become possessed, is in a schizoid relation to the facts. What stance should he assume: a pretence of objectivity and omniscience—or should he openly empathise and sympathise with his subject? Biographer and alter ego disagree heavily on this issue—while demonstrating what each approach entails—as they disagree on the relation of criticism to biography. For Owen Webster, the quality of Louisa Lawson's poetry 'would matter in a book of literary criticism or literary history' as the quality of her housekeeping would matter in a social history, but in a biography 'what is interesting is simply that the poetry and the housekeeping happened' (p.239). For the biographer also, Louisa's writings matter as part of her life but 'how can poetry matter other by being in itself the most intense and striking way possible ... Which means that it is important to determine as accurately as possible how accomplished Louisa's poetry is as poetry' (p.242).

The engaging play with such theoretical issues—contained within a metabiographical fiction that in turn contains fictional interludes: and which, even if there had never been a Louisa Lawson, could presumably still be read for affording some of the same fictional satisfactions as, say, A. S. Byatt's novel *Possession* (1990)—should not obscure Matthews's simultaneous observance of the biographical pact. Enfolded

8 Brian Matthews, *Louisa* (McPhee Gribble, Melbourne, 1987), p.107. Subsequent page references, included in the text in parentheses, refer to this edition.

within *Louisa*'s metabiographical and fictional coils is a Life that still satisfies conventional expectations, even though Matthews inverts conventional procedures by engaging openly with critical and scholarly problems that others more usually resolve within, or suppress beneath, their 'rounded periods of biographical prose'. Criticism and scholarship are also absorbed deeply into his Life-in-progress: the re-reading of Louisa's autobiography against her daughter Gertie's family memoirs and her son Henry's story 'The Drover's Wife' is an interpretative *tour de force* and an instance of what 'criticism', so often a problematical term today, can still mean—in this case, an imaginative, even inspired, insight into what is happening in such an incestuous interplay of texts.

The increasing number of Australian literary biographies and increasing interest in the form since 1980 could be interpreted as a desirable catching-up with the situation obtaining elsewhere with longer-established literatures—a catching-up akin to Australian literature's acquiring, for example, its own Oxford *History* (1981), *Companion* (1985) and *Literary Guide* (1987) during the same period. However, what might seem local and particular developments in Australian literary history can usually be correlated with those occurring elsewhere in the English-speaking world, and literary biography provides yet another example. Rather than being evidence of an often assumed cultural 'lag', the flourishing of interest here, both practical and theoretical, correlates with what has been occurring elsewhere over the same period—not only with biography itself but also with the wider reconstituting of the discourses that 'literary criticism' used to comprehend, and contain, more confidently than it does today.

The general tendency in recent literary discourse, a tendency exhibited in diverse ways within the *Penguin New Literary History*, has been to focus on areas, and genres, perceived to have been marginalised by established canons and historical overviews: women's writing, gay writing, black writing, migrant writing, regional writing. Already Australian literary biography offers a range of detailed 'case studies', and investigative models, which are broadly in keeping with, or readily assimilable to, the turn of literary-critical interest towards the social construction of gender, class and race, and consideration of how these constructions have impinged on writing at various stages. If, in the usual way of intellectual fashions, the turn in the United States from 'deconstruction' to 'new historicism' (a return to formerly repressed historical interests combining with a vogue for Geertzian 'thick description' of gender, class or race relations) is reflected here, the newly-discovered contemporaneity of Australian literary biography should see the millennium in.

# PUBLICATIONS OF THE SYDNEY ASSOCIATION FOR STUDIES IN SOCIETY AND CULTURE

No. 1 *Words and Worlds. Studies in the Social Role of Verbal Culture*, eds Stephen Knight and S. N. Mukherjee, 1983.

No. 2 *Feudalism: Comparative Studies*, eds Edmund Leach, S N. Mukherjee and J. O. Ward, 1985.

No. 3 *Semiotics, Ideology, Language*, eds Terry Threadgold, E. A. Grosz, Gunther Kress and M. A. K. Halliday, 1986.

No. 4 *The Cultural Construction of Race*, eds Marie de Lepervanche and Gillian Bottomley, 1988.

No. 5 *Revolution as History*, eds S. N. Mukherjee and J. O. Ward, 1989.

No. 6 *Words and Wordsmiths, a Volume for H. L. Rogers*, eds Geraldine Barnes, John Gunn, Sonya Jensen and Lee Jobling, 1989.

No. 7 *Disasters: Image and Context*, ed. Peter Hinton, 1992.

No. 8 *Social Visions*, by Michael Wilding, 1993.

No. 9 *Theatre and Cultural Interaction*, by Maria Shevtsova, 1993.

No. 10 *The Epic Circle*, by Zdenko Zlatar, 1993.

No. 11 *The Epic in History*, eds Lola Sharon Davidson, S. N. Mukherjee and Z. Zlatar, 1995.

No. 12 *Religious Change, Conversion and Culture*, ed. Lynette Olson, 1996.

No. 13 *The Citizen Historian: Explorations in Historiography*, by S. N. Mukherjee, 1996.

No. 14 *If Rain Doesn't Come*, by Bob Fisher, 1996.

No. 15 *History, Literature and Society: Essays in Honour of S. N. Mukherjee*, eds Mabel Lee and Michael Wilding, 1997.

No. 16 *Studies in Classic Australian Fiction*, by Michael Wilding, 1997.

No. 17 *Studies in Australian Literary History*, by Brian Kiernan, 1997.